Advances in Preventing and Treating Violence and Aggression

Series Editor

Peter Sturmey, Queens College and The Graduate Center, City University of New York, Flushing, USA

The series publishes books focused and developed across three domains. The first is understanding and explaining violence and aggression. Books in this domain address such subject matter as genetics, physiology, neurobiology, cultural evolution, biobehavioral, learning, cognitive, psychoanalytic, sociological and other explanations of violence. The second domain focuses on prevention and treatment for individuals and couples. Examples of books in this domain include cognitive behavioral, behavioral, counseling, psychopharmacological, psychosocial, couples, and family therapy approaches. They also explore extant treatment packages for individually focused treatments (e.g., mindfulness, cognitive analytic therapies). Within this domain, books focus on meeting the information needs of clinicians and professionals who work in youth facilities, emergency rooms, special education, criminal justice, and therapy settings. Finally, books in the third domain address prevention and treatment for groups and society, including topical focus on early intervention programs, school violence prevention programs, policing strategies, juvenile facility reform as well as socio-legal and ethical issues. Books in this series serve as must-have resources for researchers, academics, and upper-level undergraduate and graduate students in clinical child and school psychology, public health, criminology/criminal justice, developmental psychology, psychotherapy/counseling, psychiatry, social work, educational policy and politics, health psychology, nursing, and behavioral therapy/rehabilitation.

Angela Hattery · Earl Smith
Editors

Theories of Family Violence

Springer

Editors
Angela Hattery
Center for the Study & Prevention
of Gender-Based Violence,
Department of Women & Gender Studies
University of Delaware
Newark, DE, USA

Earl Smith
Center for the Study & Prevention
of Gender-Based Violence,
Department of Women & Gender Studies
University of Delaware
Newark, DE, USA

ISSN 2946-4757 ISSN 2946-4765 (electronic)
Advances in Preventing and Treating Violence and Aggression
ISBN 978-3-032-17094-1 ISBN 978-3-032-17095-8 (eBook)
https://doi.org/10.1007/978-3-032-17095-8

This Springer imprint is published by the registered company Springer Nature Switzerland AG
The registered company address is: Gewerbestrasse 11, 6330 Cham, Switzerland

Contents

Contributors

Negar Aghassizadeh Adelphi University, Garden City, NY, USA

John Caffaro Alliant University, San Diego, CA, USA

Lauren C. Camphausen College of Health Sciences, University of Delaware, Newark, DE, USA

Nicole E. Conroy Counseling, Human Development, and Family Science, Department College of Education and Social Services, University of Vermont, Burlington, VT, USA

Walter S. DeKeseredy West Virginia University, Morgantown, WV, USA

Katelyn E. Foltz University of Mississippi, Oxford, MS, USA

Emma Freetly Porter Adelphi University, Garden City, NY, USA

Ruthann Froberg Center for Gerontology, Virginia Tech, Blacksburg, VA, USA

Angela J. Hattery Department of Women and Gender Studies, Center for the Study and Prevention of Gender-Based Violence, University of Delaware, Newark, DE, USA

Jennifer A. Horney College of Health Sciences, University of Delaware, Newark, DE, USA

Katherine Kafonek Stockton University, Galloway, NJ, USA

Kris Marsh University of Maryland, College Park, MD, USA

Jill McCorkel School of Law and Criminology, Maynooth University, Maynooth, County Kildare, Ireland

Monica L. McCoy Converse University, Spartanburg, SC, USA

Maria Paula Mendoza University of Delaware, Newark, DE, USA

Katie Mirance University of Delaware, Newark, DE, USA

Allison E. Monterrosa California State University, San Marcos, CA, USA

Jennifer Naccarelli Department of Women and Gender Studies, Center for the Study and Prevention of Gender-Based Violence, University of Delaware, Newark, DE, USA

Janis Parker Department of History, Villanova University, Villanova, PA, USA

Karen A. Roberto Institute for Society, Culture, and Environment, Blacksburg, VA, USA

Earl Smith Department of Women and Gender Studies, Center for the Study and Prevention of Gender-Based Violence, University of Delaware, Newark, DE, USA

Peter Sturmey The Graduate Center and Queens College, City University of New York, New York, USA;
Brock University, St. Catharines, Ontario, USA;
Endicott University, Massachusetts, USA

Pamela B. Teaster Center for Gerontology, Virginia Tech, Blacksburg, VA, USA

Chapter 1
Introduction to Theories of Family Violence

Angela J. Hattery and Earl Smith

Introduction

In the summer of 2021, Dr. Peter Sturmey reached out to us to invite us to contribute a chapter on theories of family violence for a new handbook he was editing, *ADVANCES IN PREVENTING AND TREATING VIOLENCE AND AGGRESSION.* That series came out in 2022 (Sturmey, 2022), and shortly after, Dr. Sturmey reached out again, this time to gauge our interest in editing a volume focused entirely on theories of family violence.

We were initially hesitant, given our already busy writing schedule, but after speaking with Dr. Sturmey we became convinced that there was a significant need for this type of book and that we had a professional network diverse enough to assemble a volume that covered the breadth of theoretical perspectives utilized by scholars who study the range of forms of family violence.

The chapters in this volume are written by leading scholars in the field of family violence studies and are informed by their own research as well as their command of the literatures in their specific discipline or subdiscipline. However, the book is written in such a way as to be accessible to readers who are new to this field of study as well as for more seasoned scholars who wish to expand their understanding of different theoretical approaches outside of their traditional training. For example, as sociologists, we have much to learn from our colleagues in psychology or public health who approach the same areas of research guided by different theoretical frames that inform the research questions they ask, methodologies and analytical techniques they employ, and policy recommendations they propose.

A. J. Hattery (✉) · E. Smith
Department of Women & Gender Studies, Center for the Study & Prevention of Gender-Based Violence, University of Delaware, Newark, DE, USA
e-mail: hatterya@udel.edu; hatterya@gmail.com

E. Smith
e-mail: smithea@udel.edu

A. Hattery and E. Smith (eds.), *Theories of Family Violence*, Advances in Preventing and Treating Violence and Aggression, https://doi.org/10.1007/978-3-032-17095-8_1

Why Theory?

Theory is important (Bourdieu & Wacquant, 1992; Collins, 2000; Lewin, 1951; Merton, 1968)[1] not only for scholars but also for practitioners and policy makers who are seeking to better understand and address family violence from their various professional vantage points. These different theories provide the frameworks that guide the development of research questions as well as the analysis and interpretation of data. In addition, each provides a different road map for the development of policy recommendations that seek to address various forms of family violence through criminal and civil courts, institutional policies, and legislation. Though they often have overlap, indicative of their interdisciplinarity, they provide distinct and unique ways of understanding the complexities of family violence.

The field of family violence studies crosses many traditional disciplinary lines. And, though some scholars conduct research within their disciplinary bounds, much of the scholarship that is produced is interdisciplinary. Some fields and disciplines have clear applications of their major theories to the study of family violence, for example psychology. Others have been modified by scholars to study phenomena that are neglected or even ignored by their traditional disciplines; for example Black Feminist Criminology was developed in response to a lack of attention to the racialized nature of gendered violence in traditional criminology. Further, some fields are organized around one specific type of violence, such as theories of child abuse and sibling abuse. Finally, some theoretical perspectives, such as feminist theory or theories of public health, are themselves inter-disciplinary. Thus, this book was motivated by our desire, and a demonstrated need, to create a place to consider a variety of different theoretical frames as they are applied to various forms of family violence.

---

[1] 1. Kurt Lewin (1945/1951), "There is nothing so practical as a good theory." This is perhaps the most famous scholarly statement about the importance of theory, widely cited in social sciences.

2. Robert K. Merton (1968), "Theories should be clear, precise, and logically consistent … The importance of theory for sociology can scarcely be exaggerated" (p.39). Merton explicitly ties the progress of sociology to the central role of theory.

3. Patricia Hill Collins (1990/2000), "Black feminist thought demonstrates the importance of theory for empowering people who traditionally have been excluded from thinking theoretically" (p.33).

   Collins highlights how theory is not only important but transformative, especially for marginalized groups.

4. Pierre Bourdieu (1992), "Theory without empirical research is empty, empirical research without theory is blind" (p.162). Bourdieu and Wacquant underline the mutual importance of theory and empirical research.

What Is Family Violence?

For the purposes of this volume and the chapters contained within, family violence refers broadly to any type of interpersonal violence that occurs among family members and/or people living within a household who are not necessarily related. Specifically, family violence includes: (1) violence between intimate or ex-intimate partners, otherwise known as intimate partner violence, (2) abuse between siblings (sibling abuse), (3) child abuse (by parents or caregivers), and (4) elder abuse (abuse by adult children against their aging parents).

As noted, some theories presented in this text focus on a specific type of violence, e.g. child abuse, whereas others take a broader approach and attempt to explain many different forms of family violence. Several chapters focus specifically on what we refer to as "gender-based violence;" this includes intimate partner violence, sexual violence, sexual harassment and stalking. Theories that focus on gender-based violence, including feminist theory, family violence theory, Male Peer Support Theory, and Intersectional/Black Feminist criminology are concerned with the ways in which gender stratification and inequality shapes both the risk for engaging in or being victimized by interpersonal violence as well as the specific form that violence takes.

The authors of each chapter describe and define the types of violence that are relevant to their discussion. And, though the types of violence vary, the strength of the text is its breadth in covering not just a range of theoretical perspectives but also the spectrum of violence that occurs across various family forms. Indeed, the final chapter of the book offers a mandate for expanding our definitions and theories of family violence to include singlehood and chosen families.

The Organization of the Book

The book is organized into three sections: (1) major theories, (2) meso-theories, and (3) specialized theories that focus on one form of family violence. The first section of the book, (1) Major Theories, provides an overview of the primary theories that have been used to study family violence, these include Family Violence Theory (Chap. 2), Feminist Theory (Chap. 3), Criminological Theories (Chap. 4), Psychological Theories (Chap. 5), and Public Health Theories (Chap. 6). Each of these chapters is written to provide a general overview of the theory as well as consider applications of these theories to specific forms of family violence.

The second section of the book, Meso-Theories, is organized around theoretical approaches that draw upon or work at the intersections of the primary theories discussed in section one. These include Intersectional and Black Feminist Criminology (Chap. 7), which combines tenets of both feminist theory and criminological theory, Behavior Analytic Theories (Chap. 8), which is focused at the intersections of psychology and anthropology, and Male Peer Support Theory (Chap. 9) which is derived from theories prominent in sociology, psychology, and feminist studies.

The third and final section of the book, Specialized Theories, is comprised of the applications of various theoretical perspectives to specific forms of family violence, including Theories of Elder Abuse (Chap. 10), Theories of Sibling Abuse (Chap. 11), and Theories of Child Abuse and maltreatment (Chap. 12).

The book begins with the introduction, which you are reading now, and ends with two chapters that address new approaches: Chap. 13 provides an overview of Abolitionist Theories and approaches to addressing Family Violence and Chap. 14, "Where Theories of Family Violence Fall Short" identifies new directions for the field.

Prominent Themes in Family Violence Theory

As noted, each chapter in the text considers family violence from a different theoretical foundation. And yet, across various disciplinary and theoretical lenses, a set of clear and persistent themes emerge. Here we briefly identify several themes and provide examples of the ways they are interrogated across disciplinary and theoretical lines.

Individual Factors and Sociocultural Factors: Most commonly associated with psychological theories of family violence, some disciplines focus on the ways in which individual qualities interact with sociocultural factors that put some individuals at risk for perpetrating various forms of family violence. Not surprisingly, psychological theories focus on the ways in which early experiences impact the development of personality and the unconscious relational patterns. In other words, the ways in which we are socialized in childhood impacts the ways we engage in relationships as adults. And, though these perspectives predominate in psychological theories of family violence, they have been widely adopted by other disciplines as well. For example, two of the most pervasive concepts that emerge from this framework are (1) the intergenerational transmission of violence, and (2) the impact of child witnesses to violence. Criminological theories have focused on the ways in which "deviant" behavior is socialized by both family and peers (for example differential association theory). Male Peer Support Theory focuses explicitly on the ways in which hegemonic ideologies of masculinity are socialized (or not) among men and boys. Feminist theorists and theories of sibling abuse often consider the impact of witnessing violence on children. In theories of sibling abuse, this is used to explain "modeling" that is often at the root of sibling abuse, whereas feminist theories and those studying child abuse focus on the trauma that is inflicted when a child witnesses violence and the impacts that can have on their adult relationships. Psychologists lead the cacophony of voices in identifying childhood exposure to trauma—otherwise known as Adverse Childhood Experiences (ACES)—and examining their impact on mental health and relationality. And this trauma-informed lens is incorporated in many other theories, including feminist theory, intersectional theory, and abolition theory, just to name a few.

Systemic Factors: As common as the emphasis on individual and sociocultural factors may be, many theories of family violence focus on systemic factors, including demographic patterns, other systems of oppression and marginalization, and family structure. Though feminist theories, Intersectional theory, and Abolition theory each turn their attention and focus onto different sites of power and oppression, foundational to each approach is a focus on power. Feminist theorists were the first to articulate the role that gender and gender inequality plays in all forms of family violence, and their focus, at least initially, was on the experiences of women and girls. Intersectional theorists were troubled by this singular focus and demanded that theories of family violence be attentive to the role that race, sexuality and social class also played in shaping the risks for being victimized or engaging in various forms of family violence.

More recently, theories of singlehood demand that we interrogate the very construction of "family" and center the experiences of those that are often rendered invisible—in this case those whose family may be chosen rather than defined by biological or legal ties. Male Peer Support theory locates the promise for reimagining hegemonic masculinity and dismantling heteropatriarchy as one strategy for reducing family violence, and gender-based violence in particular. Finally, abolitionist theory and Black feminist criminology illuminates the role that the criminal legal system plays in perpetuating rather than preventing or even interrupting family violence.

Family violence theory and its focus on power is perhaps the best positioned to explain power across various domains of family violence, including elder abuse, child abuse, sibling abuse, and domestic violence.

Socio-Ecological approaches: Socio-ecological approaches are perhaps best known for shaping not just theory but policy approaches in the realm of public health. Today, the socio-ecological model has been applied to public health campaigns as wide-ranging as those addressing anti-smoking, cancer screenings, and anti-violence. Public health theories of family violence center the socio-ecological model which creates space for examining risks and protective factors at all levels, from the individual to the family to the community to the society. And, this model has been widely taken up by those seeking better frames for not just explaining but also preventing and intervening in all forms of family violence, but specifically child abuse, sibling abuse, and elder abuse. In each of these chapters the socio-ecological model is foregrounded as a tool for describing the data on each of these forms of abuse as well as emergent policy recommendations to address it.

Risk and Protective Factors: Each chapter in this volume in some way or another considers the factors that put individuals, families, and communities at risk for being victimized or engaging in family violence. Risk and protective factors are considered at each level of socio-ecological model. Family violence theorists identify power as a key factor in risk: those in the family with more power (men, adults) are more likely to engage in violence, whereas those with less power (women, children, elders) are more likely to become the victims. Feminist, intersectional, Black feminist, and abolitionist theoretical frames add other systems of oppression to the "power" matrix; interrogating the role that race, social class, sexuality, and adjacency to the criminal legal system play in shaping not only the likelihood that an individual will be victimized or perpetrate violence, but more so the impact on entire communities. For example, in communities with high rates of incarceration, rates of family abuse will be higher. And, in the US these communities are more often than not populated by people who are poor and racially marginalized. As noted, psychological theories—which inform much of the research on child abuse, elder abuse, and sibling abuse—center exposure to ACES and trauma in building theories of risk and protection. And, intersecting with theories of public health, this focus is extended from the individual across all levels of the socio-ecological model.

In sum, though each chapter in this volume takes a distinct approach to theorizing family violence, as a result of the interdisciplinary nature of this field of study, common themes cross a variety of theoretical frames. And, though you can (and should) read this book in any order you choose, it is organized, as noted above, to elucidate the cross-pollination and overlapping concepts that characterize the theories of family violence presented here.

Conclusion

Family violence in its various forms, including intimate partner violence, child abuse, elder abuse, and sibling abuse, pose significant threats to the health and well-being of our families, and thereby to the very fabric of our social institutions. Sadly, despite decades of research, training, and policy innovation, rates of all forms of family violence remain disturbingly high. By gathering the leading experts in the field of the study of family violence and curating this comprehensive volume that provides an overview of each of the theoretical approaches used by scholars, practitioners, and policy makers, we hope to inspire more work in these areas and vision new approaches that will ultimately reduce the prevalence of family violence in the US as well as globally.

References

Bourdieu, P., & Wacquant, L. J. D. (1992). *An invitation to reflexive sociology*. University of Chicago Press.

Collins, P. H. (2000). *Black feminist thought: Knowledge, consciousness, and the politics of empowerment* (2nd ed.). Routledge. (Original work published 1990).

Lewin, K. (1951). *Field theory in social science: Selected theoretical papers*. In D. Cartwright (Ed.), Harper & Row. (Original work published 1945).

Merton, R. K. (1968). *Social theory and social structure* (enlarged ed.). Free Press.
Sturmey, P. (2022). *Violence and aggression: Integrating theory, research, and practice (Advances in preventing and treating violence and aggression)*. Springer.

Chapter 2
Michael Johnson's Typology of Intimate Partner Violence

Nicole E. Conroy

Name of the theory: Johnson's Typology of Intimate Partner Violence
Proponents of the theory: Alison Cares, Nicole Conroy, Janel Leone, Jennifer Hardesty, Megan Haselschwerdt, Bela Nawaz, Sandra Stith
What the theory says: Unlike most intimate partner violence research and theory, Johnson's typology necessitates making distinctions between types of violence specifically determined by the presence or absence of a pattern of coercive control. Intimate terrorism is violence used as one of many tactics of coercive control, wherein the perpetrator's primary goal is to dominate their partner. Situational couple violence, on the other hand, includes the use of physical violence in response to conflict, absent the desire to control one's partner more generally. Another central tenet of the typology is that violence is gendered, with women in heterosexual relationships being more likely to experience fear and injury no matter the type of violence, and with heterosexual men being more likely to perpetrate intimate terrorism against women. Finally, to effectively test the typology, researchers must attend to inherent sampling bias, given that intimate terrorism is more likely to be found in clinical and agency samples, whereas situational couple violence is more likely to be represented in general community samples.

N. E. Conroy (✉)
Counseling, Human Development, and Family Science, Department College of Education and Social Services, University of Vermont, Burlington, VT, USA
e-mail: nconroy@uvm.edu

A. Hattery and E. Smith (eds.), *Theories of Family Violence*, Advances in Preventing and Treating Violence and Aggression, https://doi.org/10.1007/978-3-032-17095-8_2

Introduction

Michael P. Johnson's typology of violence provides a framework for making distinctions between types of intimate partner violence (IPV), rooted in different motivations, characteristics, and consequences. First published in 1995, Johnson's typology facilitated a paradigm shift in how scholars and practitioners think about intimate partner violence (Stith & Spencer, 2024). Today, the typology represents decades of theory development, including empirical testing and modification by Johnson and other scholars of IPV.

Definitions of "intimate partner violence" vary, with some conceptualizations including any act of physical violence or nonphysical abuse that can result in harm (e.g., World Health Organization, 2022).

However, Johnson (2008) specifically defines violence as—and states the intent for the typology to be used for classifying types of—*physical violence.* In Johnson's typology, a pattern of *coercive control* is the distinguishing factor between types of violence. More specifically, *situational couple violence* is used by one or both partners in the context of a particular conflict and typically the result of poor conflict management skills, whereas *intimate terrorism* (or *coercive controlling violence*) is violence used by the perpetrator as one tactic in a broader pattern of coercive control (Johnson, 2006, 2008).

Johnson's typology has been broadly utilized in both research and practice, across academic and professional disciplines. Empirical research on Johnson's typology is primarily published in journals whose disciplinary reach includes family science, psychology, criminology, and women's studies, and whose topical focus is IPV (Careset al., 2024b). Johnson's typology has also been applied in—and been informed by—the work of clinical professionals serving clients who have experienced IPV victimization and/or perpetration, as well as other IPV professionals working in service provision, the criminal justice system, and government agencies (Johnson, 2017). In this way, Johnson's typology has bridged research, policy, and practice across disciplines.

However, Johnson's typology is not universally accepted among scholars of IPV, and there has been relatively limited empirical testing of his typology. Roughly 3% of 2,793 empirical research articles citing Johnson's work incorporate the typology in a way that was central to the analysis (Careset al., 2024b). Similarly, when the typology has been applied to the study of IPV, testing its validity is not a primary aim of the study (Conroyet al., 2024a). However, when considering only empirical studies that have appropriately defined, measured, and analyzed violence and coercive control, the data supports the notion that types of individual violence can be distinguished by the dyadic nature of power and control (Conroyet al., 2024a).

History

Michael Johnson published the first iteration of his typology of IPV in 1995, with the aim of reconciling the longstanding debate among researchers regarding the role of gender in IPV (Johnson, 2006, 2008, 2017). On one side of the debate, family violence scholars conclude that IPV is *not* a gendered phenomenon but a relational problem, with data suggesting that men and women experience comparable rates of violence. On the other side, feminist scholars assert that gender *is* central to understanding IPV, with data suggesting that men disproportionately perpetrate violence against women. Following a critical review of IPV research, however, Johnson offered a unique proposition: Both groups of scholars were failing to consider that there may be two distinct types of violence.

By comparing feminist research using agency samples with family violence research relying on community samples, Johnson found that different sampling strategies corresponded to differences in the frequency, severity, escalation and directionality of violence experienced by respondents—findings that were also differentially gendered (Johnson, 1995, 2008, 2017). Different theoretical orientations and methods resulted in family violence scholars capturing what Johnson initially called *common couple violence* (later called *situational couple violence*). This body of literature evidenced comparable rates of violence for men and women. On the other hand, feminist scholars were tapping into what he called *patriarchal terrorism* (later called *intimate terrorism* or *coercive controlling violence*). This body of literature showed that men disproportionately perpetrated IPV against women. By making distinctions, the typology explicated the important gender differences in IPV that had long been debated.

Also central to the typology is that the types of violence differ based on the dynamics of power and control in the relationship. *Situational couple violence* (SCV) is characteristic of conflicts that escalate and become violent but do not include a desire to generally control one's partner. SCV is perpetrated at comparable rates by men and women and is more likely to—but not always—be relatively minor and infrequent. In contrast, *intimate terrorism* (IT) involves violence as one of many tactics used in the context of a relationship with ongoing, systematic use of *coercive control* by one partner over the other. IT is disproportionately perpetrated by men against women and is more likely to be severe, escalate over time, and result in fear and injury. Johnson's novel way of thinking about IPV was viewed by other feminist family scholars as a potential turning point in the study of violence in family science (Thompson & Walker, 1995).

Since its inception, Johnson has called for empirical testing of his typology. Over time, the typology has gone through multiple iterations, including changes in terminology and additional classifications of violence (Johnson, 2017). In 1999, Johnson published the first empirical test of his typology using data previously collected by feminist psychologist, Irine Frieze (1983), who had studied women's experiences of victimization and perpetration of both physical violence and nonviolent control among a random community sample of women as well as women who had utilized shelter and/or court services. Frieze's sampling strategy eliminated the sampling bias that Johnson argued was at the heart of the gender debate in IPV research, providing a unique opportunity to test his typology. As Johnson expected, violent relationships with the highest levels of coercive control (i.e., intimate terrorism) were captured by the agency and court samples, whereas violent relationships captured in the community sample were characterized by little to no controlling behaviors (i.e., situational couple violence).

At around the same time, Johnson also adopted new terminology. *Intimate terrorism* replaced the term *patriarchal terrorism* to clarify that not all violence paired with coercive control is rooted in patriarchal motives; there are a multitude of power structures and dynamics that can underly one's coercive control and violence against another. Despite this clarification, some researchers continue to erroneously assert that Johnson and his typology only account for patriarchal motives for IT and that IT is solely defined as male-perpetrated violence. *Common couple violence* was also changed to *situational couple violence* (SCV) in response to misinterpretation that SCV was seen by Johnson as acceptable, and to clarify that this type of violence is situation-specific and not rooted in coercive control. Shortly thereafter, Johnson expanded the typology to include two additional types of violence, *violent resistance* and *mutual violent control*, to further capture the dyadic nature of relationship power and control dynamics. In 2008, Johnson published a book detailing the development of his typology, the rationale for his conceptualizations of each type of violence, the key assumptions at the heart of the typology, and methodological recommendations for empirically testing them. What started as some "common sense" published in "an odd paper, with a bit of a literature review to it, some quirky statistical manipulations, and a lot of theoretical speculation," as Johnson describes it (2017, p. 152), the typology has evolved into a theoretical framework that has received extensive attention among researchers, practitioners, and policy makers aiming to understand and respond to IPV.

Empirical evidence also supports the extension of Johnson's typology. For example, some teens and young adults in heterosexual dating relationships report responding to their partner's *nonviolent* coercive control with physical violence, evidence of unique relationship dynamics of control and violence not originally accounted for in Johnson's definition of violent resistance (Conroy & Crowley, 2022; Zweig et al., 2014). Similarly, some scholars suggest that there is good reason to consider expanding the typology beyond its original focus on classifying types of *physical violence*, given the deleterious effects of nonviolent coercive control on its own (Careset al., 2024a; Conroy & Crowley, 2022; Crossman et al., 2016). Although not included in the typology itself, Johnson (2008) acknowledges the power of nonviolent coercive control, calling it *incipient intimate terrorism*. Additionally, *familial intimate terrorism* has been identified as an additional type of violence in Pakistan, wherein male intimate terrorists are generally controlling and rely on tactics rooted in joint family systems that legitimize and reinforce husbands' control over their wives (Nawaz & Johnson, 2024).

Despite long-lasting influence on research and practice, the empirical research testing Johnson's typology appears to be inconclusive three decades after its inception, with seemingly contradictory findings about the role of gender in IPV. However, two systematic reviews of the empirical research on Johnson's typology help to explain these findings, providing greater clarity regarding the validity of Johnson's typology and insight into the ongoing gender debate. Out of 78 empirical studies that tested Johnson's typology, more than 40% are characterized by conceptual misrepresentations and/or erroneous operationalizations of the typology (Conroy et al., 2024b). These methodological flaws, some of which are rooted in ideologically biased motivations, ultimately preclude the ability to support or refute Johnson's theoretical assumptions about IPV (Johnson, 2017; Conroy et al., 2024b).

Similarly, oversimplified conceptualizations and measurement of gender results in published research that fails to account for the nuanced ways that gender influences experiences of IPV, in general and when testing Johnson's typology specifically (Anderson, 2005). On the other hand, when studies with correct conceptualization and operationalization of the typology are considered, the empirical support for Johnson's typology is clear and validates the need for making distinctions (Conroyet al., 2024a). Nonetheless, additional research with the primary aim of testing the typology is warranted.

Key Tenets

There is more than one type of intimate partner violence, distinguishable by the context of power and control. Central to Johnson's typology is the supposition that IPV is not a unitary phenomenon; rather, there are distinct types of violence that have long been erroneously conflated with one another (Johnson, 1995, 2008). The distinctions between types of violence are rooted in relationship dynamics of power and control, specifically a pattern of coercive control or absence thereof. As a typology of *violence,* it is intended for classifying an individual's use of physical violence (Johnson, 2008). *Coercive control* is characterized by ongoing, systematic use of control tactics, such as emotional control and abuse, intimidation, monitoring and surveillance, economic abuse, isolation, and other strategies rooted in unequal power dynamics between partners (Johnson, 2008). Coercive control is distinct from other types of situation-specific emotional or psychological abuse. Of note, however, many researchers erroneously conflate violence with nonphysical acts of abuse and more minor types of emotional abuse with coercive control when testing Johnson's typology (Conroy et al., 2024b; Johnson, 2005).

Situational couple violence (SCV) is when at least one partner uses physical violence and coercive control is not present in the relationship (Johnson, 2008). *Intimate terrorism* (IT)—also called *coercive controlling violence*—refers to the perpetration of physical violence by a coercively controlling individual, capturing what is often referred to as "battering" or "domestic violence" in popular conversations and depictions of IPV (Johnson, 2008). *Violent resistance* is violence used by victims of IT (Johnson, 2008).

Violent resistance can include retributive acts of violence and/or violence used as an immediate response to their partner's abuse. Emerging research suggests that victims may also use violent resistance (physical violence) in response to a partner's perpetration of coercive control absent the use of physical violence, i.e., *nonviolent coercive control* (Conroy & Crowley, 2022; Zweig et al., 2014). *Mutual violent control* is characterized by bidirectional use of physical violence and coercive control. Mutual violent control is exceedingly rare, showing up in very small numbers in quantitative studies (Johnson, 2008). Originally conceptualized as bidirectional violence between two intimate terrorists, it is more likely to be representative of a relationship with one intimate terrorist and the partner utilizing a counter-control tactic or violent resistance (i.e., the victim is not otherwise motivated to control their partner; Johnson, 2017).

Using data from female survivors in Pakistan, an additional type of IPV has been identified, beyond what has been found in samples from the United States. *Familial intimate terrorism* (Nawaz & Johnson, 2024), as the name implies, is similar in many ways to IT, including the use of physical violence and broad use of control. However, familial intimate terrorists may be less likely to use control tactics such as intimidation, isolation, sexual control, and jealousy than other intimate terrorists, and their general attempts to control their partner are sanctioned by the joint family system; in many cases, in-laws also perpetrate physical violence against the wife. Unlike the other types of violence, familial intimate terrorism necessitates consideration of relationship dynamics beyond the dyad to include dynamics within the joint family system.

Different sampling strategies capture different types of violence. Johnson's (1995, 2008) typology is rooted in the assumption that different methods of sampling will generally capture different types of violence. Samples drawn from community samples and that typically rely on survey data are most likely to tap into SCV, whereas samples from intervention settings, such as shelters, emergency rooms, law enforcement, and courts, are most likely to capture IT (Johnson, 1995, 2008; Conroy et al., 2024b). In this way, differences in sampling strategies will result in a particular type of violence being overrepresented. Sampling strategies, however, are not intended to be used as a means of classifying types of violence. For example, victims of the most severe SCV may also utilize clinical and agency services, and participants reporting on past relationships in community samples are more likely to participate in general surveys and disclose experiences of IT compared to those currently experiencing IT (Johnson, 2008; Johnson et al., 2014).

Situational Couple Violence and Intimate Terrorism Differ in Motives, Trajectories, and Outcomes. Johnson's typology distinguishes between types of violence based on power and control dynamics in the relationship, specifically whether there is a pattern of coercive control. SCV occurs in the context of conflict that escalates to the use of physical violence by one or both partners, without attempts to more generally control one's partner (i.e., coercive control is not part of the relationship dynamic; Johnson, 2008). SCV is often the result of poor conflict resolution skills. In contrast, IT is motivated by the perpetrator's desire to control their partner and is rooted in patriarchal norms, particularly in the context of heterosexual relationships (Conroyet al., 2024a; Johnson, 2008).

Compared to SCV, IT is more likely to be frequent and severe, to escalate over time, and to result in injury, fear, and other negative physical and psychological outcomes (Conroyet al., 2024a; Johnson, 2008). These differences are not absolute, however, and should not be used to classify types of violence. For example, it is possible for SCV to be relatively frequent and so severe as to be lethal, and intimate terrorists may use infrequent and/or minor acts of violence, especially when they have established themselves as a legitimate threat to their partner's safety and wellbeing (Johnson, 2008).

Intimate partner violence is gendered. Johnson's typology has been overwhelmingly applied to IPV in heterosexual relationships, reflecting the focus of IPV research in general. In heterosexual relationships, men are disproportionately the perpetrators of IT, whereas men and women are equally likely to perpetrate SCV (Conroyet al., 2024a; Johnson, 2008). Compared to men, women are more likely to experience injury, fear, and other negative outcomes from SCV or IT victimization (Conroyet al., 2024a; Johnson, 2008). Cunningham and Anderson (2024) explain, "When we consider IPV experienced over the lifetime, the debate about gender symmetry vs. asymmetry is resolved: in different-gender relationships... the forms of restrictive violent entrapment that terrorize victims [intimate terrorism] are disproportionately perpetrated by men against women" (p. 100).

Contributions to the Study of Family Violence

Johnson's typology has changed the way people think about IPV, aiding researchers and practitioners to better understand that there is more than one type of IPV. Research that has accurately represented and tested Johnson's typology provides support for making distinctions between types of violence, as well as the effects of sampling strategies on which types of violence will be represented in participant reports (e.g., Love et al., 2020). Moreover, existing research that accurately represents the theoretical assumptions of the typology supports the premise that IPV is gendered in nuanced ways. In particular, evidence suggests that men are more likely to perpetrate IT, whereas SCV is equally likely to be perpetrated by women and men (e.g., Johnson et al., 2014). Findings also validate the assumptions that IT is more likely to be frequent, severe, and to escalate over time (Haselschwerdt et al., 2019; Leone et al., 2007) and, unlike SCV, is motivated by a desire to control one's partner (Frankland & Brown, 2014). Research also supports the idea that heterosexual men and women experience different outcomes associated with IPV (e.g., Lysova et al., 2019), and IT typically results in more deleterious outcomes for victims (e.g., Anderson, 2008; Hardesty et al., 2016).

More recently, Johnson's typology is also being applied to relationship contexts beyond white, heterosexual married couples, which has been the focus of Johnson's work and in IPV research more generally. For example, the utility of Johnson's typology has been tested in the study of teen dating violence, young adult dating violence, and same-sex couples, providing preliminary support for the validity of the typology across relationship contexts (Conroyet al., 2024a). The differential experiences of IT and SCV have also been found among racial and ethnic minorities in the United States (Bubriski-McKenzie & Jasinski, 2013; Leone, 2011) and across cultures (Graham-Kevan et al., 2012; Nawaz & Johnson, 2024; Tiwari et al., 2015). Johnson's typology has also been utilized in the study of children's exposure to IPV, which sheds light on the deleterious effects of exposure on parent–child relationships and its associations with child abuse, as well as the nuanced ways that exposure to IT and SCV can influence their own future romantic relationships (Haselschwerdt et al., 2019, 2020, 2021).

Research Methods

Since its inception, Johnson's typology has been tested qualitatively, quantitatively, and with mixed-method designs; with general community samples, clinical/agency samples, and with mixed samples; and utilizing a variety of measures to capture experiences of violence and coercive control (Conroyet al., 2024a). However, empirical tests of Johnson's typology represent only about 3% of the scholarly literature that reference Johnson's typology in some way (Careset al., 2024b). And of the limited empirical research that tests Johnson's typology, over 40% is plagued by misuses of Johnson's typology, including flawed representations of its key tenets and corresponding methodological missteps (Conroy et al., 2024b).

The most common methodological errors include (i) failing to measure coercive control or conflating other types of emotional abuse with coercive control, despite the typology's premise being that coercive control, specifically, distinguishes between types of violence; (ii) classifying types of violence based on the frequency, severity, and patterns of escalation, rather than the context of coercive control or (iii) based solely on the type of sample used; (iv) using reports of nonviolent aggression or emotional abuse to classify a relationship as violent, despite the typology being intended for use with physically violent relationships, and (v) using cluster analysis to classify respondents from community samples into low/no control and high/coercive control groups, which is then used to identify SCV, IT, violent resistance, and mutual violent control (Conroy et al., 2024b). Due to the nature of cluster analysis, a "low" and "high" group will always be found; however, in a community sample, the identification of a "high" control group, and the subsequent erroneous over-classification of IT, is an artifact of the inherent sampling bias of a group of respondents reporting relatively little to no control (Johnson, 2008, 2017).

More generally, IPV researchers also overwhelmingly fail to make distinctions between types of violence altogether, despite evidence that IPV is not a unitary phenomenon (Johnson, 2017).

As a result of these methodological errors, a cursory look at the scholarly literature might suggest that IPV is not a gendered phenomenon, with evidence for and against the idea that men and women experience IPV in different ways (Anderson, 2008; Conroy et al., 2024b; Johnson, 2017). However, the subset of empirical research with conceptual accuracy and appropriate methods for testing Johnson's typology overwhelmingly provides evidence in support of the key tenets of the typology (Conroyet al., 2024a). Moving forward, to fairly assess Johnson's typology and contribute to its development, researchers must accurately represent the tenets of the typology, conceptually and methodologically, including sampling, measurement, and analysis. In doing so, we can deepen our understanding of the distinctions between types of IPV.

Johnson (2008) provides recommendations for avoiding these methodological missteps, including:

(1) *Measuring physical violence for both partners.* Testing the typology necessitates measuring physical acts of violence. The Revised Conflict Tactics Scale (CTS2; Straus et al., 1996) is the most used measure of physical partner violence (Conroyet al., 2024a). Of the CTS2, researchers should use only the "physical assault" subscale and/or items from the "sexual coercion" subscale that measure use of physical force. While information about the nature and pattern of violence should not be used to classify types of violence, researchers should collect and analyze data regarding the frequency, severity, and escalation of violence over time if they want to test the theoretical assumption that IT and SCV typically differ on these characteristics. (2) *Measuring coercive control (correctly) for both partners.* The different types of violence in the typology are determined solely by the power and control dynamics in the relationship. This necessitates the measurement of coercive control, including questions about each partner's general use of control tactics, such as threats for noncompliance, wearing down a partner's will to resist via tactics that degrade their self-worth, monitoring their partner's behavior, isolation from support networks, and financial control (Johnson, 2008). The Psychological Maltreatment of Women Inventory (PMWI; Tolman, 1999) is the most used measure of coercive control in studies testing Johnson's typology (Conroyet al., 2024a). In quantitative studies using mixed agency samples and general community samples, cluster analysis can be useful for identifying high levels of coercive control, since true cases of IT are likely to be captured by the agency sample. In general samples, however, the likelihood of capturing IT increases if respondents can report on past relationships (Johnson et al., 2014). Otherwise, since there is no determined cut-off score for any standardized measures of coercive control, Johnson (2008) suggests using control scale scores two standard deviations above the sample mean to identify high coercive control in general samples. Hardesty et al. (2015) recommend a score of 19 as a conservative cutoff for the PMWI, as well as measuring the frequency of coercive control rather than the number of tactics, since the latter approach seems to misclassify IT in general

samples. Ultimately, however, Johnson (2008) recommends qualitative validation of coercive control in general samples.

Assessment

Johnson's typology is intended, first and foremost, to facilitate making distinctions between types of violence. Johnson (2008) argues that: "We desperately need a concerted effort to redress the imbalance of [more than] thirty years of research by hundreds of scholars who did not make distinctions vs. a few years of research by a few scholars who did" (p. 85). This remains true of IPV research today, where limited empirical testing of Johnson's typology has resulted in a continued impasse between researchers on the role of gender in IPV (Careset al., 2024a, 2024b; Conroyet al., 2024a). However, if the typology is tested with valid measures and appropriate analyses of violence and control dynamics of a relationship, it is useful for lines of inquiry related to the role of gender in IPV, in heterosexual, same-sex, and other queer relationships, and across culture. The typology also provides an appropriate framework for examining the effects of exposure to different types of violence for children and other family members, as well as for examining the effectiveness of prevention and intervention efforts across sectors, including policy and practice.

Practical Applications

Johnson's typology has had a great influence on clinical practice with individuals and couples seeking treatment. Prior to Johnson's typology, and still today, it is not uncommon for interventions to operate under the assumption that IPV is synonymous with intimate terrorism (Johnson, 2008). For example, it was common practice for mental health professionals to assess for IPV when couples sought therapy, as conjoint therapy was deemed inappropriate and unsafe for couples experiencing IPV, again operating under the assumption that clients seeking services were experiencing IT, with men as the perpetrators and women as the victims (Stith & Spencer, 2024). These assumptions reflect the tendency to erroneously treat all IPV the same without making distinctions, and they mirror the sampling bias in research discussed above, i.e., that IT victims are more likely to seek out services. Johnson's typology, however, brought to light the relative commonality of SCV and raised the possibility that conjoint therapy is an appropriate intervention for SCV (and confirming that it is unsafe for victims of IT).

In a review of research on conjoint treatment for IPV, Stith et al. (2003) determined that conjoint treatment is safe for victims of SCV and can be effective at eliminating IPV in the relationship altogether. To ensure safety, Stith et al. (2020) emphasize the need for screening to ensure that couples seeking treatment are experiencing SCV and not IT, as well as the importance of safety protocol, such as a plan for instances where conflict or violence escalates as well as therapists discussing each partner's comfortability with conjoint therapy throughout the process. These protocols are essential components of Domestic Violence Focused Couples Therapy (DVFCT), which can be adapted for effective treatment across cultural contexts (Stith et al., 2020). Others have extended this work to consider SCV through the lens of attachment theory, wherein Emotionally Focused Therapy (EFT) is proposed as an appropriate conjoint treatment model for couples whose SCV is rooted in attachment-related experiences or mismatched relationship needs (Schneider & Brimhall, 2014; Slootmaeckers & Migerode, 2020).

Regardless of the specific therapeutic intervention, practitioners agree that screening for IPV type is essential for determining the appropriateness of conjoint therapy, specifically that any concern of IT deems such therapy to be inappropriate, and that ongoing monitoring for escalation of violence and comfortability of both partners is necessary for ensuring safety (e.g., Karakurt et al., 2016; Rosenthal & Dehle, 2025). Finally, although there is broad acceptance of the need for making distinctions between types of IPV in clinical settings, there is limited empirical research on the application of Johnson's typology in therapeutic interventions. As such, empirical research on therapeutic interventions with IPV perpetrators, victims, and couples is warranted to better understand ways to best promote client safety and effectively reduce violence perpetration for both SCV and IT.

Critiques

The body of empirical research that accurately uses Johnson's typology overwhelmingly supports the basic tenets: there are meaningful differences in intimate terrorism and situational couple violence, with intimate terrorism being rooted in a desire to control one's partner, significantly more likely to be perpetrated by men in heterosexual relationships, and more likely to result in deleterious outcomes for victims (Conroyet al., 2024a). However, the typology and the research that has applied it are not without limitations. Even among its proponents, scholars have critiqued the typology for its focus on violent relationships, considering the effectiveness of and negative outcomes associated with coercive control even without the use of physical violence (Anderson, 2008; Crossman et al., 2016). Although it is not formally part of the typology, Johnson (2008) acknowledges the potential for nonviolent coercive control to be a meaningful predictor of IT ("incipient intimate terrorism") and, thus, worthy of study; others argue for the inclusion of nonviolent coercive control as an appropriate addition to the typology, in its own right (Careset al.,2024a; Conroy & Crowley, 2022).

The typology's origins are deeply rooted in an understanding of gender and patriarchal norms that reflect the experiences of cisgender people in heterosexual relationships. The emphasis on cis-heterosexual couples has been identified as a limiting factor to Johnson's typology and scholars' engagement with it (Bermea & van Eeden-Moorefield, 2024; Conroy, 2024a). For example, the typology's reliance on cis-heteronormative understandings of gendered power dynamics occludes the unique abuse tactics used in queer relationships, including but not limited to the tactics used against transgender partners by cisgender partners (Bermea & van Eeden-Moorefield, 2024).

Similarly, the typology has been criticized for its overemphasis on dynamics of power and control being tied so closely to gender, without consideration of the multiple, intersecting influences on power in any given relationship, such as race, ethnicity, culture, socioeconomic status, and disability (Careset al.,2024a). Moving forward, studying the typology's applicability across relationship contexts in ways that consider the many manifestations of power and control, including and beyond the role of gender, and across cultural contexts will deepen our understanding of how to distinguish between, prevent, and respond to different types of violence.

Conclusions

Michael Johnson's typology of violence provides a valuable theoretical framework for distinguishing between different forms of IPV based on the relationship context of power and control. Developed in 1995 to address the contentious debate over the role of gender in IPV, the typology has garnered broad attention by researchers and practitioners. Yet, despite its prominence, the gender debate endures—largely due to limited empirical testing and widespread misuses of the typology, including conceptual distortions and flawed methodologies. However, when applied with theoretical precision and empirical rigor, Johnson's framework supports the conclusion that IPV is not a monolithic phenomenon but consists of distinct types with unique causes, dynamics, and consequences. To attend to the critiques identified above and to expand the body of literature that provides evidence for validating, revising, or otherwise extending Johnson's typology—and to inform policy and practice—additional empirical research is warranted.

References

Anderson, K. L. (2005). Theorizing gender in intimate partner research. *Sex Roles, 52*, 853–865. https://doi.org/10.1007/s11199-005-4204-x

Anderson, K. L. (2008). Is partner violence worse in the context of control? *Journal of Marriage and Family, 70*(5), 1157–1168. https://doi.org/10.1111/j.1741-3737.2008.00557.x

Bermea, A. M., & van Eeden-Moorefeld, B. (2024). Conceptualizing Johnson's typology of intimate partner violence in queer relationships. *Journal of Family Violence, 39*. https://doi.org/10.1007/s10896-023-00494-x

Bubriski-McKenzie, A., & Jasinski, J. L. (2013). Mental health effects of intimate terrorism and situational couple violence among black and hispanic women. *Violence Against Women, 19*(12), 1429–1448. https://doi.org/10.1177/1077801213517515

Cares, A. C., Haselschwerdt, M. L., Hardesty, J. L., & Few-Demo, A. L. (2024a). After all this time: Clarifying misconceptions and charting clear directions for the next 25 years of Johnson's typology. *Journal of Family Violence, 39*, 1–8. https://doi.org/10.1007/s10896-023-00669-6

Cares, A., Khallouq, B. A. B., & Mukazhanova-Powell, K. (2024b). The reach of Johnson's typology of intimate partner violence: A scoping review of empirical research, 1996–2020. *Journal of Family Violence, 39*, 9–21. https://doi.org/10.1007/s10896-023-00602-x

Conroy, N. E., & Crowley, C. G. (2022). Extending Johnson's typology: Additional manifestations of dating violence and coercive control. *Journal of Interpersonal Violence, 37*, NP13315–NP13341. https://doi.org/10.1177/08862605211005149

Conroy, N. E., Crowley, C. G., & DeSanto, D. L. (2024a). Assessing the state of empirical research on Johnson's typology of violence: A systematic review. *Journal of Family Violence, 39*, 23–45. https://doi.org/10.1007/s10896-022-00416-3

Conroy, N. E., Griffin, S. M., Crowley, C. G., & DeSanto, D. L. (2024b). Conceptual misrepresentations and methodological misapplications: A systematic review of misuses of Johnson's typology of violence. *Journal of Family Violence, 39*, 47–63. https://doi.org/10.1007/s10896-023-00514-w

Crossman, K. A., Hardesty, J. L., & Raffaelli, M. (2016). He could scare me without laying a hand on me. *Violence Against Women, 22*(4), 454–473. https://doi.org/10.1177/1077801215604744

Cunningham, M., & Anderson, K. L. (2024). Union status, union dissolution, and intimate partner violence: Investigating Johnson's typology among heterosexual dating, cohabiting, and married couples. *Journal of Family Violence, 39*(1), 91–103. https://doi.org/10.1007/s10896-022-00448-9

Frankland, A., & Brown, J. (2014). Coercive control in same-sex intimate partner violence. *Journal of Family Violence, 29*(1), 15–22. https://doi.org/10.1007/s10896-013-9558-1

Frieze, I. H. (1983). Investigating the causes and consequences of marital rape. *Signs, 8*(3), 532–553. https://www.jstor.org/stable/3173950

Graham-Kevan, N., Zacarias, A. E., & Soares, J. J. F. (2012). Investigating violence and control dyadically in a help-seeking sample from Mozambique. *The Scientific World, 2012*, 590973–591012. https://doi.org/10.1100/2012/590973

Hardesty, J. L., Crossman, K. A., Haselschwerdt, M. L., Raffaelli, M., Ogolsky, B. G., & Johnson, M. P. (2015). Toward a standard approach to operationalizing coercive control and classifying violence types. *Journal of Marriage and Family, 77*(4), 833–843. https://doi.org/10.1111/jomf.12201

Hardesty, J. L., Crossman, K. A., Khaw, L., & Raffaelli, M. (2016). Marital violence and coparenting quality after separation. *Journal of Family Psychology, 30*(3), 320–330. https://doi.org/10.1037/fam0000132

Haselschwerdt, M. L., Hlavaty, K., Carlson, C., Schneider, M., Maddox, L., & Skipper, M. (2019). Heterogeneity within domestic violence exposure: Young adults' retrospective experiences. *Journal of Interpersonal Violence, 34*(7), 1512–1538. https://doi.org/10.1177/0886260516651625

Haselschwerdt, M. L., Maddox, L., & Hlavaty, K. (2020). Young adult women's perceptions of their maritally violent fathers. *Family Relations, 69*(2), 335–350. https://doi.org/10.1111/fare.12406

Haselschwerdt, M. L., Carlson, C. E., & Hlavaty, K. (2021). The romantic relationship experiences of young adult women exposed to domestic violence. *Journal of Interpersonal Violence, 36*(7–8), 3065–3092. https://doi.org/10.1177/0886260518771679

Johnson, M. P. (1995). Patriarchal terrorism and common couple violence: Two forms of violence against women. *Journal of Marriage and Family, 57*, 283–294. https://doi.org/10.2307/353683

Johnson, M. P. (2005). Domestic violence: It's not About gender—Or is it? *Journal of Marriage and Family, 67*, 1126–1130. https://doi.org/10.1111/j.1741-3737.2005.00204.x

Johnson, M. P. (2006). Conflict and control: Gender symmetry and asymmetry in domestic violence. *Violence Against Women, 12*(11), 1003–1018. https://doi.org/10.1177/1077801206293328

Johnson, M. P. (2008). *A typology of domestic violence: Intimate terrorism, violent resistance, and situational couple violence.* Northeastern University Press.

Johnson, M. P. (2017). A personal social history of a typology of intimate partner violence. *Journal of Family Theory & Review, 9*, 150–164. https://doi.org/10.1111/jftr.12187

Johnson, M. P., Leone, J. M., & Xu, Y. (2014). Intimate terrorism and situational couple violence in general surveys: Ex-spouses required. *Violence against Women, 20*(2), 186–207. https://doi.org/10.1177/1077801214521324

Karakurt, G., Whiting, K., Van Esch, C., Bolen, S. D., & Calabrese, J. R. (2016). Couples therapy for intimate partner violence: A systematic review and meta-analysis. *Journal of Marital and Family Therapy, 42*(4), 567–583. https://doi.org/10.1111/jmft.12178

Leone, J. M. (2011). Suicidal behavior among low-income, African American female victims of intimate terrorism and situational couple violence. *Journal of Interpersonal Violence, 26*(13), 2568–2591. https://doi.org/10.1177/0886260510388280

Leone, J. M., Johnson, M. P., & Cohan, C. L. (2007). Victim help seeking: Differences between intimate terrorism and situational couple violence. *Family Relations, 56*(5), 427–439. https://doi.org/10.1111/j.1741-3729.2007.00471.x

Love, H. A., Spencer, C. M., May, S. A., Mendez, M., & Stith, S. M. (2020). Perpetrator risk markers for intimate terrorism and situational couple violence: A meta-analysis. *Trauma, Violence, & Abuse, 21*(5), 922–931. https://doi.org/10.1177/1524838018801331

Lysova, A., Dim, E. E., & Dutton, D. (2019). Prevalence and consequences of intimate partner violence in Canada as measured by the national victimization survey. *Partner Abuse, 10*(2), 199–221. https://doi.org/10.1891/1946-6560.10.2.199

Nawaz, B., & Johnson, M. P. (2024). Types of domestic violence in Pakistan: Elaborating on Johnson's typology. *Journal of Family Violence, 39*, 133–141. https://doi.org/10.1007/s10896-022-00420-7

Rosenthal, M. N., & Dehle, C. (2025). Treating situational couple aggression: An integrative behavioral couple therapy approach. *Family Process, 64*(1), Article e70021. https://doi.org/10.1111/famp.70021

Schneider, C., & Brimhall, A. S. (2014). From scared to repaired: Using an attachment-based eprspective to understand situational couple violence. *Journal of Marital and Family Therapy, 40*, 367–379. https://doi.org/10.1111/jmft.12023

Slootmaeckers, J., & Migerode, L. (2020). EFT and intimate partner violence: A roadmap to de-escalating violent patterns. *Family Process, 59*(2), 328–345. https://doi.org/10.1111/famp.12468

Stith, S. M., Rosen, K. H., & McCollum, E. E. (2003). Effectiveness of couples treatment for spouse abuse. *Journal of Marital and Family Therapy, 29*, 407–426. https://doi.org/10.1111/j.1752-0606.2003.tb01215.x

Stith, S. M., Spencer, C. M., Ripoll-Núñez, K. J., Jaramillo-Sierra, A. L., Khodadadi-Andariyeh, F., Nikparvar, F., Oksman, R., & Metelinen, J. (2020). International adaptation of a treatment program for situational couple violence. *Journal of Marital and Family Therapy, 46*(2), 272–288. https://doi.org/10.1111/jmft.12397

Stith, S. M., & Spencer, C. (2024). Commentary: 25 years after Johnson's typology of intimate partner violence: The impact of Johnson's typology on clinical work. *Journal of Family Violence, 39*, 143–148. https://doi.org/10.1007/s10896-023-00654-z

Straus, M. A., Hamby, S. L., Boney-McCoy, S., & Sugarman, D. B. (1996). The revised Conflict Tactics Scales (CTS2): Development and preliminary psychometric data. *Journal of Family Issues, 17*(3), 283–316. https://doi.org/10.1177/019251396017003001

Thompson, L., & Walker, A. J. (1995). The place of feminism in family studies. *Journal of Marriage and the Family, 57*, 847–965. https://doi.org/10.2307/353407

Tiwari, A., Chan, K. L., Cheung, D. S. T., Fong, D. Y. T., Yan, E. W., & Tang, D. H. M. (2015). The differential effects of intimate terrorism and situational couple violence on mental health outcomes among abused Chinese women: A mixed-method study. *BMC Public Health, 15*(1), 314. https://doi.org/10.1186/s12889-015-1649-x

Tolman, R. M. (1999). The validation of the psychological maltreatment of women inventory. *Violence and Victims, 14*(1), 25–37. https://doi.org/10.1891/0886-6708.14.1.25

World Health Organization. (2022). *Intimate partner violence*. https://apps.who.int/violence-info/intimate-partner-violence/

Zweig, J. M., Yahner, J., Dank, M., & Lachman, P. (2014). Can Johnson's typology of adult partner violence apply to teen dating violence? *Journal of Marriage and Family, 76*(4), 808–825. https://doi.org/10.1111/jomf.12121

Chapter 3
Feminist Theories of Family Violence

Jennifer Naccarelli

Name of the theory: Feminist Theories
Proponents of the theory: Liberal Feminism: Susan B. Anthony, Cynthis Fuchs Epstein, Betty Friedan, Arlie Hochschild, Lucrecia Mott, Barbara Risman, Elizabeth Cady Stanton, Mary Wollstonecraft.
Radical Feminism: Mary Daly, Andrea Dworkin, Shulamith Firestone, Carol Hanish, Liz Kelly, Catharine MacKinnon, Kate Millet.
Intersectional Feminism: Gloria Anzaldúa, Kimberly Crenshaw, Patricia Hill Collins, bell hooks, Beth Richie, Barbara Smith, Rebecca Walker.
Postmodern/Queer Feminism: Judith Butler, Donna Haraway, Judith Lorber, Julia Kristeva, Hélène Cixous, Luce Irigaray, Gayle Rubin.
What the theory says: Feminism is both a social movement and a theoretical approach focused on the origins of gender inequality and approaches to reducing its prevalence and impact. In the simplest of terms, the goal of feminism is to achieve equality between men and women (Lorber, 2010). Critical to the persistence of inequality is the utilization of physical, sexual, and psychological violence, predominantly perpetrated by men against women. Feminist theories provide us with the language to understand and potentially prevent such violence as they demonstrate how violence against women is central to establishing and sustaining male dominance. Feminist understandings of gender, patriarchy, and power are critical to understanding the role that violence plays in sustaining gender inequality. "Feminist Theor(ies)" include liberal feminism, radical feminism, intersectional feminism, and post-modern and queer feminism.

J. Naccarelli (✉)
Department of Women & Gender Studies, Center for the Study & Prevention of Gender-Based Violence, University of Delaware, Newark, DE, USA
e-mail: jnacc@udel.edu

A. Hattery and E. Smith (eds.), *Theories of Family Violence*, Advances in Preventing and Treating Violence and Aggression, https://doi.org/10.1007/978-3-032-17095-8_3

Introduction

Feminism is both a social movement and a theoretical approach focused on the origins of gender inequality and approaches to reducing its prevalence and impact. In the simplest of terms, the goal of feminism is to achieve equality between men and women (Lorber, 2010). Critical to the persistence of inequality is the utilization of physical, sexual, and psychological violence, predominantly perpetrated by men against women. Feminist theories provide us with the language to understand and potentially prevent such violence as they demonstrate how violence against women is central to establishing and sustaining male dominance. Feminist understandings of gender, patriarchy, and power are critical to understanding the role that violence plays in sustaining gender inequality.

The Context

In 1987 sociologist Liz Kelly introduced the concept of the "continuum of sexual violence" arguing that women experience multiple forms of violence across the lifespan that range from harassment to sexual assault (Kelly, 1987). The most pervasive form is relationship violence, commonly referred to as Domestic Violence (DV) or Intimate Partner Violence (IPV). Along with child abuse, elder abuse and sibling abuse, DV/IPV is a primary form of family violence (Hattery et al., 2023). DV/IPV is "a pattern of abusive behavior in any relationship that is used by one partner to gain or maintain power and control over another intimate partner" (Office on Violence Against Women, 2025). This abusive behavior includes "physical, sexual, emotional, economic, psychological, or technological actions or threats of actions" that combine and escalate over time, leaving an individual isolated and embedded in a cycle of abuse (Office on Violence Against Women, 2025). Along with sexual assault, feminist activists and theoreticians view these forms of violence as outcomes of male domination and mechanisms of its perpetuation. While a many forms of family violence, sexual and intimate partner violence are not limited to the context of the family; nonetheless, family violence theory, as developed by Gelles and Straus, shares two elements with feminist theoretical approaches to the problem (Gelles, 1972; Gelles & Straus, 1979; Straus, 1979; Straus et al., 1996). The first is the centrality of power and control, individuals with more power engage in violence over others to control behavior, and the second is the acknowledgement that most violence takes place in the private sphere and is perpetuated by individuals known by the victim. However, feminists critique the techniques developed by Gelles and Straus used to measure family violence (namely the conflict tactics scale or CTS) as their focus on conflict both (1) fails to capture the scope of coercive behavior existing outside of a moment of conflict and (2) fails to capture extent that this is a gendered phenomenon (Hattery et al., 2023). Feminist theories are critical to understanding how this form of family violence functions to sustain gender inequality (Anderson, 1997).

Critics of the feminist theory and activism often focused on division, difference, and moments of stalled momentum within the movement. However, while differing in emphasis and priority, simultaneously applying diverse feminist frameworks is an essential strategy to understand and confront the problem of intimate partner and sexual violence. Feminist theories enable scholars to understand the problem both on interpersonal and systemic levels. Exploring violence on both micro and macro levels, feminist theories provide useful frameworks for scholars investigating the problem in a variety of disciplines. For example, scholars in the disciplines of Women and Gender Studies, Sociology, Psychology, and Public Health most frequently integrate the insights of feminist theoreticians into their own disciplinary frameworks to address intimate partner and sexual violence.

History of the Theory/Key Tenents

Making sense of the past, feminist theories provide us with explanations of how gender inequality evolved. Looking to the future, feminist theories give rise to the tools and interpretive lenses necessary to end gender inequality. They each in their own way explain how intimate partner and sexual violence works to sustain power-based relationships and systems. This section connects historical moments in the feminist movement to useful frameworks emerging from distinct varieties of feminist theory, notable among them liberal, radical, intersectional, and postmodern feminism. It highlights the most prominent feminist theoretical concepts for understanding, documenting, and preventing gender-based violence.

Liberal Feminism: Both feminist activism and feminist theory is generally organized utilizing the metaphor of waves (Lear, 1968; Lerner, 1993). Despite the critiques of this metaphor, its use persists among historians and in the common vernacular. Building upon one another, each wave responds to the dominant issues, perspectives, and strategies of its time.

The first wave of American feminism emerged in the early nineteenth century and continued until the middle of the twentieth century. Its focus was acquiring rights and access for women. The feminism of the first wave is primarily classified as liberal feminism. Liberal feminism emerges from liberal political philosophy emphasizing that all individuals should be equal in the eyes of the law (Cott, 1987). From 1848 through 1920 early liberal feminist activists focused on acquiring voting rights, but they also advocated for access to education, property ownership, and the ability to earn and control income (Lorber, 2010). This agenda had important implications for reforming marriage laws, *a critical first step for enabling abused women to potentially leave an abusive relationship*. The agenda of the Seneca Falls Convention (1848) included ending the practice of coverture establishing women a separate legal identity from their husbands (Mann, 2012). First wave activists worked to acquire access to divorce, sustain custody of children, and retain property (Kraditor, 1981). During the early first wave issues such as marital rape and spousal abuse were most often considered private problems, a static designation that persists as a barrier to ending violence. However, the crossover between suffrage activists and the temperance movement highlighted the public harms that come from private behavior and the role that alcohol can play in violence within the home (Gordon, 1988).

Liberal feminism continued to flourish during the second wave of feminism from the 1960s through the early 1990s. While first wave liberal feminist activists were successful in achieving US voting rights in 1920, gender inequality continued to persist. Second wave liberal feminists focused their efforts on access to education, opportunities in the workplace, restructuring the division of labor in the home, and the disruption of traditional gender roles through the socialization of children.

During the late 1960s women began to share their experiences with one another in small settings known as "consciousness raising" groups and as a result they identified the commonalities among their lives (Kinnamon, 2024). Doing so women of the second wave intentionally pushed private issues into the public sphere, a move that coincided with the emergence of radical feminism. One of the most glaring commonalities expressed in these consciousness-raising groups was the nearly universal experience of sexual, physical, and psychological violence.

Speaking publicly of these private matters gave rise to the rally cry that the "personal is political" (Firestone, 1970; Hanish, 1969). Recognizing the public relevance of private matters demonstrates the persistence of the liberal feminist prioritization of rights and access, as Sweet articulates, "'private" violence was in fact a public (sic) issue of women's citizenship" (Sweet, 2021, p. 33).

Radical Feminism: As women began to share the details of their lives and map common experiences of oppression a new variety of feminist thought and activism emerged. While focused on the secondary status of women in general, emerging activists and theoreticians articulated different priorities and foci as they worked against inequality. The radical feminists of the second wave made violence against women an explicit focus and doing so articulated the key feminist concepts of patriarchy and control.

Radical feminists identified and fought against *the mechanisms of control that ensured the continued subordination of women.* They revealed how men sustain control over women not only through gender norms, family structures, institutions and cultural productions, but also through violence (Daly, 1978; Dowrkin, 1974, 1981; MacKinnon, 1987, 1989). Naming violence against women, including the threat of violence, as a critical component of sustaining control over women, second wave radical feminists were the first to make violence against women a central theme in their work (DeKeseredy, 2021; Renzetti, 2018). Doing so they not only developed theoretical frameworks but built an infrastructure to support women experiencing violence. The "battered women's movement" in the U.S. combined the radical feminist theoretical analysis of patriarchal control with political mobilization and grass roots activism.

Radical feminists designed public awareness campaigns highlighting the pervasiveness of domestic violence. They created female centered spaces like bookstores and cultural events. These activists established networks of support for those attempting to leave abusive relationships and by 1975 there were 300–500 grass roots shelters in operation (Sweet, 2021). Through the 1980s and 1990s these efforts would coalesce into an industry of social services bound closely to the state.

Forcing the "recognition of the 'private' sphere as central to social and political life" radical feminist anti-violence activists intentionally "recast women's homelives as dangerous spaces of unfettered patriarchal power" (Sweet, 2021, p. 39). Recasting homelife in this manner was a critical step in mobilizing public and political support against intimate partner and sexual violence, as was the rise of consciousness raising groups, but both often resulted in a false homogenous depiction of domestic life.

Intersectional Feminism: During the 1960s and 1970s both liberal and radical feminists of the second wave tended to universalize the experiences of white middle class women, failing to account for the ways in which expressions of gender are shaped by other social locations such as race, class, ethnicity, sexuality and ability. Generating public support against widespread violence against women relied upon what Richie calls the "everywoman analysis" and she argued that this framing resulted in a race and class neutral understanding of physical, psychological, and sexual violence (Richie, 2000, p. 1135). Furthermore, early theories of violence against women failed to extend analysis beyond social location to consider how identities interact with broader structures and institutions in important ways. Emphasizing inequality based on sex, mid twentieth century liberal and radical feminists overlooked the persistence of inequalities based on other social locations. This hindered the potentially transformative power of feminist anti-violence theory and activism and worse, "the assumed race class neutrality of gender violence led to the erasure of low-income women and women of color from the dominant view" (Richie, 2000, p. 1135). Despite this dominant erasure, Black and Indigenous women established critical practices in anti-violence activism and the social services that emerged from them. For example, during the 1970s and 1980s organizations such as the National Black Women's Health Project modeled a strategy for connecting the experiences of violence to health outcomes. They highlighted the interplay of the multiple oppressions of violence sexism, racism and classism and elevated the practice of consciousness raising to a systematic tool that could be harnessed to combat violence in communities of color (Caitlin, 2022). Theoretical constructions emerging from feminists of color, international feminists and lesbian feminists flourished during the 1980s and 1990s. Concepts such as standpoint and intersectionality were developed by scholars including Patricia Hill Collins and Kimberly Crenshaw and marked a critical shift in the study of domination and marginalization (Collins, 1990, 2004; Crenshaw, 1989, 1991; Hooks, 1984; Smith, 1983). Ushering in the third wave, as declared by Rebecca Walker in 1992, activists and theoreticians now demanded scholarship and advocacy that explores the multifaceted nature of violence against women (Walker, 1992). Their work demonstrated the ways that victimization is caused not only by individuals but is perpetuated by institutions and structures as well. This intersectional approach reveals how interpersonal violence reenforces structural inequality (Hattery, 2022). De Coster and Heimer explain, "understanding IPV requires a perspective that considers how culture, structure, and situations shape experiences for individuals and groups differentially situated in multiple hierarchies of power and control" (De Coster & Heimer, 2021, p. 287). Yet, such an approach makes it difficult to view experiences of violence in strictly binary terms.

Postmodern Feminism and Queer Theory: As the mid-20th-century radical feminists broke down the barrier between the public and the private, and the intersectional feminists deny the universal and static nature of identities and structures, postmodern feminist and queer theoreticians concurrently expanded our understanding of intimate partner and sexual violence by viewing seemingly fixed identities as fluid categories existing on a continuum (Butler, 1990). In general, postmodern thought challenges universal theories, and works against monolithic categories such as "patriarchy" (Mann, 2012). This shift enables the movement away from essentialist and static notions of patriarchy toward understanding the ways in which physical, psychological, and sexual violence appear among different "varieties of patriarchy" (Hunnicut, 2009). Postmodern feminism also grants considerable attention to the ways in which meaning is constructed through narratives, languages, and discourse (Bartky, 1997; Foucault, 1975). This approach has valuable applications for how we understand the terminology surrounding abuse, victimization, trauma, and recovery (Hattery, 2022; McPhail et al., 2007). Challenging a gender binary and fixed identities, postmodernism moves away from oversimplified constructions of who is a perpetrator and victim, a move that expands the investigation of LGBTQ+ and non-binary experiences of violence (De Coster & Heimer, 2021). Equally important, a postmodern feminist approach calls into question the process of knowledge building by highlighting the positionality of the researcher relative to their subject and explores the ways in which power is manifest in the research process.

Contributions to the Study of Family Violence

Patriarchy: Building upon the work of Karl Marx and Friedrich Engles, feminist theoreticians elaborated upon his concept of patriarchy (Daly, 1978; Firestone, 1970; Lerner, 1986; Millett, 1970). For Engles, patriarchy was "institutionalized male domination of women and children" (Mann, 116). Among different varieties of feminism, the origins of this domination vary from the rise of private property to the division of labor based on biological sex. Put simply patriarchy is a set of "social arrangements that privilege males, where men as a group dominate women as a group both structurally and ideologically" (Hunnicut, 2009). Under patriarchy it is gender then, that determines who is privileged and who is dominated. As Renzetti summarizes, "At the heart of feminism is the recognition that *gender* (sic) is a central organizing principle of social life" (Renzetti, 2018, p. 74). It follows that violence too is gendered, and gendered violence plays an important role in maintaining the patriarchal system of privileging men. In fact, some feminist scholars argue that gender-based violence is not just the outcome of the patriarchal order but instead a deliberate strategy to ensure continued gender segregation and its resulting inequality. As Hattery argues, "gender-based violence is not a *product* of gender inequality;

rather, it is a *tool* for ensuring gender segregation and thus perpetuating gender inequality" (Hattery, 2022, p. 791).

The Sex/Gender Distinction: Acts of domination within patriarchy rely on a hierarchical arrangement which infuses value and privileges upon one group over another. Debates during the second wave centered upon the origins of this secondary status and many radical feminists identified biological sex and the obligations of reproduction as its source. However others, such as Marxist feminists, argued that these distinctions were cultivated through social systems, such as economics and the division of labor (Mann, 116). This challenged the assumption that biological categories of sex are fixed at birth and introduced the idea that the characteristics of masculinity and femininity known as gender are socially constructed. As early as 1949 Simone De Beauvoir argued that "One is not born but, rather becomes, woman" (Beauvoir, 1949). Gender differs from a biological determination and instead refers to a set of characteristics, behaviors, and roles that are socially constructed, reified by structures, and whose markers vary according to time, place, and culture (Rubin, 1979). Some of these roles are connected to biological necessities related to reproduction but as Epstein argues, "all social statuses and the roles attached to them are socially prescribed" (Epstein, 2007, p. 3). For liberal feminists this distinction serves as foundational proof that inequality is not inherent in the differences between men and women but rather cultivated through socialized gender roles. For radical feminists this distinction exposes how the system of male dominance relies on gender roles which serve to reinforce male power. The social construction of gender is of great consequence for the study of intimate partner and sexual violence because the essentialized gender roles that align masculinity with violence and aggression often provide an excuse to ignore or minimize the prevalence of physical, sexual and psychological violence. Focusing on the socialization of children, liberal feminists argue that if these characteristics were not cultivated in men, then there would be a decline in rates of sexual and physical violence against women. Additionally, the failure to live up to the ideal of an essentialized gender role often provides the justification for violence in abusive relationships.

Referred to as "role and rule enforcement" by Hattery and Smith, violence is a punishment for both violating the rules of a relationship and for failing to enact essentialized gender roles properly (Hattery, 2022; Hattery & Smith, 2020).

Evolution of Feminist Theory in the Study of Family Violence

As noted above, the story of feminist theory, which is somewhat unique to approaches utilized to study family violence is iterative. Each new generation of feminist theorists, scholars and activists offered critique (as articulated above) and feminist theory shifted and expanded to absorb and respond to these critiques. As feminist theories of violence against women evolved over time the focus on the control of women by men in intimate relationships soon expanded beyond interpersonal relationships. The evolutions in the concepts of patriarchy, the social construction of gender, and intersectional understandings of social location and social structures revealed how power is produced and reinforced through all institutions that shape our lives.

Interwoven into traditional disciplines, contemporary scholarship reveals how the criminal-legal system, religious organizations, educational institutions, and the delivery of health services, to name a few, sustain a complex system of domination and marginalization. Expanding this conceptual focus, feminist scholars such as Paige Sweet encourage the field of family violence to move beyond understanding violence as individual incidents but instead as "power relations rooted in gendered institutions" (Sweet, 2020, p. 935). This shift offers family violence scholars a pathway to avoid the "public–private divide" that prevents alignment of family violence within broader "patterns of gender-based exclusion and discrimination" (Sweet, 2020, p. 935). As articulated by Sweet, "it is the relational web of power that has defined feminists approach to abuse" (Sweet, 2020, p. 938).

From Theory to Praxis: Feminist theory goes beyond simply conceptualizing patriarchy and power and offers an epistemological frame for praxis guiding the strategies that feminist scholars use to empirically document the outcomes of these structural inequalities. Attentive to dynamics of power and marginalization, feminist theoreticians raise some important methodological considerations for scholars documenting the experiences of intimate partner and sexual violence. In 1987 Sandra Harding asked the question, "Is there a Feminist Method?" as she explored feminist knowledge building in the social sciences. Answering this question, she argued that while there is not a "distinctive feminist method of research," there are distinctive characteristics of feminist analyses: they are centered upon the experiences of women, they investigate and problematize the relationship between the researcher and the researched, and they provide explanations and solutions defined by women as problems (Harding, 1987). Current feminist scholarship, while expanding its focus from women to marginalized populations more broadly, a move contested by some, reveals the persistence of Harding's characteristics. Centering the experiences of the marginalized, feminist scholars often utilize methods such as in-depth interviews, open-ended survey questions, and focus groups to collect qualitative data.

Quantitative data too has its place and when placed in conversation with the experiences of victims informing the development of policy and interventions that provide solutions to the problems identified by the research participants themselves. For example, feminist participatory action-based research projects further challenge the power differentials between researcher/researched as victims and survivors engage in the data collection, analysis, and solution generation to resolve problems of the subject or communities' own identification (Hesse-Biber, 2014). Such techniques sustain attentiveness to the dynamics of power. Whether primarily utilizing quantitative, qualitative, or mixed methods of generating data the practice of reflexivity is a hallmark of feminist research praxis. Reflexivity is a process for scholars to identify and examine the implications of their own social locations, assumptions, and context of their inquiry for the research project (Hesse-Biber, 2014). This is not intended to be a self-indulgent announcement of positionality but rather the learning acquired through this process should be integrated at every phase of the research project from conception to data collection, to publication. First articulated in the

1980s by scholars such as Harding, Haraway, Collins and others, feminist scholars remain attentive to the ways in which their own understandings shape investigations and outcomes (Collins, 2004; Haraway, 1991; Harding, 2004). In fact, some argue that the practice of reflexivity, when conducted thoroughly, results in "feminist objectivity." This concept argues that more complete forms of knowledge are generated if operating from the perspective that "knowledge and truth are always partial and inseparable from the lived experience of the researched" (Hesse-Biber, 2014, p. 5). This emphasis on the lived experience of victim/survivors is a central practice for feminist anti-violence advocates and scholars. All scholarship, interventions and prevention techniques operating from a feminist perspective must be rooted in the practice of examining the dynamics of power, centering marginalized experiences and voices, and investigating not only interpersonal dynamics but also critically analyzing the structural and social contexts that enable violence and intentionally ensure inequality.

Conclusions

Focusing on the problem of physical and sexual violence, liberal, radical, intersectional, and postmodern feminisms prioritize an examination of power as it relates to gender and its resulting hierarchical relationships and structures, even if they vary in their emphasis and approaches to combating gender inequality. Foundational concepts such as patriarchy, control, and the sex/gender distinction, while developed through specific branches of feminism, at specific moments in time, broadly inform feminist approaches to physical, emotional, and sexual violence.

Moreover, feminist epistemology provides a toolkit for feminist scholars to empirically document the everyday experiences of gender oppression, including all forms of gendered violence.

References

Anderson, K. L. (1997). Gender, status, and domestic violence: An integration of feminist and family violence approaches. *Journal of Marriage and Family, 59*, 655–669.

Bartky, S. L. (1997). Foucault, femininity, and the modernization of patriarchal power. In K. Conboy, N. Medina, & S. Stanbury (Eds.), *Writing on the body: Female embodiment and feminist theory* (pp. 129–154). Columbia University Press.

Butler, J. (1990). *Gender trouble: Feminism and the subversion of identity*. Routledge.

Caitlin, R. W. (2022). "The first thing we cry about is violence": The National Black Women's Health Project and the fight against rape and battering. *Journal of Women's History, 34*(1), 71–92.

Collins, P. H. (1990). *Black feminist thought: Knowledge, consciousness, and the politics of empowerment*. Unwin Hyman.

Collins, P. H. (2004). Some group matters: Intersectionality, situated standpoints, and Black feminist thought. In V. Taylor, N. Whittier, & L. J. Rupp (Eds.), *Feminist frontiers* (pp. 66–84). McGraw-Hill.
Cott, N. F. (1987). *The grounding of modern feminism*. Yale University Press.
Crenshaw, K. (1989). Demarginalizing the intersection of race and sex: A Black feminist critique of antidiscrimination doctrine, feminist theory and antiracist politics. In *University of Chicago Legal Forum* (pp. 140–167.)
Crenshaw, K. (1991). Mapping the margins: Intersectionality, identity politics, and violence against women of color. *Stanford Law Review, 43*(6), 1241–1299.
Daly, M. (1978). *Gyn/Ecology: The metaethics of radical feminism*. Beacon Press.
de Beauvoir, S. (1949). *The second sex* (H. M. Parshley, Trans.). Cape.
De Coster, S., & Heimer, K. (2021). Unifying theory and research on intimate partner violence: A feminist perspective. *Feminist Criminology, 16*(3), 286–303.
DeKeseredy, W. S. (2021). Bringing feminist sociological analyses of patriarchy back to the forefront of the study of woman abuse. *Violence Against Women, 27*(5), 621–638.
Dowrkin, A. (1974). *Woman hating*. E.P. Dutton.
Dworkin, A. (1981). *Pornography: Men possessing women*. Perigee.
Epstein, C. F. (2007). Great divides: The cultural, cognitive, and social bases of the global subordination of women. *American Sociological Review, 72*(1), 1–22.
Firestone, S. (1970). *The dialectic of sex: The case for feminist revolution*. William Morrow.
Foucault, M. (1975). *Discipline and punish: The birth of the prison*. Vintage Books.
Gelles, R. J. (1972). *The violent home: A study of physical aggression between husbands and wives*. Sage.
Gelles, R. J., & Straus, M. A. (1979). Violence in the American family. *Journal of Social Issues, 35*(2), 15–39.
Gordon, L. (1988). *Heroes of their own lives: The politics and history of family violence*. Viking Penguin.
Haraway, D. J. (1991). *Simians, cyborgs, and women: The reinvention of nature*. Free Association Books.
Hanish, C. (1969). The personal is political. In S. Firestone & A. Koedt (Eds.), *Notes from the second year: Women's liberation*.
Harding, S. (1987). Is there a feminist method? In S. Harding (Ed.), *Feminism and methodology* (pp. 1–14). Indiana University Press.
Harding, S. G. (Ed.). (2004). *The feminist standpoint theory reader: Intellectual and political controversies*. Routledge.
Hattery, A. J. (2022). Re-imagining gender-based violence as a strategy for enforcing institutional segregation and reproducing structural inequalities. *Gender & Society, 36*(6), 789–812.
Hattery, A. J., & Smith, E. (2020). *The social dynamics of family violence* (3rd ed.). Routledge.
Hattery, A. J., Kafonek, K., Monterrosa, A., Freetly Porter, E., & Smith, E. (2023). Theories of family violence: Implications for prevention and treatment. In P. Sturmey (Ed.), *Violence in families* (pp. 155–175). Springer Nature Switzerland AG.
Hesse-Biber, S. N. (Ed.). (2014). *Feminist research practice: A primer* (2nd ed.). SAGE Publications.
Hooks, B. (1984). *Feminist theory: From margin to center*. South End Press.
Hunnicutt, G. (2009). Varieties of patriarchy and violence against women: Resurrecting patriarchy as a theoretical tool. *Violence Against Women, 15*(5), 553–573.
Kelly, L. (1987). The continuum of sexual violence. In J. Hanmer & M. Maynard (Eds.), *Women, violence, and social control* (pp. 46–60). Macmillan.
Kraditor, A. S. (1981). *The ideas of the woman suffrage movement, 1890–1920*. W. W. Norton.
Kinnamon, L. (2024). "We Stayed Up All Night Rapping': Toward a history of feminist consciousness-raising, 1964–1986." *Signs: Journal of Women in Culture and Society, 50*(1).
Lear, M. W. (1968). The second feminist wave: What do these women want? *The New York Times Magazine*, SM24.
Lerner, G. (1986). *The creation of patriarchy*. Oxford University Press.

Lerner, G. (1993). *The creation of feminist consciousness*. Oxford University Press.

Lorber, J. (2010). *Gender inequality: Feminist theories and politics* (4th ed.). Oxford University Press.

MacKinnon, C. A. (1987). *Feminism unmodified: Discourses on life and law*. Harvard University Press.

MacKinnon, C. A. (1989). *Toward a feminist theory of the state*. Harvard University Press.

Mann, S. A. (2012). *Doing feminist theory: From Modernity to Postmodernity*. Oxford University Press.

McPhail, B. A., Busch, N. B., Kulkarni, S., & Rice, G. (2007). An integrative feminist model: The evolving feminist perspective on intimate partner violence. *Violence Against Women, 13*(8), 817–841.

Millett, K. (1970). *Sexual politics*. Doubleday.

Office on Violence Against Women. (2025). Domestic violence. U.S. Department of Justice. https://www.justice.gov/ovw/domestic-violence

Richie, B. (2000). A Black feminist reflection on the antiviolence movement. *Signs, 25*(4), 1133–1137.

Renzetti, C. M. (2018). Feminist perspectives. In W. S. DeKeseredy & M. Dragiewicz (Eds.), *Routledge handbook of critical criminology* (2nd ed., pp. 74–82). Routledge.

Rubin, G. (1979). The traffic in women: Notes on the 'political economy' of sex. In R. Reiter (Ed.), *Toward an anthropology of women* (pp. 157–210). Monthly Review Press.

Smith, B. (1983). *Home girls: A Black Feminist anthology*. Women of Color Press.

Straus, M. A. (1979). Measuring intrafamily conflict and violence: The Conflict Tactics (CT) scales. *Journal of Marriage and the Family, 41*(1), 75–88.

Straus, M. A., Hamby, S. L., Boney-McCoy, S., & Sugarman, D. B. (1996). The revised Conflict Tactics Scales (CTS2): Development and preliminary psychometric data. *Journal of Family Issues, 17*(3), 283–316.

Sweet, P. L. (2020). Who knows? Reflexivity in feminist standpoint theory and Bourdieu. *Gender & Society, 34*(6), 922–950.

Sweet, P. L. (2021). *The politics of surviving*. University of California Press.

Walker, R. (1992). Becoming the third wave. *Ms. Magazine, 7*(1), 39–41.

Chapter 4
Criminological Theories

Katherine Kafonek, Katie Mirance, and Maria Paula Mendoza

Name of the theory: Criminological Theories.
Proponents of the theory:
Traditional theorists: Ronald Akers, Robert Agnew, Robert K. Merton, John Laub, Robert Sampson, Edwin Sutherland.
Contemporary theorists: Amanda Burgess-Proctor, Patricia Hill Collins, Kimberlé Crenshaw, Meda Chesney-Lind, Kathleen Daly, Walter DeKeseredy, Vanessa Panfil, Hillary Potter, Ian Taylor, Paul Walton, Jordan Blair Woods, Jock Young.
What the theory says: Traditional criminological theories focus on the individual act of a crime and the appropriate punishment for the crime. Strain theories, learning theories, and life course theories share a focus on studying risk factors for crime but disagree on which individual characteristics, experiences, or neighborhood-level factors are most significant in predicting crime. Contemporary perspectives expand on traditional theories by introducing the role of social, political, and economic inequality to study crime and victimization. Victimology, Feminist Criminology, Critical Criminology, and Queer Criminology propose alternative analytic frameworks for responding to committing crime and victimization, particularly by examining how social institutions uphold systems of power at the expense of marginalized groups.

K. Kafonek (✉)
Stockton University, Galloway, NJ, USA
e-mail: katherine.kafonek@stockton.edu

K. Mirance · M. P. Mendoza
University of Delaware, Newark, DE, USA
e-mail: kmirance@udel.edu

M. P. Mendoza
e-mail: mendozam@udel.edu

A. Hattery and E. Smith (eds.), *Theories of Family Violence*, Advances in Preventing and Treating Violence and Aggression, https://doi.org/10.1007/978-3-032-17095-8_4

Introduction

Criminological theories have, for decades, focused on predicting "criminal" and "deviant" behavior. Generally, these theories attempt to answer questions such as "why?" and "what are the causes?" of crime/criminal behavior. Before the 1950s, theories of criminology (e.g., crime and societal response to crime) and criminal justice (e.g., the application and enforcement of laws) were restricted to theorizing men as victims and perpetrators of crime. Starting in the 1960s and throughout the 1970s, social movements such as the Anti-Violence Movement shed light on the mistreatment of racialized minorities, women, and children in the United States. Thus, the focus of contemporary criminological theories shifted vis-à-vis increased attention on women, racialized minorities, and crime. Contemporary perspectives expanded the realm of inquiry to explore victimization generally and the role of social inequalities in influencing such victimization. However, studying family violence through a criminological lens is still relatively new. Indeed, it was not until the 1980s, with the emergence of the sub-field of Victimology and the codifying of family violence as "criminal," that there was a focus on using criminological theory to explain family violence. Contemporary perspectives included in this chapter address shortcomings of traditional theories that are necessary for a comprehensive understanding of family violence, such as the role of *power* in gender-based violence. This chapter provides a discussion of traditional and contemporary criminological theories and frameworks, each with a focus on family violence.

Traditional Criminological Theories/Perspectives

Modern criminology is generally divided into two main schools of thought: classical and positivist. Whereas Classical criminology focuses on the individual's decision to engage in crime, the Positivist school of thought considers sociological factors in explaining the probability of criminal behavior. In the eighteenth century, classical theorists, including Cesare Beccaria and Jeremy Bentham, proposed that crime was a rational act motivated by an individual's pursuit of self-interest. For these theorists, crime occurred when an individual believed the rewards of crime outweighed the potential costs. Thus, Classical criminology emphasizes the role of swift, certain, and proportionate punishment in theorizing how to control crime.

Positivist criminology emerged during the nineteenth century and applied a more scientific view of human behavior to the study of crime. Cesare Lombroso (1876) is known for his theories of criminality based on physical characteristics, though these ideas were quickly debunked as biased and unscientific. However, Lombroso's later contributions, published in 1911, are more relevant to our understanding of crime. Using the scientific method, Lombroso proposed that social and environmental factors were necessary to understand increases or decreases in the likelihood that someone would engage in criminal behavior. The traditional criminological theories that arose during this time focused on the role of macro-level factors and aggregate-level data (e.g., social structures and neighborhoods) as well as micro-level factors (e.g., experiences and interactions). Some of these theories have been used to explain family violence. This chapter will overview three examples of theoretical perspectives used in Criminology to understand family violence: (1) strain theories, (2) learning theories, and (3) life course theories.

Strain Theories

The strain tradition originated from structural-functionalist Robert Merton (1938), who theorized that crime occurs when societies place great emphasis on monetary success (goals) while alienating individuals who cannot achieve success through legitimate means.

Decades later, Robert Agnew (1992) proposed General Strain Theory (GST), which argues that failure to achieve societal values can lead to strain, though GST expands on where these stressors come from (Cloward & Ohlin, 1960; Cohen, 1955). According to GST, strain is caused by: (1) the failure to achieve positively valued stimuli, (2) the presence of negative stimuli, and (3) the removal of positive stimuli. When these elements are present, individuals may experience negative emotions, such as frustration or anger. If an individual does not have positive mechanisms to cope with these negative emotions, they may turn to crime to alleviate strain.

Research demonstrates there are specific strains most conducive to crime that fall under the purview of family violence: child abuse and neglect, unemployment, and intimate partner violence (IPV) (Agnew, 2006; Agnew & Brezina, 2019). Following the tenets of GST, when children are abused in the home, this can influence later involvement in crime (Sigfusdottir et al., 2008; Watts & McNulty, 2013) and an increased use of substances (Carson et al., 2009). Evidence also demonstrates that, as a response to parental violence, children may cope by using violence against their parents (Brezina, 1999). Finally, financial strains, including unemployment, can lead to both child abuse and IPV.

Differential Association/Social Learning Theories

Certain aspects of family violence can also be explained by learning theories of criminal behavior. First, differential association theory (DAT) contends that criminal behavior is learned (just like any other behavior) through interactions with others, most commonly peer groups (Sutherland, 1947). Through interactions with intimate groups, Edwin Sutherland theorized that individuals are exposed to and acquire definitions (i.e., attitudes or meanings) that are 'favorable' and 'unfavorable' toward crime. DAT argues that when an individual's favorable definitions of crime are in excess to unfavorable definitions towards crime, crime is likely to occur. In other words, crime is the result of individuals learning meanings and attitudes favorable toward engaging in criminal behavior, especially when they are exposed to groups (1) early in life, (2) for a long period of time, (3) on a frequent basis, and (4) from intimates they respect, such as family or peers.

Ronald Akers' (1973) social learning theory (SLT) expands Sutherland's DAT. Like Sutherland, Akers asserts that an individual's criminal *and* conforming behavior is learned from other intimate individuals (i.e., peers and family) and this learning takes place through four principles: (1) differential associations (interaction with others), (2) definitions (attitudes, judgments, or meaning), (3) differential reinforcement (rewards and punishments for the behavior), and (4) imitation (engaging in behavior you observed). According to Akers, criminal behavior occurred due to interactions and exposure to intimate others (differential association) who teach an individual about the appropriateness of criminal behaviors (definitions) by modeling (imitation) criminal behavior that is positively reinforced (differential reinforcement).

SLT, as one of the most widely used theories in Criminology with substantial empirical support (Pratt et al., 2010), offers implications for studying family violence. Specifically, SLT can be used to explain perpetration within the family whereby individuals (e.g., a child) learn how to commit violence (*imitation*) by someone (e.g., a parent) they admire (*differential associations*) who holds beliefs that approve of violence (*definitions*) and subsequently see rewards (*differential reinforcement*) for that violence (Sellers et al., 2005). Existing research on SLT and domestic violence demonstrates that this may be the case, whereby individuals who are exposed to abuse in the home may learn and perpetuate this violence, creating a cycle of domestic violence (Powers et al., 2017; Wareham et al., 2009).

Life Course Perspective/Developmental Theories

Unlike other traditional criminological theories that typically focus on offending during a discrete time period, the life course perspective focuses on the pattern of engaging in criminal activity *over the life course*, arguing that criminal and deviant behavior varies across an individual's life due to the interplay between social, biological, psychological, and other individual- and structural-level processes (Laub & Sampson, 2003). It is well-documented that criminal behavior is highly correlated with age, as engaging in criminal activity peaks in adolescence and decreases in early adulthood (Farrington, 1986; Moffitt, 1993). To explain this age-crime curve, John Laub and Robert Sampson's (2003) *Shared Beginnings, Divergent Lives* studied the lives of 500 men through age 70, starting when they were delinquent boys. Findings revealed that an individual's relationship to others shaped their engagement in antisocial behavior, as different relationships across the life course exerted informal social control that decreased the likelihood of criminal behavior. This is because individuals with stronger bonds to other individuals, or institutions such as work or family, have "more to lose" if they engage in crime (Laub & Sampson, 1990, 2003).

Other research identifies peer influence (Warr, 1998) and employment status (Uggen, 2000) as significant predictors of declining engagement in criminal behavior.

In examining family violence, the life course perspective also sheds light on the influence of childhood experiences on future crime. Family violence researchers have found that witnessing domestic violence as a child significantly increases the risk of perpetrating such violence as an adult due to weakened child-parent bonds, which have lasting effects on adult intimate relationships (Dutton & Kropp, 2000). Further, this perspective illuminates how age may also "affect the type, severity, and frequency of the violence committed" (Payne & Gainey, 2014, p. 8); For example, individuals are more likely to perpetrate IPV in young adulthood, while elder abuse perpetration is more common in adulthood (Hattery & Smith, 2026). The life-course perspective can explain any type of offense, including all forms of family violence, in addition to victimization (Macmillan, 2001).

Critiques of Traditional Criminological Theories

Strain, learning, and life course theories seek to understand motivations for committing crime over time. These theories generally explain family violence by identifying the life circumstances, individual characteristics, and peer interactions that may contribute to one's inclination to participate in criminal behavior. In this vein, most traditional criminological theories fall short as they do not consider structural contexts of violence. Further, most traditional criminology theories do not coherently explain victimization, especially among marginalized groups. While imperfect, contemporary criminological frameworks expand on traditional perspectives by incorporating race, gender, and Queer theories. Family violence frameworks supplement criminological theories by reinforcing the role of interpersonal power imbalances in conflict (Straus, 1979; Straus et al., 2017).

Contemporary Criminological Frameworks

Contemporary criminology encompasses a growing body of theories, epistemologies, and research methods that encourage interdisciplinary collaboration to reduce disparities. As highlighted previously, most traditional criminological theories predominantly focus on those who commit crime, subsequently leaving victims-survivors invisible, rarely addressing, among other things, the violence women suffer at the hands of men, and often blaming women for their victimization (Chesney-Lind & Morash, 2013). Further, when women were considered in traditional criminological theories, they were considered *in relation to men*. Fortunately, this began to change in the 1960s and 1970s in part due to the Anti-Violence Movement.

The Anti-Violence Movement was largely a response to systemic issues, especially violence committed by men against women, such as domestic violence and sexual assault. At the time, anything that occurred between a man and woman within the home, including domestic violence, was considered a private matter. The Anti-Violence Movement helped change this perception and is significant to our discussion of family violence for several reasons. First, it sought to raise public awareness and thus remove family violence from the private sphere. Second, it sought to conceptualize family violence as being more than just physical (e.g., also economic, emotional, and mental). And, third, it advocated for the development of victim services as well as increased police response to address harm (Daigle, 2022).

Early development of contemporary perspectives, however, failed to serve the needs of marginalized groups, including communities of color and the Queer community. This gap paved the way for theoretical contributions by Black feminist scholars, which have been instrumental in creating more comprehensive frameworks that address family violence. For example, Kimberlé Crenshaw's (1989) intersectionality framework highlights the distinct but overlapping phenomena of racism and sexism experienced by Black women in society. Sociologist Patricia Hill Collins (1990) also informs our understanding of how race, class, and gender interact to maintain systems of oppression. Finally, Hillary Potter (2015) situates these theoretical frameworks in a criminological context, describing how policies and practices embedded in our criminal legal system sustain racialized, gendered, and class disparities in victimization and engagement in crime. Intersectionality is crucial for understanding why marginalized groups are uniquely vulnerable to individual victimization and state-sanctioned violence.

Specific to family violence, contemporary criminological frameworks examine power and control dynamics, the role of social structures in upholding disparities across race, class, the sex/gender system, and implications for social services. In the following sections, we explore four examples of contemporary criminology perspectives: (1) Victimology, (2) Feminist Criminology, (3) Critical Criminology, and (4) Queer Criminology.

Victimology

One major critique of applying criminological theories to family violence is that most traditional theories seek to explain why people commit crime, rather than understand victimization (Hattery et al., 2023). This led to the development of sub-field Victimology, which is broadly defined as the scientific study of victims-survivors of crime, the extent, nature, and causes of criminal victimization, and the treatment of victims-survivors (Karmen, 2020; Kirchoff, 1994). Victimology is interdisciplinary in nature and helpful for understanding individual- and structural-level risk factors for victimization and perpetration of family violence, the provision of victim services, and theorizing the prevention of family violence. Rather than focusing exclusively on motivations for committing crime, victimologists are interested in victims'-survivors' treatment in the criminal legal system, the role of social institutions in shaping the victimization experiences (e.g., government, child welfare system, education, media), victims'-survivors' resilience, and violence education/prevention (Daigle,

2022). One example of victimological research involves interrogation of women's use of violence as a form of self-defense in violent relationships (Goodmark, 2008; Miller, 2005). A Victimology lens applied to family violence brings attention to victims'-survivors' reasons for and against help-seeking, including the perceptions of the power and control dynamics of their relationship.

Although Victimology revolutionized the field of Criminology, ongoing tensions exist between criminologists' interest in research and theory and victimologists' goals of facilitating sociopolitical change (Sebba & Berenblum, 2014). For example, Victimology research is intertwined with victim's rights and services, including rape shield laws, help-seeking processes for victims-survivors of IPV such as protection orders, and the nature of mandatory reporting for child maltreatment (Sebba & Berenblum, 2014). Aside from these tensions in the fight to produce material change, Victimology's focus on driving practical interventions to improve outcomes for victims-survivors highlights its significant contributions to Criminology.

Feminist Criminology

As a response to the male-dominated focus of traditional criminological theories, Feminist Criminology emerged in the 1970s to examine how gender inequality contributes to victimization and criminal behavior (Burgess-Proctor, 2006). As defined by Kathleen Daly and Meda Chesney-Lind (1988), Feminist Criminology is both "a set of theories about women's oppression *and* a set of strategies for change" (p. 502). Multiple types of feminism offer different explanations for women's oppression, including well-known approaches such as liberal and radical feminism (see Burgess-Proctor, 2006, for an overview of feminist perspectives). Feminist perspectives share the viewpoint that women's oppression and marginalization in society contribute to crime; the difference across perspectives lies in the source of the oppression (Becker et al., 2020). Although these perspectives differ in their approaches to ending women's victimization and oppression, they share a common focus on patriarchy—a social structure that upholds male dominance—as a key factor in explaining family violence, societal attitudes toward women, and inequitable criminal legal responses to family violence.

Feminist criminologists also emphasize the role of agency in women's experiences. Agency describes one's sense of control over their life, influence over their thoughts and behaviors, and capacity to make decisions in the face of conflict or otherwise negative circumstances (Lerner, 1986). In the case of IPV, the question 'Why doesn't she leave?' is a common misinterpretation of the complex and varied reasons someone may remain in a violent relationship. This question conflates women's agency with weakness if they do not follow the socially prescribed assumption that it is easy to leave—an assumption that feminist criminologists have long challenged. Relatedly, feminist criminologists advocate for a nuanced understanding of victimization, emphasizing how victim versus survivor binaries are problematic, evident in public discourse that associates the term "victim" with weakness and powerlessness (Kelly et al., 1996; O'Shea et al., 2024).

While Feminist Criminology adds value and depth to theorizing family violence, limitations exist. Although Feminist Criminology considers the role of gender in crime, the field largely reflects and centers on the experiences of cisgender, heterosexual women and girls, and at times, has been dismissive of and even harmful toward the transgender community (Buist & Lenning, 2022; Snipes et al., 2024; Valcore et al., 2021; Woods, 2014). Moreover, feminist criminological perspectives tend to focus on middle-to-upper-class white women, ignoring the reality that violence not only affects everyone but also has disproportionate impacts on marginalized women and/or transgender non-binary people (Richie, 2012; Valentine et al., 2017). Feminist criminologists draw attention to the nuanced experiences of women who do not fit into that narrow frame of reference. However, feminist criminologists have also been criticized for focusing solely on the experiences of the "powerless", which can inadvertently pathologize crime and preserve power imbalances between the researcher and subject (Mallicoat, 2011).

Critical Criminology

Responding to criticisms of traditional criminological theories in ignoring the role of social inequality as a driving force of crime, Critical Criminology offers a comprehensive framework for understanding the dynamics of violence and oppression (Taylor et al., 1973). Unlike traditional criminological theories, which focus on the individual and crime, Critical Criminology is interested in the role of systems in producing and sustaining social inequalities; thus critical criminologists analyze unequal social and economic conditions, power imbalances, and the interconnectedness of race, class, and/or gender in upholding oppressive structures of crime control (DeKeseredy, 2021; Dragiewicz & DeKeseredy, 2012). This shifts the perception away from crime as an individual act and instead offers a more radical perspective. In this view, crime is seen as a product of the larger capitalist system wherein laws are created by dominant classes to protect their interests, thereby maintaining a power imbalance (Quinney, 1977). Critical criminologists also advocate for the expansion of the definition of "crime" to include racism, sexism, poverty, unemployment, inadequate social services, and other social inequalities (DeKeseredy, 2021; Taylor et al., 1973).

Critical Criminology is particularly useful for studying responses to family violence, such as divorce and custody hearings during the process of terminating a violent relationship, because systems can be wielded in ways that sustain power and control and contribute negatively to victimization experiences and/or outcomes (Hattery et al., 2023). For these reasons and more, Critical Criminology provides a comprehensive analysis of family violence by shifting focus away from individual criminality and towards broader structural inequalities as well as the failure of systems in protecting victims-survivors.

Queer Criminology

Historically, Criminology has excluded gender and sexuality from analysis (Chesney-Lind & Morash, 2013; Peterson & Panfil, 2014). This is especially true when examining lesbian, gay, bisexual, transgender, queer, questioning, intersex, and asexual (LGBTQIA+) people and their experiences with crime, victimization, and the criminal legal system. Moreover, Criminology has, at times, conflated sexuality with deviance and focused less attention on LGBTQIA+ victimization than on committing crime (Snipes et al., 2024). Even when those who identify as part of the Queer community are included in the research, "their sexual and/or gender identities are not interrogate[d] as salient characteristics, as these are likely not recognized at all" (Peterson & Panfil, 2014, p. 3). Due to this shortcoming, scholars argued for the integration of Queer theory and more explicit engagement with LGBTQIA+ topics and populations in Criminology and Criminal Justice, resulting in the subfield of Queer Criminology (Ball, 2016; Buist & Lenning, 2022; Panfil, 2018). At the same time, family violence research has been criticized for heteronormativity (Ristock, 2012). As such, scholars have begun to center Queer families in family violence research (Workman & Dune, 2019).

Existing research demonstrates that rates of IPV in Queer relationships are relatively similar or even higher compared to heterosexual relationships. Xavier L. Guadalupe-Diaz's (2019) book, titled *Transgressed: Intimate Partner Violence in Transgender Lives,* follows the lives of transgender survivors of IPV. Guadalupe-Diaz (2019) found that abusers used genderist abuse, such as claims relating to what being a "real man" or "real woman" looks like, as well as transphobic abuse, where disgust is associated with trans people, to oppress their trans partners. These findings underscore the gendered nature of IPV while amplifying the experiences of transgender survivors navigating an inherently transphobic society (Guadalupe-Diaz, 2019). Overall, research on family violence among Queer relationships remains limited but is growing in the sub-field of Queer Criminology.

Conclusion

For decades, Criminology has focused exclusively on the criminal behavior patterns of white heterosexual men. Arguably, such androcentrism remains; however, criminological perspectives have evolved greatly in their depth of analysis and even centered the unique experiences of previously ignored groups and types of "crime." Additionally, Criminology has expanded to study family violence and the ways victims-survivors of violence are treated within the criminal and civil legal systems. However, one limitation of criminological theories, as a whole, relates to Criminology's proximity to social institutions, particularly the punitive criminal legal system. Contemporary criminological frameworks advocate for addressing violence outside of harmful institutions such as the criminal and civil legal systems, given their failures to ensure equity and safety (DeKeseredy, 2021; Goodmark, 2023; Richie, 2012). More often than not, this may involve a restorative justice approach, community-based safety strategies, and provision of services rather than punishment. To fully understand the nuances of family violence and make strides to reduce such violence, we must continue to center victims-survivors in our analyses and explore the role of structural inequalities in causing harm.

References

Agnew, R. (2006). General strain theory: Current status and directions for further research. In F. T. Cullen, J. P. Wright, & K. R. Blevins (Eds.), *Taking stock: The status of criminological theory* (pp. 121–123). Transaction Publishers.

Agnew, R. (1992). Foundation for a general strain theory of crime and delinquency. *Criminology, 30*(1), 47–88. https://doi.org/10.1111/j.1745-9125.1992.tb01093.x

Agnew, R., & Brezina, T. (2019). General strain theory. In M. Krohn, N. Hendrix, G. Penly Hall, & A. Lizotte (Eds.), *Handbook on crime and deviance* (pp. 145–160). Springer International Publishing. https://doi.org/10.1007/978-3-030-20779-3_8

Akers, R. (1973). *Deviant behavior: A social learning approach.* Wadsworth.

Ball, M. (2016). *Criminology and queer theory: Dangerous bedfellows?* SpringerLink.

Becker, P., Kafonek, K., & Manzer, J. L. (2020). Feminist perspectives of intimate partner violence and abuse (IPV/A). In R. Geffner, J. W. White, L. K. Hamberger, A. Rosenbaum, V. Vaughan-Eden, & V. I. Vieth (Eds.), *Handbook of interpersonal violence and abuse across the lifespan* (pp. 2–24). Springer.

Brezina, T. (1999). Teenage violence toward parents as an adaptation to family strain: Evidence from a national survey of male adolescents. *Youth & Society, 30*(4), 416–444. https://doi.org/10.1177/0044118X99030004002

Buist, C. L., & Lenning, E. (2022). *Queer criminology* (2nd ed.). Routledge.

Burgess-Proctor, A. (2006). Intersections of race, class, gender, and crime: Future directions for feminist criminology. *Feminist Criminology, 1*(1), 27–47. https://doi.org/10.1177/1557085105282899

Carson, D., Sullivan, C. J., Cochran, J., & Lersch, K. (2009). General strain theory and the relationship between early victimization and drug use. *Deviant Behavior, 30*(1), 54–88. https://doi.org/10.1080/01639620802050023

Chesney-Lind, M., & Morash, M. (2013). Transformative feminist criminology: A critical rethinking of a discipline. *Critical Criminology, 21*(3), 287–304. https://doi.org/10.1007/s10612-013-9187-2

Cloward, R. A., & Ohlin, L. E. (1960). *Delinquency and opportunity: A theory of delinquent gangs.* Free Press.

Cohen, A. K. (1955). *Delinquent boys.* Free Press.

Collins, P. H. (1990). *Black feminist thought: Knowledge, consciousness and the politics of empowerment.* Routledge.

Crenshaw, K. (1989). Demarginalizing the intersection of race and sex: A Black feminist critique of antidiscrimination. *University of Chicago Legal Forum, 1*(8), 139–167. Doctrine, Feminist Theory and Antiracist Politics.

Daigle, L. E. (2022). *Victimology: The essentials* (3rd ed.). Sage.

Daly, K., & Chesney-Lind, M. (1988). Feminism and criminology. *Justice Quarterly, 5*(4), 497–538. https://doi.org/10.1080/07418828800089871

DeKeseredy, W. S. (2021). Bringing feminist sociological analyses of patriarchy back to the forefront of the study of woman abuse. *Violence Against Women, 27*(5), 621–638. https://doi.org/10.1177/1077801220958485

Dragiewicz, M., & DeKeseredy, W. S. (2012). Claims about women's use of non-fatal force in intimate relationships: A contextual review of Canadian research. *Violence Against Women, 18*(9), 1008–1026. https://doi.org/10.1177/1077801212460754

Dutton, D. G., & Kropp, P. R. (2000). A review of domestic violence risk instruments. *Trauma, Violence, & Abuse, 1*(2), 171–181. https://doi.org/10.1177/1524838000001002004

Farrington, D. P. (1986). Age and crime. *Crime and Justice, 7*, 189–250. https://doi.org/10.1086/449114

Goodmark, L. (2008). When is a battered woman not a battered woman? When she fights back. *Yale Journal of Law and Feminism, 20*(75), 76–128.

Goodmark, L. (2023). *Imperfect victims: Criminalized survivors and the promise of abolition feminism* (Vol. 8). University of California Press.

Guadalupe-Diaz, X. L. (2019). *Transgressed: Intimate partner violence in transgender lives*. NYU Press.

Hattery, A. J., Kafonek, K., Monterrosa, A., Porter, E. F., & Smith, E. (2023). Theories of family violence: Implications for prevention and treatment. In P. Sturmey (Ed.), *Violence in families: Integrating research into practice* (pp. 155–175). Springer Nature Switzerland AG. https://doi.org/10.1007/978-3-031-31549-7_7

Hattery, A., & Smith, E. (2026). *The social dynamics of family violence* (4th ed.). Routledge.

Karmen, A. (2020). *Crime victims: An introduction to victimology* (10th ed.) Cengage.

Kelly, L., Burton, S., & Regan, L. (1996). Beyond victim or survivor: Sexual violence, identity and feminist theory and practice. In L. Adkins & V. Merchant (Eds.), *Sexualizing the social: Power and the organization of sexuality* (pp. 77–101). Palgrave Macmillan.

Kirchhoff, G. F. (1994). Victimology: History and basic concepts. In Kirchhoff, G. F., Kosovski, E. & Schneider, H. J. (Eds.). *International Debates of Victimology* (pp. 1–81). WSV Publishing.

Laub, J. H., & Sampson, R. J. (1990). Crime and deviance over the life course: The salience of adult social bonds. *American Sociological Review*, 609–627.

Laub, J. H., & Sampson, R. J. (2003). *Shared beginnings, divergent lives: Delinquent boys to age 70*. Harvard University Press.

Lerner, E. (1986). Immigrant and working-class involvement in the New York City woman suffrage movement, 1905–1917. In J. Friedlander (Ed.), *Women in culture and politics: A century of change* (pp. 223–236). Indiana University Press.

Lombroso, C. (1876). *L'Uomo delinquente*. Hoepli.

Macmillan, R. (2001). Violence and the life course: The consequences of victimization for personal and social development. *Annual Review of Sociology, 27*(1), 1–22. https://doi.org/10.1146/annurev.soc.27.1.1

Mallicoat, S. L. (2011). *Women and crime: A text/reader*. Sage

Merton, R. K. (1938). Social structure and anomie. *American Sociological Review, 3*(5), 672–682. https://doi.org/10.2307/2084686

Miller, S. L. (2005). *Victims as offenders: The paradox of women's violence in relationships*. Rutgers University Press.

Moffitt, T. E. (1993). Adolescence-limited and life-course-persistent antisocial behavior: A developmental taxonomy. *Psychological Review, 100*(4), 674–701. https://doi.org/10.1037/0033-295X.100.4.674

O'Shea, B., Feicht, R., Brown, M., & Numer, M. (2024). Rethinking sexual violence labels: Exploring the impact of 'victim' and 'survivor' discourse. *European Journal of Psychotraumatology, 15*(1), 2296329. https://doi.org/10.1080/20008066.2023.2296329

Panfil, V. R. (2018). Young and unafraid: Queer criminology's unbounded potential. *Palgrave Communications, 4*(1), 1–5. https://doi.org/10.1057/s41599-018-0165-x

Payne, B., & Gainey, R. (2014). *Family violence and criminal justice: A life-course approach*. Routledge.

Peterson, D., & Panfil, V. R. (2014). Introduction: Reducing the invisibility of sexual and gender identities in criminology and criminal justice. In D. Peterson & V. R. Panfil (Eds.), *Handbook of LGBT communities, crime, and justice* (pp. 3–13). Springer.
Potter, H. (2015). *Intersectionality and criminology: Disrupting and revolutionizing studies of crime*. Routledge.
Powers, R. A., Cochran, J., Maskaly, J., & Sellers, C. (2017). Social learning theory, gender, and intimate partner violent victimization: A structural equations approach. *Journal of Interpersonal Violence, 35*(17–18), 3554–3580. https://doi.org/10.1177/0886260517710486
Pratt, T. C., Cullen, F. T., Sellers, C. S., Winfree Jr., L. T., Madensen, T. D., Daigle, L. E., Fearn, N. E., & Gau, J. M. (2010). The empirical status of social learning theory: A meta-analysis. *Justice Quarterly, 27*(6), 765–802. https://doi.org/10.1080/07418820903379610
Quinney, R. (1977). *Class, state, and crime: On the theory and practice of criminal justice*. D. McKay Company.
Richie, B. E. (2012). *Arrested justice: Black women, violence, and America's prison nation*. New York University Press.
Ristock, J. (2012). *No more secrets: Violence in lesbian relationships*. Routledge.
Sebba, L., & Berenblum, T. (2014). Victimology and the sociology of new disciplines: A research agenda. *International Review of Victimology, 20*(1), 7–30. https://doi.org/10.1177/0269758013511657
Sellers, C. S., Cochran, J. K., & Branch, K. A. (2005). Social learning theory and partner violence: A research note. *Deviant Behavior, 26*(4), 379–395. https://doi.org/10.1080/016396290931669
Sigfusdottir, I. D., Asgeirsdottir, B. B., Gudjonsson, G. H., & Sigurdsson, J. F. (2008). A model of sexual abuse's effects on suicidal behavior and delinquency: The role of emotions as mediating factors. *Journal of Youth and Adolescence, 37*, 699–712 (2008). https://doi.org/10.1007/s10964-007-9247-6
Sutherland, E. (1947). *Principles of criminology*. Lippincott.
Snipes, J. B., Bernard, T. J., & Trinkner, R. (2024). *Vold's theoretical criminology* (9th ed.). Oxford University Press.
Straus, M. A., Gelles, R. J., & Stenmetz, S. K. (2017). *Behind closed doors: Violence in the American family*. Routledge.
Straus, M. A. (1979). Measuring intrafamily conflict and violence: The Conflict Tactics (CT) Scales. *Journal of Marriage and the Family, 41*(1), 75–88. https://doi.org/10.2307/351733
Taylor, I., Walton, P., & Young, J. (1973). *The new criminology: For a social theory of deviance*. Routledge and Kegan Paul. https://doi.org/10.4324/9780203405284
Uggen, C. (2000). Work as a turning point in the life course of criminals: A duration model of age, employment, and recidivism. *American Sociological Review, 65*(4), 529–547. https://doi.org/10.2307/2657381
Valcore, J., Fradella, H. F., Guadalupe-Diaz, X., Ball, M. J., Dwyer, A., DeJong, C., Walker, A., Wodda, A., & Worthen, M. G. (2021). Building an intersectional and trans-inclusive criminology: Responding to the emergence of "gender critical" perspectives in feminist criminology. *Critical Criminology, 29*, 687–706. https://doi.org/10.1007/s10612-021-09590-0
Valentine, S. E., Peitzmeier, S. M., King, D. S., O'Cleirigh, C., Marquez, S. M., Presley, C., & Potter, J. (2017). Disparities in exposure to intimate partner violence among transgender/gender nonconforming and sexual minority primary care patients. *LGBT Health, 4*, 260–267. https://doi.org/10.1089/lgbt.2016.0113
Wareham, J., Boots, D. P., & Chavez, J. M. (2009). A test of social learning and intergenerational transmission among batterers. *Journal of Criminal Justice, 37*(2), 163–173. https://doi.org/10.1016/j.jcrimjus.2009.02.011
Warr, M. (1998). Life-course transitions and desistance from crime. *Criminology, 36*(2), 183–216. https://doi.org/10.1111/j.1745-9125.1998.tb01246.x
Watts, S. J., & McNulty, T. L. (2013). Childhood abuse and criminal behavior: Testing a general strain theory model. *Journal of Interpersonal Violence, 28*(15), 3023–3040. https://doi.org/10.1177/0886260513488696

Workman, A., & Dune, T. (2019). A systematic review on lgbtiq intimate partner violence from a western perspective. *Journal of Community Safety and Well-Being*, *4*(2), 22–31. https://doi.org/10.35502/jcswb.96

Woods, J. B. (2014). "Queering criminology": Overview of the state of the field. In D. Peterson & V. Panfil (Eds.), *Handbook of LGBT communities, crime, and justice* (pp. 15–41). Springer Science + Business Media. https://doi.org/10.1007/978-1-4614-9188-0_2

Chapter 5
Psychological Theories

Emma Freetly Porter and Negar Aghassizadeh

Name of the theory: Psychoanalytic Theories; Social Learning Theories, Intergenerational Theories, Neurobiological Theories.
Proponents of the theory: Psychoanalytic Theory: Sigmond Freud, Melanie Klein, Mary Ainswoth, John Bowlby; Social Learning Theory: Albert Bandura, Intergenerational Theories: epigeneticists, psychologists, biologists, public health scholars; Neurobiological Theories: neuropsychologists, psychologists, psychiatrists, behavioral neuroscientists, neuroendocrinologists.
What the theory says: Psychoanalytic theories focus on the impact of early experiences on the development of personality and the unconscious relational patterns. Attachment theory is a specific theory within the psychoanalytic realm that focuses on the development of relational schema in childhood that govern future relational interactions. Social Learning theories focus on the role of observation and reinforcement in shaping behavior. Intergenerational theories focus on how patterns of violence and the impact of trauma are passed from one generation to the next via behavioral and epigenetic pathways. Neurobiological theories focus on the impact of brain function in promoting or inhibiting violence.

E. Freetly Porter (✉) · N. Aghassizadeh
Adelphi University, Garden City, NY, USA
e-mail: efreetlyporter@adelphi.edu

N. Aghassizadeh
e-mail: naghassizadeh@adelphi.edu

A. Hattery and E. Smith (eds.), *Theories of Family Violence*, Advances in Preventing and Treating Violence and Aggression, https://doi.org/10.1007/978-3-032-17095-8_5

Introduction

This chapter explores the nuances of family violence through psychological theories and frameworks using individual, relational, and sociocultural lenses. Psychoanalytic theories emphasize the role of early childhood experiences, unconscious processes, and personality development in shaping abusive behaviors. Attachment theory is another prominent lens through which family violence and its impacts on relational development can be understood. Next, social learning theory is included to explore the role of learning in contributing to violence. The theory of intergenerational transmission of trauma and violence, which illustrate how experiences of violence and adversity can be perpetuated across generations, will also be reviewed. Finally, neurobiological theories will be discussed to explain the role of neuropsychological and neurobiological processes in violence. Factors such as executive function, impulse control, traumatic brain injuries, and difficulties in emotion regulation can impact aggression and anger management leading to increased risk of family violence occurrence. Together, these theories provide a comprehensive framework for understanding the psychological mechanisms underlying family violence.

Psychoanalytic and Personality Theories

Family violence is a widespread phenomenon, and despite clinical and research attention, this issue continues to be a frequent occurrence with devastating consequences (Chan et al., 2021). While there are several lenses through which family violence can be conceptualized, psychological theories offer unique advantages, including a focus on both individual personality formation and broader sociocultural influences. In the first section of this chapter, we aim to explore the relationships between personality traits and family violence. Then, we will turn to reviewing relational psychoanalytic theories, such as attachment theory.

Personality Traits

Despite earlier notions within the field of psychology that infants are blank slates that can learn to adopt whatever tendencies are reinforced, there is now substantial evidence that while some traits are modifiable, personality and temperament also play a major role in influencing behavior (Chess & Thomas, 1977). While psychoanalytic theories and personality theories are not one in the same, they often intersect in their exploration of the development of identity and personality traits; therefore, we present them together. In the realm of family violence, there is evidence that certain personality traits may influence an individual's tendencies toward either experiencing or perpetrating abuse.

First, it bears mentioning the distinctions between personality traits versus clinical personality disorders, although research on both uncovers telling trends in family violence. There are several theoretical models of general personality traits in psychology that differ in important ways, but theorists tend to agree that personality is a set of stable traits that develop early in life and often remain consistent into adulthood, governing emotional reactions, interpersonal style, and behaviors (McRae & Costa, 1996). One prominent model is the five factor model (FFM; McRae & Costa, 1996) which suggests that the following five traits serve as reliable categories explaining much of the personality variation in the population: (1) extraversion, (2) agreeableness, (3) conscientiousness, (4) neuroticism, and (5) openness to experience. On the other hand, personality pathology, or personality disorders, are conceptualized as personality types that are exceedingly rigid and cause clinically significant distress and harm for the individual with the personality disorder and/or those with whom they have relationships (American Psychological Association, 2013).

In terms of general traits, there is evidence that neuroticism is associated with perpetration of intimate partner violence (Dorling et al., 2024; Ulloa et al., 2016). Given that neuroticism is often associated with high emotional reactivity and difficulty regulating emotions, it stands to reason that this trait may be associated with violence and aggression, specifically reactive violence (discussed more below), which is a common typology in family violence.

Although not as widespread, there is also evidence that lower levels of agreeableness is associated with the perpetration of violence, as this trait can be associated with empathy and cooperation in relationships (Dorling et al., 2024). On the more pathological end of the personality spectrum, disorders such as narcissistic personality disorder, borderline personality disorder, and antisocial personality disorder, have also been linked with perpetration of violence within relationships (Collison & Lynam, 2021).

One model of subclinical personality pathology that is prominent in the family violence literature is that of the dark tetrad (formerly the dark triad) model of personality traits (Bonfá-Araujo et al., 2022). In other words, these traits are not considered to be signs of full personality disorders in and of themselves, but they are associated with pathological behavior, such as violence. Machiavellianism, narcissism, and psychopathy were referred to as the "dark triad" due to their socially aversive nature (Furnham et al., 2013; Jonason et al., 2012; Paulhus & Williams, 2002). The dark triad traits are associated with a range of antisocial behaviors such as artificially inflated self-views (narcissism) and a tendency to manipulate others to achieve goals (Machiavellianism) with little empathy or remorse (psychopathy) (Crysel et al., 2013). Further, these traits have been found to be associated with intimate partner violence perpetration (Carton & Egan, 2017). The fourth trait that has been included in this model is sadism due to its association with patterns of physical/emotional harm towards others (Buckels et al., 2013).

The concept of Machiavellianism comes from the writings of political strategist Niccolo Machiavelli (1527). In fact, a selection of statements from Machiavelli's original books (see Christie et al., 2014) were turned into a personality assessment by demonstrating reliable differences in respondents' agreement with the items. Further research showed that participants who agreed with these Machiavellian statements were more likely to show a cold and manipulative behavior in laboratory and real world studies (Christie et al., 2014; Paulhus & Williams, 2002). Within the dark triad/tetrad context, narcissism is defined by entitlement and exploitativeness, as well as a grandiose sense of oneself and one's authority and a tendency to draw the attention toward oneself (Ackerman et al., 2011). Psychopathy is characterized by lack of affect, with guiltlessness, dishonesty, cynicism, and insensitivity. Personality descriptors for psychopathy include: interpersonally charming, (absence of) nervousness, unreliability, insincerity, (lack of) shame, poor judgment, and egocentricity, affectively impoverished and interpersonally unresponsive (Patrick, 2007).

Taken together, these traits paint the picture of an individual who is self-concerned, lacking in empathy, willing to and skillful at taking advantage of others, and ultimately, taking pleasure in engaging in violence towards others. With this personality composite in mind, the connection with family violence perpetration is clear. However, unlike the above mentioned personality traits, such as neuroticism, it may be that these dark tetrad traits are more associated with intimate terrorism, a type of violence characterized by systematic control, rather than the reactive violence associated with emotional dysregulation (Dorling et al., 2024).

Relational Patterns

Psychoanalytic theories emphasize the impact of relationships on development. That is, besides the traits we are born with, our earliest relationships with our caregivers shape our understanding of ourselves and the world. These early interactions form the basis of our relational schemas that along with our innate traits, form the structure of our personality. Indeed psychoanalytic theories suggest that early relationships form our expectations for future relationships and can thereby become relational patterns that are repeated, whether consciously or otherwise. Early relational experiences may leave behind intrapsychic conflicts, and according to psychoanalytic theory, one way to resolve such conflicts is through reenactments.

Reenactments are thought to occur when individuals unconsciously seek to resolve conflicted early relational experiences by unconsciously recreating such experiences in subsequent relationships, thus explaining how these early experiences can transform into ongoing relational patterns. In the context of family violence, one common application of this theory is to explain how children exposed to violence in their families may be at risk for perpetrating and being victimized in future relationships (Herman, 2015). One of the foundational psychoanalytic concepts that explains these relational phenomena is attachment theory.

Attachment Theory

From the first day of life, in order for the infant to survive, a caregiver is present not only to take care of biological and safety needs, but also to mirror the child's emotional state.

Attachment styles are formed based on the repetition of each interaction we have with our primary caregiver(s) (Kourti et al., 2023; Zosky, 1999). Attachment theory was developed by John Bowlby (1969) as well as by Mary Ainsworth, and it has become an instrumental theory in understanding the dynamics in adult relationships, where attachment styles are categorized as secure, avoidant, and anxious/ambivalent (Ainsworth & Bowlby, 1991; Goldberg et al., 2009). People with secure attachment find it relatively easy to get close to others and are comfortable with interdependence in the relationship, feeling secure that their needs will be met. People categorized with avoidant attachment style feel uncomfortable being close to others. For example, they may agree with statements like "I find it difficult to trust [others] completely, difficult to allow myself to depend on them." Anxious/ambivalently attached people tend to worry about losing their connections with others, often feeling others are not as close with them as they would like (Ainsworth & Bowlby, 1991).

Attachment theory suggests that individuals form their attachment styles based on the quality and consistency of their interactions with their primary caregivers, and this subsequently forms the basis for how people interpret relational experiences, engage in communication, and form relationships in the future. From the perspective of these theories, therefore, childhood experiences can be said to have a profound impact on relationships functioning, which ultimately applies to family violence in several ways. First, there is evidence that exposure to family violence in childhood tends to be associated with greater attachment insecurity (Unger & De Luca, 2014), which suggests that early exposure to this violence may lead to greater impairment in relational functioning in the future. Furthermore, empirical evidence suggests that insecure attachment style mediates the relationship between exposure to family violence in childhood and adulthood perpetration of family violence (Banford et al., 2015), thus suggesting that attachment is one mechanism through which abusive relational patterns are repeated. Finally, employing attachment theory to understand the entire family system, individuals with insecure attachment may turn to violence and aggression as a way to cope with complex feelings about closeness and distance in family relationships (Doumas et al., 2008). For example, those with attachment insecurity may find it particularly difficult to navigate the needs for both closeness and independence in their relationships, and thus, violence may be one mechanism for attempting to control and manage those challenges, albeit a maladaptive one.

Critiques of Psychoanalytic Theories

There are several notable critiques of the aforementioned theories within the psychoanalytic realm. First, psychoanalytic theories are often questioned due to the lack of empirical evidence supporting their claims. On the one hand, there is credence to this critique insofar as certain claims of psychoanalytic theory would be difficult to test empirically. For example, the premise of unconscious reenactment would be challenging to definitively prove given the very nature of the unconsciousness of the processes. On the other hand, there is strong empirical evidence supporting certain aspects of psychoanalytic thinking, such as attachment styles and personality formation. Psychoanalytic theories have also been criticized for being overly focused on the experience of the individual, rather than emphasizing the role of systems and structures.

Social Learning Theory

Next, we present social learning theory (SLT; Bandura, 1971, 1977; Bandura & Barab, 1971). While this theory is not considered to fall under the psychoanalytic umbrella, it bears resemblance to attachment theory in its emphasis on learning within relationships. Indeed, learning theories understand family violence as a behavioral pattern that is observed, internalized, and in some cases, repeated. A foundational tenet of social learning theory is that all behaviors, whether maladaptive or not, are learned through experience and/or observation. SLT emphasizes that parents are often primary sources of learning (Bandura, 1977). When learning through experience, behaviors are primarily shaped by the reinforcing or punishing responses that follow their enactment. For example, children may learn that emotional expression (e.g., crying) may lead to a parent criticizing them (e.g., punishment), thereby learning that this behavior is not acceptable and likely reducing the future occurrence of that behavior. Social learning theory also contends that people learn vicariously, through observation, without having to experience consequences directly (Bandura, 1971; Bandura & Barab, 1971). Bandura and Barab (1971) argue that this type of learning goes beyond mere imitation in that cognitive interpretations intervene between what is observed and what is ultimately internalized to help the individual make meaning of their surroundings and their own behaviors. For example, a child who observes family violence may not only recreate this violent behavior in their future partnerships because they are imitating, but also because they have internalized the belief that this is an effective way to navigate familial disputes. In addition to learning through experience, social learning theory suggests that individuals' thoughts and behaviors are influenced by observation and vicarious learning (Bandura & Barab, 1971; Bandura, 1971). Though not all children who witness family violence go on to become violent themselves, they may instead *vicariously* learn that it is acceptable, thus making them vulnerable to experience future violence in relationships. Indeed, authors have found an empirical association between exposure to family violence in childhood and more accepting attitudes towards violence, thus lending evidence to SLT (Copp et al., 2019). Further, even children who reject the violence they have observed from their parents may still be at risk for inadvertently perpetuating violence if they have not been given opportunities to learn/observe alternatives. For example, a child exposed to family violence may vow never to replicate this experience for their own children; however, they may still find themselves at a loss for the positive, alternative skills needed to resolve family disputes and conflict, thus highlighting how gaps in social learning can also play role in perpetuating violence (Abbassi & Aslinia, 2010). Unfortunately, these skill deficits and maladaptive learning may be passed from one generation to the next, if there is not adequate intervention, which is further explored in our review of intergenerational transmission of violence theories.

Critiques of Social Learning Theory

Despite the prominence of SLT as a psychological theory to explain how violence is learned by children and subsequently replicated, there are also several notable limitations of its explanatory power. First, although SLT can be used to understand intergenerational patterns, the theory has historically focused on the individual as the primary unit of analysis, thereby neglecting the impact of learning that occurs from broader social and structural influences (Copp et al., 2019). Extending SLT to conceptualize learning on a broader scale could help account for instances wherein children develop violent tendencies without directly observing it at home.

On the other hand, there are limitations in terms of SLT's ability to account for the fact that the majority of those exposed to family violence do not go on to be violent in adulthood (Smith et al., 2011). While internalizing violent scripts can be a risk factor for victimization in adulthood, SLT cannot account for examples wherein family violence exposure led to neither future perpetration nor victimization.

Intergenerational Theories Within Psychology

Although prominent psychological theories of family violence emphasize individual and interpersonal notions of violence, there are also psychological theories that conceptualize family violence as a behavioral pattern that is transmitted from one generation to the next. Examining family violence in this way allows for the conceptualization of family violence as a multigenerational phenomenon.

Intergenerational Transmission of Violence and Trauma

In addition to the overt learning that is conceived of as essential from the SLT perspective, intergenerational transmission psychological theories explain family violence as a pattern that can be passed from one generation to the next through various pathways. The present section will draw upon two interrelated frameworks: the intergenerational transmission of violence and the intergenerational transmission of trauma.

The intergenerational transmission of trauma (ITT) effect was first identified among Holocaust survivors and their descendents, with observations suggesting that the offspring of Holocaust survivors presented with negative mental health effects despite not being directly impacted by the event themselves (Sigal & Rakoff, 1971). Though there have been some methodological critiques of ITT as a framework, it has become widely accepted (Yehuda & Lehrner, 2018). ITT explains that trauma-related symptoms may be present in subsequent generations even if they were never directly exposed to the original traumatizing event; further, when offspring generations are also exposed to their own trauma, these symptoms may be magnified based on their intergenerational history (Yehuda & Lehrner, 2018). Multiple pathways have been implicated as mechanisms through which trauma responses are passed down from one generation to the next. Some of these proposed mechanisms are behavioral, such as traumatized parents' struggling to teach their children emotion regulation given their own trauma symptoms (Lang & Garstein, 2018). Other proposed mechanisms are biological, involving epigenetic changes-that is, changes to gene expression- that have the potential to affect development and eventual mental and physical health outcomes (Yehuda & Lehrner, 2018).

The intergenerational transmission of violence (ITV) framework extends the intergenerational transmission of trauma framework into the specific realm of family and domestic violence. That is, this framework attempts to explain the ways in which violence is passed from one generation to the next. While not entirely separate from SLT, which also explains that violence is taught by parents to children, ITV emphasizes traumatic reactions among the parent generation as the key avenue through which violence is conveyed from one generation to the next, rather than solely through observation and learning. For example, individuals exposed to violence in childhood may develop posttraumatic stress disorder, with one of the primary symptoms being hypervigilance, a state of heightened arousal wherein one is scanning the environment for potential threats. This hypervigilance could persist through adulthood, thus rendering the individual more on-edge and hyper-aware of danger. While this can manifest in many ways, one such way is through anticipating violence. One way to cope with constantly anticipating violence is to enact violence preemptively as a means to protect oneself. In the context of family violence, this may look like: Roger was exposed to family violence and develops PTSD with hypervigilance, angry outbursts, and negative alterations in his beliefs about the world (other common PTSD symptoms). Roger tends to anticipate threats even when they are not there and assume the world is "out to get him." In his adult intimate partnership Roger is on-guard for slights and harms from his partner, thus leading to him lashing out angrily, preemptively, and disproportionately at the slightest perceived harm. Roger's children witness these violent outbursts and themselves are at risk for developing PTSD, thus the cycle is perpetuated.

Critiques of Intergenerational Transmission of Trauma and Violence

Similar critiques are leveled against the ITT and ITV frameworks as social learning theory. First, these theories also emphasize symptoms and patterns that develop in the home environment, thus not accounting for outside influences and thereby also lacking explanations for those who enact family violence without their own history of trauma. One potential rebuttal to this critique is the concept of historical trauma, which is a related framework explaining that broader experiences such as slavery, colonization, and imperialism can have a traumatic impact on entire people groups, and that this trauma may also be transmitted intergenerationally. For example, the HT framework has been used to conceptualize health disparities that persist among Indigenous peoples (Brave Heart, 1998). Another critique of the intergenerational transmission of violence paradigm is that it cannot account for the inconsistency with which childhood exposure to family violence is empirically linked with adulthood family violence (Smith et al., 2011). There are several factors that may complicate the empirical study of the link between childhood and adulthood family violence such as variability in how family violence is conceptualized and studied, specifically the extent to which power and coercion are captured within research, as well as the different ways in which children are exposed to family violence (Haselschwerdt et al., 2019).

Neurobiological Theories

The study of family violence in the field of psychology also draws heavily upon related disciplines, such as neuroscience and neurobiology, to explain the role of body and brain processes in violence. Neuroimaging evidence in conjunction with evidence from psychological/behavioral studies suggest several patterns of aggressive behavior, ranging from: (1) aggression that is driven by negative emotions and impulsivity, (2) aggression driven by delusional thinking, (3) premeditated aggression driven by deficits in empathy and personality pathology, to (4) hyperarousal-based aggression triggered by cues of a past trauma (Siever, 2008). Several neurobiological studies focus on two primary pathways to violence: proactive violence and reactive violence. Proactive violence is associated with individuals who engage in manipulation and calculation, using violence as a form of control over others. On the other hand, reactive violence occurs when an individual experiences negative emotions based on an environmental stimulus, has difficulty managing those emotions, and engages in violence as a maladaptive coping and expression strategy (Romero-Martínez et al., 2022). In the realm of family violence, both typologies are prevalent, and further, these varying types of violence involve several brain areas in different ways.

The prefrontal cortex is an important brain area that is associated with executive functioning, impulse control, and future planning. Deficits in this area secondary to legion, injury, or neurotransmitter dysfunction have been associated with violence and aggression (Dugré & De Brito, 2024; King, 2012; Yang & Raine, 2009). In the context of reactive violence, individuals with prefrontal cortex impairment may perceive an environmental trigger, experience negative emotions, struggle to regulate this emotional response, fail to engage in long-term decision making, and ultimately act impulsively motivated by the negative affective state. There are several factors that influence the function and dysfunction of the prefrontal cortex, and by extension, have the capacity to impact violent behaviors. For example, serotonin activity in the prefrontal cortex helps with modulating behaviors, especially aggressive ones (Sievers, 2008). Further, reductions in grey matter volume in the prefrontal cortex are associated with violence, specifically the reactive type (Dugré & De Brito, 2024). There are certain psychiatric disorders associated with prefrontal cortex deficits, including but not limited to: attention deficit/hyperactivity disorder and antisocial personality disorder. Thus, while no single psychiatric diagnosis predicts violent behavior, and there are many diagnosed with a given disorder that are non-violent, there may be underlying characteristics associated with certain psychiatric disorders (i.e., impulsivity) that could put an individual at risk for perpetrating violence.

The limbic system, which is often referred to as the emotion center of the brain, is also implicated in violent behavior (George et al., 2004; Göttlich et al., 2022). Specifically, hyperactivity in the limbic system is associated with violence. Hyperactivity in this region can increase an individual's sensitivity to emotional cues in the environment, thus potentially contributing to reactive aggression (Sievers, 2008). For instance, given that anger is typically perceived as a threat within the brain, an individual with limbic system dysfunction may readily interpret the facial expression of another as angry, even if the expression is in fact neutral. This then triggers the cascade of physiological responses within the limbic system and autonomic nervous system signaling that the person ought fend off this perceived threat. This can lead to the activation of the "fight" response, as part of the autonomic nervous system survival response, which could feasibly manifest as aggression/violence. Moreover, activation of the limbic system itself tends to override the prefrontal cortex, thereby nullifying its long-term planning and emotion regulation capacities.

It also bears mentioning the General Aggression Model (GAM; Anderson & Bushman, 2002), which is a framework that consolidates social, cognitive, personality, developmental, and biological factors that contribute to aggressive behavior. While this is not a theory that falls exclusively within the neurobiological realm, it is reviewed here given that it is the only model summarized in this chapter that significantly emphasizes biological factors. GAM identifies proximate processes, including situational factors that increase risk for violence (e.g., social stress, intoxication) and personal factors (i.e., individual differences) (Anderson & Bushman, 2002). Other proximal processes include the routes through which these personal and situational factors influence behaviors. These include: affect, cognition, and arousal. Authors also note that priming can occur whereby frequent exposure to social scripts that involve violence, whether by past exposure to violence directly or even indirectly via social media, can make violent cognitions more accessible to an individual (Allen et al., 2018). Distal processes are factors that are ongoing and explain biological and environmental factors that may predispose an individual towards violence. Biological factors include those such as low serotonin levels, high testosterone levels, high levels of impulsivity (Allen et al., 2018). Environmental factors capture those such as family norms and cultural beliefs about violence (Allen et al., 2018).

Conclusion

In sum, psychological theories emphasize a range of individual, relational, and sociocultural factors that contribute to family violence. Generally, most of the theories reviewed here emphasize the intersection of individual factors (e.g., personality traits, neurobiological traits) interacting with relational factors (e.g., attachment style, family environment) that contribute to family violence. There is also some emphasis on the way in which family violence is transmitted from one generation to the next via learning and genetic changes. Psychological theories specifically contribute to understanding risk factors for violence at the individual and family level, which can support intervention and prevention strategies. Further, psychological theories have been expanded to work in tandem with feminist and public health theories to develop intervention/prevention strategies that are focused on not only individual factors, but also systems and sociocultural beliefs that contribute to violence.

References

Abbassi, A., & Aslinia, S. D. (2010). Family violence, trauma and social learning theory. *Journal of Professional Counseling: Practice, Theory & Research, 38*(1), 16–27. https://doi.org/10.1080/15566382.2010.12033863

Ackerman, R. A., Witt, E. A., Donnellan, M. B., Trzesniewski, K. H., Robins, R. W., & Kashy, D. A. (2011). What does the narcissistic personality inventory really measure? *Assessment, 18*(1), 67–87. https://doi.org/10.1177/1073191110382845

Allen, J. J., Anderson, C. A., & Bushman, B. J. (2018). The General aggression model. *Current Opinion in Psychology, 19*, 75–80. https://doi.org/10.1016/j.copsyc.2017.03.034

Ainsworth, M. D. S., & Bowlby, J. (1991). An ethological approach to personality development.

American Psychiatric Association. (2013). *Diagnostic and statistical manual of mental disorders* (5th ed.). American Psychiatric Association. https://doi.org/10.1176/appi.books.9780890425596

Anderson, C. A., & Bushman, B. J. (2002). Human aggression. *Annual Review of Psychology, 53*(1), 27–51. https://doi.org/10.1146/annurev.psych.53.100901.135231

Bandura, A. (1977). Self-efficacy: Toward a unifying theory of behavioral change. *Psychological Review, 84*(2), 191–215. https://doi.org/10.1037/0033-295X.84.2.191

Bandura, A., & Barab, P. G. (1971). Conditions governing nonreinforced imitation. *Developmental Psychology, 5*(2), 244–255. https://doi.org/10.1037/h0031499

Banford, A. J., Brown, M. D., Ketring, S. A., & Mansfield, T. R. (2015). The relationship between family-of-origin experience and current family violence: A test of mediation by attachment style and mental health symptom distress. *The American Journal of Family Therapy, 43*(1), 84–96. https://doi.org/10.1080/01926187.2014.954491

Bonfá-Araujo, B., Lima-Costa, A. R., Hauck-Filho, N., & Jonason, P. K. (2022). Considering sadism in the shadow of the dark triad traits: A meta-analytic review of the Dark Tetrad. *Personality and Individual Differences, 197*, Article 111767. https://doi.org/10.1016/j.paid.2022.111767

Bowlby, J. (1969). *Attachment and loss: Vol. 1. Attachment*. Basic Books.

Brave Heart, M. Y. H. (1998). The return to the sacred path: Healing the historical trauma and historical unresolved grief response among the Lakota through a psychoeducational group intervention. *Smith College Studies in Social Work, 68*(3), 287–305. https://doi.org/10.1080/00377319809517532

Buckels, E. E., Jones, D. N., & Paulhus, D. L. (2013). Behavioral confirmation of everyday sadism. *Psychological Science, 24*(11), 2201–2209. https://doi.org/10.1177/0956797613490749

Carton, H., & Egan, V. (2017). The dark triad and intimate partner violence. *Personality and Individual Differences, 105*, 84–88. https://doi.org/10.1016/j.paid.2016.09.040

Chan, K. L., Chen, Q., & Chen, M. (2021). Prevalence and correlates of the co-occurrence of family violence: A meta-analysis on family polyvictimization. *Trauma, Violence, & Abuse, 22*(2), 289–305. https://doi.org/10.1177/1524838019841601

Chess, S., & Thomas, A. (1977). Temperamental individuality from childhood to adolescence. *Journal of the American Academy of Child Psychiatry, 16*(2), 218–226. https://doi.org/10.1016/S0002-7138(09)60038-8

Christie, R., Geis, F. L., Festinger, L., & Schachter, S. (2014). *Studies in Machiavellianism*. Elsevier Science.

Collison, K. L., & Lynam, D. R. (2021). Personality disorders as predictors of intimate partner violence: A meta-analysis. *Clinical Psychology Review, 88*, Article 102047. https://doi.org/10.1016/j.cpr.2021.102047

Copp, J. E., Giordano, P. C., Longmore, M. A., & Manning, W. D. (2019). The development of attitudes toward intimate partner violence: An examination of key correlates among a sample of young adults. *Journal of Interpersonal Violence, 34*(7), 1357–1387. https://doi.org/10.1177/0886260516651311

Crysel, L. C., Crosier, B. S., & Webster, G. D. (2013). The dark triad and risk behavior. *Personality and Individual Differences, 54*(1), 35–40. https://doi.org/10.1016/j.paid.2012.07.029

Dorling, E., Onifade, H., & Browne, K. (2024). Intimate partner violence perpetration and the five-factor model of personality: A systematic review. *Trauma, Violence, & Abuse*, 15248380241299432. https://doi.org/10.1177/15248380241299431

Doumas, D. M., Pearson, C. L., Elgin, J. E., & McKinley, L. L. (2008). Adult attachment as a risk factor for intimate partner violence: The "mispairing" of partners' attachment styles. *Journal of Interpersonal Violence, 23*(5), 616–634. https://doi.org/10.1177/0886260507313526

Dugré, J. R., & De Brito, S. A. (2024). Unraveling the morphological brain architecture of human aggression: A systematic review and meta-analysis of structural neuroimaging studies. *Aggression and Violent Behavior, 79*, Article 102003. https://doi.org/10.1016/j.avb.2024.102003

Furnham, A., Richards, S. C., & Paulhus, D. L. (2013). The dark triad of personality: A 10 year review. *Social and Personality Psychology Compass, 7*(3), 199–216. https://doi.org/10.1111/spc3.12018

George, D. T., Rawlings, R. R., Williams, W. A., Phillips, M. J., Fong, G., Kerich, M., Momenan, R., Umhau, J. C., & Hommer, D. (2004). A select group of perpetrators of domestic violence: Evidence of decreased metabolism in the right hypothalamus and reduced relationships between cortical/subcortical brain structures in position emission tomography. *Psychiatry Research: Neuroimaging, 130*(1), 11–25. https://doi.org/10.1016/S0925-4927(03)00105-7

Goldberg, S., Muir, R., & Kerr, J. (2009). *Attachment theory: Social, developmental, and clinical perspectives*. Routledge.

Göttlich, M., Buades-Rotger, M., Wiechert, J., Beyer, F., & Krämer, U. M. (2022). Structural covariance of amygdala subregions is associated with trait aggression and endogenous testosterone in healthy individuals. *Neuropsychologia, 165*, Article 108113. https://doi.org/10.1016/j.neuropsychologia.2021.108113

Haselschwerdt, M. L., Savasuk-Luxton, R., & Hlavaty, K. (2019). A methodological review and critique of the "intergenerational transmission of violence" literature. *Trauma, Violence, & Abuse, 20*(2), 168–182. https://doi.org/10.1177/1524838017692385

Herman, J. (2015). *Trauma and recovery: The aftermath of violence—From domestic abuse to political terror*. Basic Books/Hachette Book Group.

Jonason, P. K., Webster, G. D., Schmitt, D. P., Li, N. P., & Crysel, L. (2012). The antihero in popular culture: Life history theory and the dark triad personality traits. *Review of General Psychology, 16*(2), 192–199. https://doi.org/10.1037/a0027914

King, B. (2012). Psychological theories of violence. *Journal of Human Behavior in the Social Environment, 22*(5), 553–571. https://doi.org/10.1080/10911359.2011.598742

Kourti, A., Stavridou, A., Panagouli, E., Psaltopoulou, T., Spiliopoulou, C., Tsolia, M., Sergentanis, T. N., & Tsitsika, A. (2023). Domestic violence during the COVID-19 pandemic: A systematic review. *Trauma, Violence, & Abuse, 24*(2), 719–745. https://doi.org/10.1177/15248380211038690

Lang, A. J., & Gartstein, M. A. (2018). Intergenerational transmission of traumatization: Theoretical framework and implications for prevention. *Journal of Trauma & Dissociation, 19*(2), 162–175. https://doi.org/10.1080/15299732.2017.1329773

McCrae, R. R., & Costa, P. T., Jr. (1996). Toward a new generation of personality theories: Theoretical contexts for the five-factor model. In J. S. Wiggins (Ed.), *The five-factor model of personality: Theoretical perspectives* (pp. 51–87). Guilford Press.

Paulhus, D. L., & Williams, K. M. (2002). The dark triad of personality: Narcissism, Machiavellianism, and psychopathy. *Journal of Research in Personality, 36*(6), 556–563. https://doi.org/10.1016/S0092-6566(02)00505-6

Patrick, C. J. (Ed.). (2007). *Handbook of psychopathy* (Paperback ed.). Guilford Press.

Romero-Martínez, Á., Sarrate-Costa, C., & Moya-Albiol, L. (2022). Reactive vs proactive aggression: A differential psychobiological profile? Conclusions derived from a systematic review. *Neuroscience & Biobehavioral Reviews, 136*, Article 104626. https://doi.org/10.1016/j.neubiorev.2022.104626

Siever, L. J. (2008). Neurobiology of aggression and violence. *American Journal of Psychiatry, 165*(4), 429–442. https://doi.org/10.1176/appi.ajp.2008.07111774

Sigal, J. J., & Rakoff, V. (1971). Concentration camp survival: A pilot study of effects on the second generation. *Canadian Psychiatric Association Journal, 16*(5), 393–397. https://doi.org/10.1177/070674377101600503

Smith, C. A., Ireland, T. O., Park, A., Elwyn, L., & Thornberry, T. P. (2011). Intergenerational continuities and discontinuities in intimate partner violence: A two-generational prospective study. *Journal of Interpersonal Violence, 26*(18), 3720–3752. https://doi.org/10.1177/0886260511403751

Ulloa, E. C., Hammett, J. F., O'Neal, D. N., Lydston, E. E., & Leon Aramburo, L. F. (2016). The big five personality traits and intimate partner violence: Findings from a large, nationally

representative sample. *Violence and Victims, 31*(6), 1100–1115. https://doi.org/10.1891/0886-6708.VV-D-15-00055
Unger, J. A. M., & De Luca, R. V. (2014). The relationship between childhood physical abuse and adult attachment styles. *Journal of Family Violence, 29*(3), 223–234. https://doi.org/10.1007/s10896-014-9588-3
Yang, Y., & Raine, A. (2009). Prefrontal structural and functional brain imaging findings in antisocial, violent, and psychopathic individuals: A meta-analysis. *Psychiatry Research: Neuroimaging, 174*(2), 81–88. https://doi.org/10.1016/j.pscychresns.2009.03.012
Yehuda, R., & Lehrner, A. (2018). Intergenerational transmission of trauma effects: Putative role of epigenetic mechanisms. *World Psychiatry, 17*(3), 243–257. https://doi.org/10.1002/wps.20568
Zosky, D. L. (1999). The application of object relations theory to domestic violence. *Clinical Social Work Journal, 27*(1), 55–69. https://doi.org/10.1023/A:1022861331105

Chapter 6
Public Health Theories of Violence

Lauren C. Camphausen and Jennifer A. Horney

Name of the theory: Public Health Theories of Violence: Socio-Ecological Systems Theory and Model, Social Cognitive Theory, Transtheoretical Model, and the Health Belief Model.

Proponents of the theory: U.S. Centers for Disease Control and Prevention, Urie Bronfenbrenner, Albert Bandura, James Prochaska and Carlo DiClemente, and social psychologists Irwin M. Rosenstock, Godfrey M. Hochbaum, S. Stephen Kegeles, and Howard Leventhal at the U.S. Public Health Service.

What the theory says: As public health is focused on populations, rather than individuals, the public health approach to violence is focused on the implementation of evidence-based interventions that have the most significant benefit for the largest number of people. An inherently multi-disciplinary field, the public health approach, which includes defining and monitoring problems using data, identifying risk and protective factors, implementing and evaluating evidence-based strategies, and disseminating best practices for widespread adoption, uses many theoretical frameworks. Fundamental theoretical frameworks include the social-ecological model, social cognitive theory, transtheoretical model, and the health belief model. This distinct perspective and population-based approach has much to offer to those seeking to understand why the incidence of violence varies among groups and how to prevent it.

L. C. Camphausen (✉) · J. A. Horney
College of Health Sciences, University of Delaware, Newark, DE, USA
e-mail: campl@udel.edu

J. A. Horney
e-mail: horney@udel.edu

A. Hattery and E. Smith (eds.), *Theories of Family Violence*, Advances in Preventing and Treating Violence and Aggression, https://doi.org/10.1007/978-3-032-17095-8_6

Introduction

This chapter takes a bit of a departure from the rest of the book as the public health theories of violence are not a single theory but rather a framework or approach for understanding and addressing family violence influenced by a number of theories common to various disciplines that make up public health. As a multidisciplinary field, public health is guided by theories from health behavior, health education, communications, sociology, psychology, and economics (National Cancer Institute, 2018). In fact, in describing the mission of the Centers for Disease Control and Prevention's (CDC) Division of Violence Prevention, Hammond et al. (2006) pointed out that success in the prevention of violence required the collaboration of public health specialists with psychologists, sociologists, epidemiologists, criminologists, economists, and others (Hammond et al., 2006).

The public health theories of violence are both a paradigm and a process. As a paradigm, the theories position violence as a preventable health issue. Public health theories characterize violence as having a major impact on the health and well-being of populations in the same way that smoking cessation prevents cancer or regulatory policies and laws protect water quality. Public health theories position violence as a leading driver of suboptimal health and mortality, prioritize prevention, and view society as both a contributor to violence and as responsible for addressing violence. As a process, public health theories promote addressing violence systematically using the established tools and methods of public health practice. Public health theories are applied to violence through the *public health approach* (Fig. 6.1). The public health approach includes four main elements: problem identification, understanding risk and protective factors, developing interventions, and promoting widespread adoption of best practices (Centers for Disease Control and Prevention, 2021). Public health theories, both as a paradigm and a process, provide an entirely new way of thinking about, and addressing, family violence.

Public health is hard to succinctly define, but its central focus is on populations, in contrast to the focus on individuals generally practiced in clinical medicine, social welfare, and criminal justice. As such, public health does not generally engage in targeted interventions or risk-based strategies with individuals. Rather, public health interventions target groups or communities where there is a high incidence (i.e., number of new cases) or a high prevalence (i.e., overall burden) of violence community wide. In considering the social determinants of the incidence and prevalence of violence, successful public health interventions can have a larger overall impact on structural, societal, and policy-based prevention efforts (Perry, 2013). Because of this "prevention paradox," it can be difficult for public health to demonstrate the benefit of public health interventions that prevent violence to individuals who never directly experience the violence that these interventions were designed to address. However, both public health and targeted individual-level approaches should be seen as complementary and necessary to reach violence prevention goals through the reduction of risk factors and the support of protective factors (U.S. Department of Health and Human Services, n.d.). For example, reducing violence in the U.S. requires both

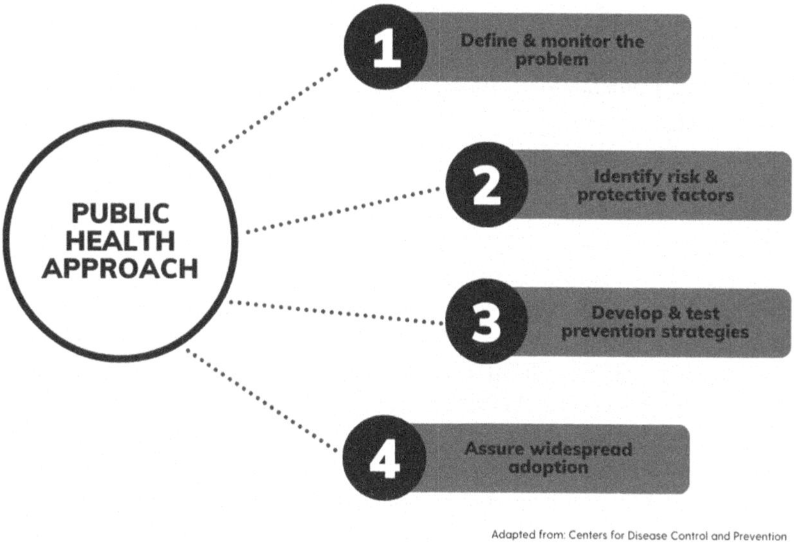

Fig. 6.1 The public health approach to violence prevention

risk-based approaches like domestic violence protection orders issued by courts to protect victims and their families and "red flag" laws that temporarily remove firearms from individuals as well as community violence prevention programs focused on safe and healthy communities.

History of the Public Health Approach to Violence

In 2009, the CDC issued a report *The History of Violence as a Public Health Issue*, which recounted the historical evolution of the recognition of violence as a public health problem and made the case that violence could be addressed from a "public health perspective" (Dahlberg & Mercy, 2009). The report details the success of public health measures like vaccination and sanitation to prevent and treat many of the leading infectious diseases, which led to the so-called "epidemiologic transition." As a result of the epidemiologic transition, the share of morbidity and mortality that could be attributed to infectious diseases decreased, resulting in chronic diseases, homicides, and suicides rising in the rankings as leading causes of death in the U.S.

The theory of the epidemiologic transition was first proposed in the 1970s and focused on changing patterns of health and disease as they relate to advances in socioecological systems (Omran, 1998). The response to these changing patterns can be seen in the evolution of violence being constructed as a public health issue. In 1979, the U.S. Surgeon General declared violence a public health problem and stated that violence should not be ignored as part of efforts to improve the public's health (Dahlberg & Mercy, 2009). This call to action around violence spurred significant accomplishments over the next two decades, including the establishment of the CDC's Violence Epidemiology Branch in 1983. Although the Branch was charged with addressing the determinants of violence broadly and assuring the conditions of a violence-free society, there was a focus on the application of epidemiologic methods and causal inference—previously used to study communicable diseases—to the identification of the determinants and consequences of violence. This demonstrated that the public health and epidemiologic methods previously used to characterize illness and disease could be applied to understanding violence.

In 1990, violence was added to the list of public health priority areas and the CDC launched the Youth Risk Behavior Surveillance System, the first surveillance system to include violence-related measures (Dahlberg & Mercy, 2009). In 1993, the CDC's Division of Violence Prevention was established to lead efforts around the public health approach to violence. This included the establishment of surveillance systems to collect data, evaluation programs, and violence prevention research. For example, early public health approaches to address youth violence transitioned into support for a more comprehensive public health focus on violence to include intimate partner violence (IPV), sexual violence, and child maltreatment (Centers for Disease Control and Prevention, 2016). Reports from the Institute of Medicine of the National Academies (Baum et al., 2013; Bonnie et al., 1999) continued to support the development of solutions to address identified data needs, to establish research priorities, and to build the governmental infrastructure needed to continue to advance the public health approach to violence prevention and intervention.

Key Tenets

Understanding Public Health

Public health is the "science of protecting and improving the health of people and their communities" (CDC Foundation, n.d.). Complementary to an individual or clinical approach focused on individuals, public health focuses on health at the population level. As applied to violence, public health broadens our approach to consider the upstream or social determinants, such as access to education, financial resources, safe and affordable housing, or the status of women and discrimination based on gender or sexual orientation to develop a deeper understanding of the socioecological connections between violence and health (Niolon et al., 2017). The public health approach uses data and surveillance to identify and monitor health concerns; to understand risk and protective factors; to develop, implement, and evaluate theoretically based interventions that address these factors; and to create programs that can be promulgated through policymaking, legislation, advocacy, law enforcement, and healthcare to ensure widespread adoption of best practices. This approach is a systematic way of understanding and addressing health issues while moving sequentially from problem identification to response. The following sections will discuss each aspect of the public health approach to violence, as well as some public health theories of violence, in more detail.

Define and Monitor the Problem

Public health surveillance is defined as the "systematic collection, analysis, and interpretation of health-related data essential to planning, implementation, and evaluation of public health practice (Thacker & Berkelman, 1988). Public health surveillance has generally been seen as a public good. After the anthrax attacks of 2001, public health surveillance expanded to include public health monitoring that focused on early warning signals from a compilation of various data sources—emergency rooms, poison control centers, electronic health records—to rapidly identify outbreaks or bioterrorist attacks. Some public health practitioners questioned the cost of syndromic surveillance as well as the data quality. However, there is not always a clear connection between data collected via syndromic surveillance and public health action. Since public health is obligated to perform surveillance as an essential service, and to appropriately respond to data with suitable public health control measures, some also saw this type of surveillance as more of a national security issue than a public health measure. During the COVID-19 pandemic, these tensions heightened, both within and external to public health noting the potential for surveillance to be "targeting, stigmatizing, discriminating, and otherwise harming individuals and groups" (Francis & Francis, 2021, p. 5). The application of critical public health theory to public health surveillance in the context of the COVID-19 pandemic placed public health in the futile position of weighing the value of data sharing, compliance, and structural injustices (Francis & Francis, 2021). For example, critical public health highlights the privilege and marginalization inherent in public health systems (Pillan, 2023), such as the racial injustice of a mostly low-wage, frontline workforce who faced higher risks of infection from COVID while having access to fewer resources to protect themselves (e.g., personal protective equipment, paid sick leave, health insurance). That the injustice was not directly accounted for in surveillance data demonstrated public health surveillance's failure to be responsive to inequalities (Blau , 2021).

The first public health surveillance system focused on population-level violence was developed in Latin America in the 1960s to understand the distribution of homicide (Briceño-Leon et al., 2008). Later adapted by the World Health Organization as part of its *Typology of Violence*, this early system focused on classifying and counting self-directed, interpersonal, and collective physical, sexual, and psychological violence (Krug et al., 2002). Over the last several decades, data and surveillance programs have evolved to focus more specifically on collecting data that can be used for public health action, such as the National Network to End Domestic Violence's Domestic Violence Counts annual survey on services provided and unmet needs, CDC's National Violence Death Reporting System, and CDC's National Intimate

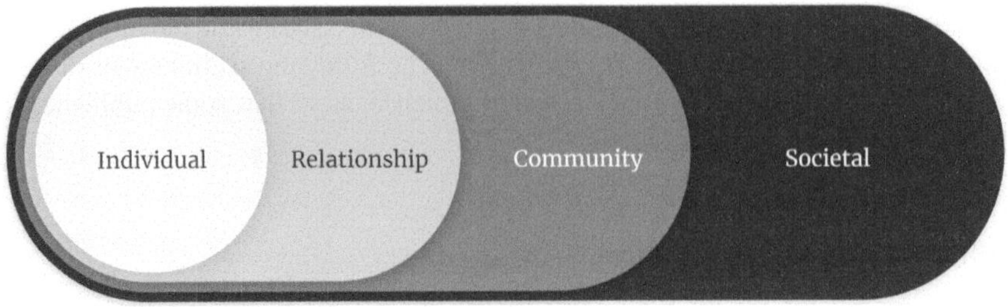

Fig. 6.2 The social-ecological model. *Source* Centers for Disease Control and Prevention (2021)

Partner and Sexual Violence Survey, which collects state- and national-level data on intimate partner and sexual violence.

Identify Risk and Protective Factors

Once violence data are collected via surveillance systems, other factors must be considered to enhance violence prevention. To do this, public health often uses the socioecological framework, adapted from Bronfenbrenner's (1979) seminal work, to identify risk and protective factors (Centers for Disease Control and Prevention, 2021). Put simply, the socioecological model (SEM) focuses on the role that factors at various levels—individual, community, and environmental—play in health and well-being. The SEM integrates research and theories from a variety of disciplines into an explanatory framework focused on theorizing the causes of violence as multifaceted and attributable to dynamic and interconnected individual, relationship, community, and societal factors (Kelly, 2011). As applied to the work of Briceño-Leon et al. (2008) on violence in Latin American mentioned above, it positions the causes of violence as originating (e.g., poverty, inequity, a lack of social support), promoting (e.g., built environments, culture of masculinity, drugs), and facilitating (e.g. easy access to alcohol and firearms) (Briceño-Leon et al., 2008). The SEM (Fig. 6.2) as applied in this context considers the complex interplay between factors at various socio-ecological levels and illustrates the necessity to act across multiple levels when addressing causes of violence. The classification of these root causes and risk factors into a public health framework brings validation to decades of theoretical and scholarly understanding of violence as being rooted in our societal structures, communities, and social conditions. This is especially central to our understanding of gender-based violence (i.e., intimate partner violence and sexual violence).

Develop and Test Interventions

Public health addresses violence by planning and implementing approaches that seek to stop violence from ever happening in the first place. These may occur at any level of the "public health impact pyramid," (Fig. 6.3) but the interventions with the most population impact are included in the widest sections at the bottom of the pyramid (Friedan, 2010). Just above the interventions that address the social determinants of health (e.g., reduced poverty, improved educational opportunities) in the pyramid are interventions that change the context for health. Sometimes known as primary prevention, these types of interventions are designed to mitigate negative impacts and avoid negative outcomes by reducing risk and building resilience at the population level. Examples of primary prevention may include neighborhood planning that improves health and security, legislative restrictions on access to firearms, or social marketing programs that address gender stereotypes (Perry, 2013).

There are several public health theories that are routinely applied to the development and testing of public health interventions. Social cognitive theory is based on the idea that thoughts, feelings, and behaviors—social and cognitive processes—are contributions to aggression and subsequent violence. For example, school-based programs that are based on social cognitive theory focus on improving coping skills and mitigating interpersonal violence by improving self-efficacy and normative beliefs (Hawkins et al., 2023). Social cognitive theory has also been a mainstay of bullying research and interventions to prevent bullying, such as programs that engage peers, parents, and teachers to address both individuals and social factors that have

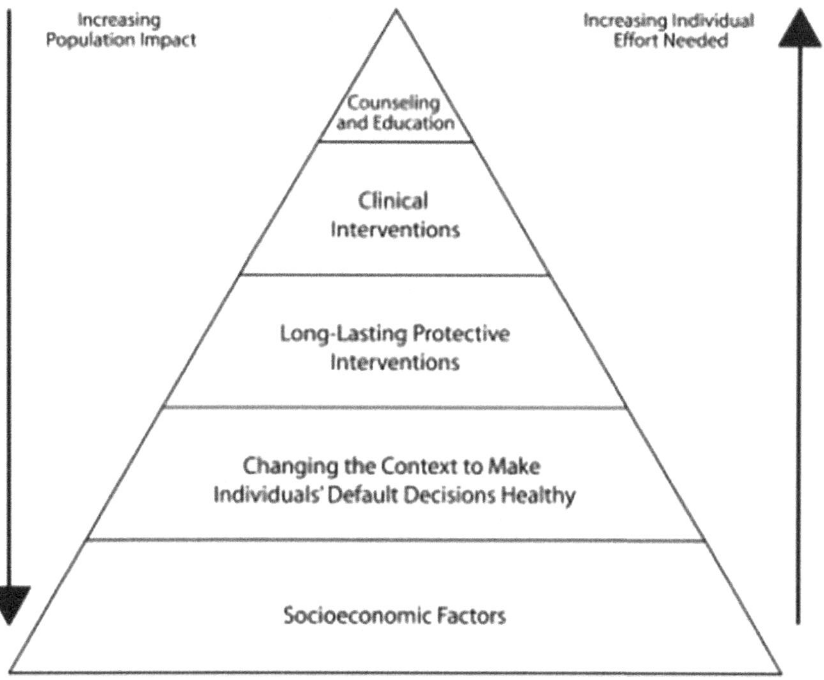

Fig. 6.3 The public health pyramid applied to violence. Adapted from Frieden (2010). *Source* Frieden (2010)

been found to be risk factors for engaging in bullying behaviors (Bussey, 2023). The transtheoretical model (TTM), which is also known as the stages of change model, is focused on processes of change (Prochaska & DiClemente, 1983). Interventions based in this model have been part of primary prevention programs that focus on changing social norms and environments and TTM has frequently been used in the development of intimate partner violence interventions. For example, a shelter-based study of the relationship between social support and engagement in change processes led to findings that suggest "tailor[ed] interventions to meet survivors where they are in the process of change" (Zapor et al., 2018, p. 1052),

Assure Widespread Adoption

Finally, the prevention of violence requires that interventions that are effective are implemented broadly and with fidelity. Both evidence from quantitative research and informal and formal qualitative evaluations must be used to continually assess the acceptability of interventions in the communities where they are applied as well as an intervention's progress towards reaching the overall goal of preventing violence. Widespread adoption of effective prevention programs is necessary to ensure success in changing the societal perspective on violence from reaction (e.g., victim safety and perpetrator accountability) to prevention (Hammond et al., 2006).

The Health Belief Model (HBM) focuses on perceptions of risks and benefits (Glanz & Bishop, 2010). As such, one application of the HBM is in identifying factors associated with intention to participate in violence prevention programs. For example, a program based on HBM showed that participants' perceptions of their susceptibility to experiencing dating violence and their perceptions of the benefits of dating violence prevention programs were the strongest predictors of participation (Cornelius et al., 2009).

However, sometimes HBM-based interventions become widespread without empirical evidence. The prevention of school shootings through enhanced building security infrastructure and personnel, while based on the benefits and barriers of the HBM, has not been shown to make schools safer (Price & Khubchandani, 2019).

Key Contributions to the Study of Family Violence

The public health approach and public health theories of violence have been applied to a plurality of violence types. As outlined in *The History of Violence*, the public health approach was first employed to examine potential causes of sudden increases in youth violence-related mortality (Dahlberg, 1998). Over time, this work has broadened to include intimate partner violence, sexual violence, child abuse, and self-harm (suicide). This comprehensive application of the public health approach and theories to a multitude of violence types has also led to an examination of the overlap across violence types by focusing on population-level impacts, understanding common root causes, and prioritizing prevention efforts that focus on shared impacts (Centers for Disease Control and Prevention, 2017).

The applications of the four phases of the public health approach to violence provides a systematic, scientifically based process for understanding and addressing family violence and shifts the focus from response to prevention. The public health approach also recognizes that efforts must (1) consider systemic inequity in data collected for public health action (e.g., critical public health); (2) focus across all levels of influence including moving beyond individual and interpersonal factors to address community and societal structures, policies and legislation, and social determinants and conditions that contribute to violence (e.g., SEM); (3) design and implement interventions like bystander response that increase feeling of responsibility among those students and teachers who see bullying (e.g., social cognitive theory) and (4) adopt evidence-based programs and policies that can prevent violence before it happens by scaling up and integrating attitudes, beliefs, and perceptions around violence reduction for both individuals (e.g., HBM) and communities. Limitations and challenges associated with traditional theories in health promotion and disease prevention (as described above) have required that public health adopt prevailing theories in family violence, many of which are included in this book, to guide their application to the public health approach to family violence.

Application of the Public Health Approach to Gender-Based Violence Prevention

Violence in Disaster Settings

Disasters occur when there is a disruption that exceeds the capacity of a community to respond. However, it is important to remember that disasters are not natural, though they are frequently referred to in that way. Due to the complex interactions of natural (e.g., climate change, extreme weather events, geophysical hazards), anthropocentric, and social systems that create hazard, risk, vulnerability, and resilience, there are rarely measures that could be taken to prevent a disaster and its socioecological impacts (Modica & Zoboli, 2016). For example, these factors can include housing segregation, deferred maintenance and a lack of investment in protective infrastructure, and the failure of policy makers to address the future risk of these events. The health and other social outcomes from emergencies and disasters are determined by community structures and resources allocation. Preparedness planning, the status and maintenance of infrastructure, and the ways in which social services and other elements of communities are able to respond all play a role in disaster outcomes. These may include the failure of institutional or other supports, the loss of opportunities for paid work, and the lack of sustainable supports for vulnerable subgroups.

Disasters often have gendered impacts due to both societal roles and inequalities. Women may face higher morbidity and mortality rates because they often have less access to resources, information, and decision-making processes during emergencies.

Women-led businesses face significant challenges during disasters, and typically have fewer financial resources, less access to loans, and increased caregiving responsibilities, all of which can hinder their ability to respond to and recover from disasters. Research also indicates that women bear the brunt of many aspects of disaster response and recovery. Given the unique perspectives that come from these responsibilities, humanitarian response efforts are more successful when women are involved in decision-making roles. Women often bring otherwise overlooked lived experiences and needs to the forefront, leading to more effective planning and response strategies for all.

Although it was unique in scope, scale, and duration, the COVID-19 pandemic public health emergency was a disaster that illustrated many of these points. The negative impacts of increased caregiving due to the closure of schools, daycares, and eldercare facilities had a far greater impact on women, who had lost 12 million jobs by February of 2022. Minority and low socioeconomic status mothers and women guardians were most severely impacted (Simien, 2020), and these impacts will be multigenerational. Minority children are 5 times as likely to have experienced the death of a parent or grandparent caregiver during the pandemic (Hillis et al., 2021). Women also saw reduced access to screenings of all types, including for domestic violence.

Low levels of social support led to worse birth outcomes, higher rates of postpartum depression, later vaccination, and higher levels of anxiety related to infection among women. All of these considerations also negatively contributed to higher rates of domestic and interpersonal violence among women throughout the pandemic. Social and structural inequities, including those that contribute to gender-based violence, were magnified during the COVID-19 pandemic and called attention to the ways in which these societal risk factors intersect with other public health issues such as disasters.

The frequency and severity of disasters is increasing, with the U.S. experiencing a record number of billion-dollar disasters over each year of the last decade. However, even with intensifying and more frequent disasters, there are evidence-based approaches to mitigating risk to women during disasters. These include engagement with global frameworks, more equitable access to supports, and the continuation of evidence-based practices from the inter-disaster to the disaster period.

Critiques of the Public Health Approach

There are many valid critiques to the public health approach and the public health theories of violence. Behavior change theories central to health promotion and disease prevention, such as the health action process model or the social cognitive theory, focus on an individual's motivation for change, risk perception, and self-efficacy.

While theories that are focused on changing individual beliefs and behaviors are viewed as an important component of a comprehensive approach to violence prevention, they do not account for the socialized power and control dynamics of gender-based violence and have been criticized for inadvertently promoting victim-blaming (Gielen & Sleet, 2003).

Furthermore, gender-based violence practitioners have pushed back on what they see is an outsized focus on behavior change interventions rather than promoting strategies that address the social and structural conditions that contribute to violence (Townsend, 2017). Relatedly, public health interventions that draw primarily from models of behavior change (e.g., HBM) are likely insufficient to effectively address the wide range of types of gender-based violence (Orr et al., 2022).

Public health theories of violence can also be too focused on the iterative, science-based public health approach, which prioritizes process over considerations included in feminist theory, such as the critical interaction of gender and power (Brubaker, 2021). Finally, many public health theories may not adequately apply, or prioritize, a health equity lens. Theoretical frameworks that do not center equity are not adequate for preventing violence. More recently, critical public health theory has emerged as a response to the lack of focus on equity available through other theories and frameworks (Pillan, 2023). Critical public health seeks to provide a set of values, techniques, and practices for challenging the status quo in public health to better align public health policy and practice with the everyday experiences of those most impacted by health inequities (Center for Critical Public Health, n.d.).

Conclusion

Public health is an inherently interdisciplinary field that incorporates core disciplines of epidemiology, biostatistics, health policy, environmental health, and health promotion with both social and hard sciences more broadly. The public health approach to violence integrates theories from across these disciplines (e.g., social-ecological model, social cognitive theory, transtheoretical model, and the health belief model) to create strong, evidence-based approaches for understanding risk factors; for modifying these risks through practice, programs, and policy; and for evaluating the uptake and utility of interventions for reducing violence. One of the hallmarks of the public health approach to violence is that it shifts our belief of violence as an inherent part of the human condition to the belief that violence is preventable—employing many of the same tools and resources that have been successfully used to address the more traditional public health issues motor vehicle and occupational safety, tobacco control, or improved maternal and child health (Centers for Disease Control and Prevention, 2021).

References

Baum K, Blakeslee KM, Lloyd J, Petrosino A (2013) Violence prevention: Moving from evidence to implementation. *NAM Perspectives*.

Blau, F. D., Koebe, J., & Meyerhofer, P. A. (2021). Who are the essential and frontline workers? *Business Economics (Cleveland, Ohio), 56*(3), 168.

Bonnie, R. J., Fulco, C. E., & Liverman, C. T. (Eds.). (1999). *Reducing the burden of injury: Advancing prevention and treatment*. National Academies Press.

Briceño-León, R., Villaveces, A., & Concha-Eastman, A. (2008). Understanding the uneven distribution of the incidence of homicide in Latin America. *International Journal of Epidemiology, 37*(4), 751–757.

Bronfenbrenner, U. (1979). *The ecology of human development*. Harvard University Press.

Brubaker, S. J. (2021). Embracing and expanding feminist theory: (Re)conceptualizing gender and power. *Violence Against Women, 27*(5), 717–726.

Bussey, K. (2023). The contribution of social cognitive theory to school bullying research and practice. *Theory Into Practice, 62*(3), 293–305.

Center for Critical Public Health (n.d.) What is critical public health?. https://criticalpublichealth.org/about/#:~:text=Critical%20Public%20Health%20is%20an,in%20which%20they%20are%20created

Centers for Disease Control and Prevention (2016) A comprehensive technical package for the prevention of youth violence and associated risk behaviors. Centers for Disease Control and Prevention.

Centers for Disease Control and Prevention (2017) Connecting the dots. https://vetoviolence.cdc.gov/apps/connecting-the-dots/content/home

Centers for Disease Control and Prevention (2021) The public health approach to violence prevention. U.S. Department of Health & Human Services. https://www.cdc.gov/violence-prevention/about/about-the-public-health-approach-to-violence-prevention.html?CDC_AAref_Val=

CDC Foundation (n.d) What is public health?. https://www.cdcfoundation.org/what-public-health

Choden, P., Armstrong, K., & Sendall, M. C. (2022). Intimate partner violence (IPV) in Bhutan: Understanding women's responses to IPV using the transtheoretical model of behavior change. *Journal of interpersonal violence, 37*(19–20), NP18238–NP18265.

Cornelius, T. L., Sullivan, K. T., Wyngarden, N., & Milliken, J. C. (2009). Participation in prevention programs for dating violence: Beliefs about relationship violence and intention to participate. *Journal of Interpersonal Violence, 24*(6), 1057–1078.

Dahlberg, L. L. (1998). Youth violence in the United States major trends, risk factors, and prevention approaches. *American Journal of Preventive Medicine, 14*(4), 259–272.

Dahlberg, L. L., & Mercy, J. A. (2009). History of violence as a public health issue. *AMA Virtual Mentor, 11*(2), 167–172. http://virtualmentor.ama-assn.org/2009/02/mhst1-0902.html

Francis, J. G., & Francis, L. (2021). *Sustaining surveillance: The importance of information for public health*. Springer.

Frieden, T. R. (2010). A framework for public health action: The health impact pyramid. *American Journal of Public Health, 100*(4), 590–595.

Gielen, A. C., & Sleet, D. (2003). Application of behavior-change theories and methods to injury prevention. *Epidemiologic Reviews, 25*, 65–76.

Glanz, K., & Bishop, D. B. (2010). The role of behavioral science theory in development and implementation of public health interventions. *Annual Review of Public Health, 31*, 399–418. https://doi.org/10.1146/annurev.publhealth.012809.103604

Hammond, W. R., Whitaker, D. J., Lutzker, J. R., Mercy, J., & Chin, P. M. (2006). Setting a violence prevention agenda at the centers for disease control and prevention. *Aggression and Violent Behavior, 11*(2), 112–119.

Hawkins, M. M., Florez-Garcia, V., Guevara-Romero, E., Santacruz-Salas, E., & Ruiz, A. (2023). Social cognitive theory-based interventions to address interpersonal violence among Hispanic Youth—A systematic review. *Hispanic Health Care International, 21*(4), 228–234.

Hillis, S. D., Blenkinsop, A., Villaveces, A., Annor, F. B., Liburd, L., Massetti, G. M., Demissie, Z., Mercy, J. A., Nelson, C. A., Cluver, L., Flaxman, S., Sherr, L., Donnelly, C. A., Ratmann, O., & Unwin, H. J. T. (2021). COVID-19–associated orphanhood and caregiver death in the United States. *Pediatrics, 148*(6), e2021053760.

Kelly, U. A. (2011). Theories of intimate partner violence: From blaming the victim to acting against injustice: Intersectionality as an analytic framework. *Advances in Nursing Science, 34*(3), E29–E51.

Krug, E. G., Mercy, J. A., Dahlberg, L. L., & Zwi, A. B. (2002). The world report on violence and health. *The Lancet, 360*(9339), 1083–1088.

Modica, M., & Zoboli, R. (2016). Vulnerability, resilience, hazard, risk, damage, and loss: A socio-ecological framework for natural disaster analysis. *Web Ecology, 16*(1), 59–62.

National Cancer Institute. (2018). *Theory at a glance: A guide for health promotion practice* (2nd ed.). U.S. Department of Health and Human Services.

Niolon, P. H., Kearns, M., Dills, J., Rambo, K., Irving, S., Armstead, T., & Gilbert, L. (2017). *Intimate partner violence prevention resource for action: A compilation of the best available evidence.* National Center for Injury Prevention and Control, Centers for Disease Control and Prevention.

Omran, A. R. (1998). The epidemiologic transition theory revisited thirty years later. *World Health Statistics Quarterly, 51*(2–4), 99–119.

Perry, I. (2013). Violence: A public health perspective. In *Rethinking violence* (pp. 76–103). Routledge.

Pillan, H. (2023) Critical public health. In Liamputtong, P. (Ed.), *Handbook of social sciences and global public health.* Springer.

Price, J. H., & Khubchandani, J. (2019). School firearm violence prevention practices and policies: Functional or folly? *Violence and Gender, 6*(3), 154–167.

Prochaska, J. O., & DiClemente, C. C. (1983). Stages and processes of self-change of smoking: Toward an integrative model of change. *Journal of Consulting and Clinical Psychology, 51*(3), 390–395.

Simien, E. M. (2020). COVID-19 and the "strong Black woman". *The Gender Policy Report, University of Minnesota.*

Thacker, S. B., & Berkelman, R. L. (1988). Public health surveillance in the United States. *Epidemiologic Reviews, 10*(1), 164–190.

Townsend, S. M. (2017). *Innovations in community-level prevention.* National Sexual Violence Resource Center.

U.S. Department of Health and Human Services (n.d.) *Healthy people 2030: Violence prevention.* https://odphp.health.gov/healthypeople/objectives-and-data/browse-objectives/violence-prevention

Zapor, H., Wolford-Clevenger, C., & Johnson, D. M. (2018). The association between social support and stages of change in survivors of intimate partner violence. *Journal of Interpersonal Violence, 33*(7), 1051–1070.

Chapter 7
The Explanatory Power of Intersectionality and Black Feminist Criminology in Understanding Family Violence

Allison E. Monterrosa

Name of the theory: Intersectionality is a theoretical framework that examines how various forms of social stratification, such as race, gender, class, sexuality, ability, and nationality, interact simultaneously to shape individuals' experiences of oppression, privilege, and identity in relation to systems of power. It emphasizes that systems of power are interdependent and cannot be understood in isolation from one another.

*Relatedly, Black Feminist Criminology (BFC) is a theoretical framework that examines how race, gender, class, and other social identities intersect to shape the experiences of Black women and other racial-ethnic marginalized people's experiences within the criminal legal system as both victims and offenders.

Proponents of the theory: Kimberlé Crenshaw, Patricia Hill Collins, Combahee River Collective, Hillary Potter.

What the theory says: The theory of intersectionality argues that social identities such as race, gender, class, sexuality, and ability do not exist separately but intersect and overlap, creating interconnected experiences of oppression and privilege in relation to power structures. It emphasizes that experiences of inequality cannot be fully understood by examining each identity in isolation, as multiple forms of oppression often reinforce one another, especially for people who embody multiple marginalized identities.

Crenshaw states, "Intersectionality is a lens through which you can see where power comes and collides, where it interlocks and intersects" (Crenshaw 2017, para 3).

A. E. Monterrosa (✉)
California State University, San Marcos, USA
e-mail: amonterrosa@csusm.edu

A. Hattery and E. Smith (eds.), *Theories of Family Violence*, Advances in Preventing and Treating Violence and Aggression, https://doi.org/10.1007/978-3-032-17095-8_7

Introduction

One of the primary critiques of theories of gender-based violence, including those in this text, is that they are not attentive to the diversity of experiences of people who hold marginalized racial and ethnic identities, particularly Black women. And, yet, Black women experience disproportionately high rates of violence at the hands of their current and ex-intimate partners, eclipsed only by Indigenous women. Violence is widespread among American Indian and Alaska Native women, with more than four in five experiencing some form of violence and over half experiencing sexual violence (Duthu, 2008; Indian Law Resource Center, 2025). Nearly half (43%) of Black women, report experiencing violence in their intimate relationships (Leemis et al., 2022). Additionally, Black women are overrepresented in rates of femicide, defined as the homicide of women. In 2020, the Violence Policy Center reported that Black women were murdered by men at a rate of 3.0 per 100,000—nearly three times the rate for white women (1.1 per 100,000). Among Black women murdered by a known offender, 60% were killed by a current or former intimate partner (2023). Black transgender women also experience disproportionately high rates of gendered violence, including intimate partner abuse, shaped by the intersection of anti-Black racism, transmisogyny, poverty, and criminalization (Human Rights Campaign Foundation, 2024). Rather than receiving protection, Black trans women are frequently subjected to surveillance, punishment, and exclusion from formal systems of support. As Bierria and Lens (2022) argue in *Survived and Punished*, state responses to violence often further harm Black trans survivors by prioritizing carceral control over survivor safety, underscoring the urgent need for non-punitive, survivor-centered approaches to addressing gender-based violence. Thus is it critical that we have theoretical frameworks that better explain the experiences of Black women and women with marginalized racial and ethnic identities who are abused by their intimate partners.

Both intersectionality and Black Feminist Criminology provide important advances in our understanding of the lived experiences of marginalized survivors of domestic violence. Thus, it is critical to have a deeper understanding of these theoretical frames in order to center the voices of survivors who are racially and ethnically marginalized as well as develop prevention and intervention approaches that meet their distinct and complex needs.

Intersectionality

Intersectionality is a theoretical framework introduced by legal scholar Kimberlé Crenshaw that explores how social identities such as race, class, gender, sexuality, ability, and citizenship status intersect to shape experiences of privilege and oppression. Rather than treating these identities as separate or additive, intersectionality highlights their interconnected and mutually constitutive nature (Crenshaw, 1989, 1991). Central to this framework is the recognition that power structures, including racism, sexism, classism, ableism, xenophobia, and other forms of systemic inequality, interact and reinforce one another, producing unique and often compounded forms of marginalization for individuals who hold multiple oppressed identities (Crenshaw, 1989).

Rooted in Black feminism and Critical Race Theory, intersectionality operates as a methodology, a theoretical orientation, and an analytic tool for understanding how interlocking systems of power shape lived experiences (Carbado et al., 2013). While the term is frequently cited, it is often misapplied. Intersectionality is not merely about identifying multiple identities (e.g., Black, working class, woman); rather, it is a theory of power that interrogates broader systems such as white supremacy, heteropatriarchy, and capitalism (Collins, 1998, 2015, 2019; Crenshaw, 1989). As a framework, intersectionality centers the experiences of those structurally marginalized in society and has informed much of the research on domestic violence within these communities.

Applying an intersectional lens requires a sustained focus on individuals' relationships to systems of power. Without this orientation, analyses risk overlooking the structural dimensions of inequality, weakening the explanatory power of the framework, and erasing the lived realities of survivors and those most affected by violence and marginalization.

Many scholars of racial-ethnic historically marginalized backgrounds have advanced our understanding of the impact of embodying multiply marginalized identities in relation to systems of power (Baca Zinn & Zambrana, 2019; Combahee River Collective, 1986; Collins, 1990; Crenshaw, 1991; Moraga & Anzaldua, 1981; Romero, 2008). Kimberlé Crenshaw, who coined the term "intersectionality," does so in her path-breaking paper, *Mapping the Margins*, which utilizes a critical race theoretical lens to interrogate Black women victim/survivors of domestic violence experiences with the criminal legal system (Crenshaw, 1991). Crenshaw's pioneering paper expanded the theory of intersectionality as it had been conceived by the Combahee River Collective (1986) and built upon the foundational insights of earlier Black women scholars and activists. Truth's (1851) speech "Ain't I a Woman?" forcefully challenged both racism and sexism, offering an early articulation of the unique oppression faced by Black women. Wells-Barnett (1895) provided one of the first detailed analyses of how racialized sexual violence against Black women was systematically ignored or justified, highlighting the intertwined oppressions of racism and misogyny in lynching narratives and broader social structures. Hamer (1964) similarly emphasized the intersections of race, gender, and systemic violence in her speeches. Crenshaw (1991) built on these legacies by applying and expanding intersectional analysis to the experiences of Black women abused by their partners, demonstrating how white supremacy and patriarchy shaped their treatment within the legal system.

As a critical race theory scholar, Crenshaw focused on the differential treatment Black women faced within the legal system, centering their experiences with domestic violence as a key case study. She argued that Black women's experiences with the law and their citizen status were profoundly shaped by the intersections of white supremacy and heteropatriarchy, leading to their experiences with domestic violence being routinely ignored or dismissed.

The Emergence of Black Feminist Criminology

Building on this rich history of Black women scholars centering Black women and theorizing the influences of structural power on their lived experiences, Black Feminist Criminology emerged through the scholarship of Potter (2006). Potter (2006) draws on the scholarship of Patricia Hill Collins, Black Feminist thought, and specifically the frame of the matrix of domination (1990). The matrix of domination illustrates the interlocking systems of oppression imbued within power structures in relation to those who embody stigmatized identities, such as race, class, gender, sexuality, (dis)ability and other marginalized identities (Collins, 1990).

BFC utilizes a nuanced intersectional framework for understanding the intersections of race, gender, class, sexuality, and citizenship within the criminal legal system. BFC highlights the epistemological aspects of positionality, power, and reflexivity to underscore Black women's unique experiences with violence. BFC critiques mainstream criminology for ignoring the unique social contexts of Black women and challenges the racial and gender biases embedded in legal institutions, policing, sentencing, and incarceration. Further, BFC illuminates how the criminal legal system functions as a structural barrier for Black women, as both victims and offenders of crime. BFC moves beyond individualistic explanations of violence to emphasize systemic and institutional factors that shape patterns of abuse and victimization within families.

Specific to domestic violence, Black Feminist Criminology (BFC) analyzes domestic violence among women who experience racialized and gendered systemic oppression. Feminist theorists like Johnson (1995), De Coster and Heimer (2021) and Sweet (2021) theorize that domestic violence is more than an exercise of male privilege, it is fueled by systemic inequality that is produced by the foundation of heteropatriarchy. Feminist scholars have long identified unilateral power and control within personal relationships as a hallmark of abuse, recognizing it as a microcosm of larger systems of social domination (Mckay, 2023; Stark, 2010). The strength of the framework provided by BFC lies in how it incorporates the intersectional feminist study of domestic violence with the historical sociology of abuse and power relations (Potter, 2015; Monterrosa, 2021a, 2021b; Therbon, 1980).

Intimate Partner Violence (IPV) and Structural Inequalities

BFC's strength is that it was envisioned to highlight the ways in which structural inequalities (poverty, housing instability) and systemic racism influence Black women's susceptibility to IPV (Potter, 2006). Further, it specifically interrogates the role that economic dependence and lack of institutional support play in exacerbating risks for exposure to domestic abuse. Moreover, societal stereotypes depicting Black women as "strong" and resilient reduce the empathy and resources they receive from social services and law enforcement. Black women are often subject to dehumanizing stereotypes that render them illegible as victims and are misread as inherently angry and aggressive, even when they initially call law enforcement for help or are using formal help-seeking institutions to leave an abusive relationship (Collins, 2005).

Monterrosa's (2021a, 2021b) work applies a BFC framework that reveals how systemic factors and cultural perceptions uniquely impact women's decisions to seek assistance and underscores the importance of considering intersecting identities and societal stereotypes when addressing help-seeking behaviors in IPV cases. BFC takes these factors into account and creates space for Black women to be visible and "seen" appropriately within the criminal legal sphere.

Furthermore, the field of gender-based violence studies is increasingly intersecting with research on the carceral state, examining how state power shapes the experiences of individuals navigating intimate and interpersonal relationships. Studies have documented that women impacted by the criminal-legal system, particularly those living in hyper-surveilled neighborhoods heavily affected by mass incarceration, face heightened risks of intimate partner violence (IPV) (Mckay, 2023) and intimate carceral violence (ICV)—a form of IPV in which the state becomes the abusive actor (Monterrosa, 2023). ICV often follows acts of coercive violence (CV) by an intimate partner who deliberately weaponizes state systems against their partner, for example by making false allegations of child abuse to child protective services (CPS) or reporting them to social services for minor infractions such as selling food stamps for cash to cover essential expenses (Monterrosa & Hattery, 2023; Monterrosa, 2023).

The emphasis on punitive measures, presumptions of wrongdoing, and systemic distrust of Black mothers embedded in policies and practices create fertile ground for abusers to exert control without direct physical violence, positioning the state as the abusive actor by proxy and further disempowering victims and survivors. Meanwhile, the state's preoccupation with identifying alleged benefit fraud or "gaming the system" diverts critical attention and resources away from enacting structural reforms needed to genuinely support mothers and strengthen families and keep victims/survivors safe. Additionally, the state creates conditions that enable abusive behaviors such as stonewalling, coercive control, (Stark, 2010) and coercive violence (Monterrosa, 2023; Monterrosa & Hattery, 2023), while simultaneously undermining victims' agency and their ability to maintain safety, placing them at greater risk of harm from both the abuser and the state.

These dynamics make it extremely difficult to build and sustain healthy romantic relationships, as individuals chronically exposed to mass criminalization and incarceration often experience profound post-traumatic stress (Comfort, 2008). Living in a state of hypervigilance and struggling to trust others, even those closest to them, can undermine intimacy, since in violent or punitive environments, vulnerability can be exploited to cause harm in various ways, especially in settings like prisons and jails. This dynamic reflects what I have theorized as *prisonized romance*, where the conditions of incarceration and systemic surveillance fundamentally distort the possibilities for safe and trusting intimate connections (Monterrosa, 2023; Monterrosa & Hattery, 2023).

Additionally, women who are in relationships with men who are navigating correctional control (e.g. probation, parole, incarceration) thus experience the long arm of the state intervening in their intimate partnerships with the coerced labor associated with navigating their partner's Post Traumatic Stress and the omnipresent threat of state violence, which is expressed and experienced as abuse (Monterrosa, 2021a, 2021b, 2023). Thus, it is crucial to include a structural lens which examines the state apparatus of racialized-gendered oppression as a key contributor to destabilizing Black families and other marginalized racal-ethnic groups.

Child Welfare Policy as State-Sanctioned Family Violence

State-sanctioned family violence (SSFV) includes violence that is enacted through policies and practices that separate Black families, such as punitive welfare policies and aggressive child protective interventions. These systems often criminalize poverty rather than addressing its root causes. As a result, Black mothers are frequently scrutinized, criminalized (Goodmark, 2023; Roberts, 2022) and penalized for poverty-related "neglect" in cases where state and social welfare policies systematically fail to provide economic stability, affordable childcare, adequate housing, and healthcare access, needs that disproportionately affect Black communities due to historical and ongoing racial discrimination (Roberts, 2022). For example, women who are victims of domestic violence are often referred to child protective services for investigation when they call 911 during a violent episode or seek safety in a shelter when fleeing an abuser (Monterrosa & Hattery, 2023; Roberts, 2022). Racially and ethnically marginalized and poor mothers are disproportionately subject to failure-to-protect laws, which are rooted in carceral logics that seek to hold victims accountable for their abusers' violence (Bierra & Lens, 2019; Trozzo, 2022).

By framing structural poverty as individual parental failure, state agencies divert attention from institutional responsibility and place the burden on already marginalized mothers.

This punitive approach increases the likelihood of Black children entering the foster care system, which serves as yet another form of state intervention in family life that perpetuates intergenerational trauma (Roberts, 2022; Harp & Bunting, 2020). Research shows that Black children are removed from their families at higher rates than white children for similar allegations, often stemming from conditions of economic deprivation rather than overt abuse (Dettlaff & Boyd, 2020; Roberts, 2022). The foster system not only severs critical familial and cultural bonds but also exposes children to potential abuse and instability in state care, increasing the risk of long-term negative outcomes such as involvement with the criminal legal system, mental health struggles, lower educational attainment, and increased risk for IPV (Roberts, 2002; Wildeman & Emanuel, 2014).

Historically, Black motherhood has been constructed as inherently deviant, rendering Black children as suspect and deviant by association. This framing is rooted in racist and sexist ideologies that have evolved from slavery, Jim Crow, and the war on poverty, portraying Black mothers as irresponsible, hypersexual, and incapable of providing adequate care for their children (Roberts, 1997, 2002). This stereotype has been institutionalized in public policy and media representations, which fuel a narrative of Black maternal unfitness and normalize harsh surveillance and intervention (Roberts, 1997, 2022).

Such constructions also create what scholars call "racialized risk discourses," where Black mothers' parenting is presumed dangerous or deficient, leading to higher rates of investigations and removals compared to white families experiencing similar or worse material hardships (Roberts, 1997, 2002, 2022). These discourses allow child welfare systems to operate with a racialized double standard that prioritizes control and punishment of Black mothers over supportive, preventative measures that could address poverty-related factors (Dettlaff & Boyd, 2020; Roberts, 2022).

BFC examines how racialized poverty and systemic inequities lead to increased surveillance of Black families, highlighting the ways child protective services can act as an extension of the carceral state, funneling Black families into cycles of trauma, separation, and criminalization (Potter, 2015). Rather than supporting family stability, these state practices reflect a broader agenda of social control, where state institutions intervene in marginalized communities under the guise of "protection," yet ultimately reinforce structural violence and white supremacist social hierarchies (Zuberi & Bonilla-Silva, 2008; Richie, 2012; Roberts, 2002).

Expanding a BFC lens to interrogate child welfare policy calls for shifting away from punitive approaches toward policies that provide economic, educational, and social supports designed to keep families together. BFC underscores the necessity of reimagining child welfare systems in ways that center the dignity, agency, and cultural resilience of Black families—challenging the harmful stereotypes and structural inequities that currently drive disproportionate state surveillance and separation.

Mass Incarceration as State-Sanctioned Family Violence

Mass incarceration functions as a form of state-sanctioned family violence (SSFV) by systematically destabilizing families and communities, particularly within Black and marginalized populations. SSFV refers to the harm inflicted on families and interpersonal relationships by governmental policies and institutions, often through punitive measures rather than protective or supportive interventions. For example, the violence of mass incarceration has disproportionately disrupted many racial-ethnic marginalized families and families navigating poverty (Alexander, 2011). The incarceration of a parent is especially destabilizing and creates an enormous set of challenges for children. Research shows that nearly 1 in 9 Black children have an incarcerated parent (Horton, 2022; Wildeman & Western, 2010), leading to developmental and emotional challenges linked to trauma and attachment disruptions (Geller et al., 2012). Studies show that children of incarcerated parents experience psychological trauma, stigma, and diminished life outcomes, perpetuating cycles of state-inflicted violence, and creating intergenerational trauma among criminal legal system impacted families (Clear, 2009; Salinas, 2023).

Further, mass incarceration has disproportionately affected fathers in Black families and separated children from their primary caregivers, creating emotional and financial instability, which are significant risk factors for violence (Richie & Eife, 2021). Mass incarceration imposes financial burdens on families through legal fees, lost income, and increased dependence on social services.

Post-incarceration barriers to employment further perpetuate poverty (Pager, 2007). Each of these impacts increases the risk for violence in intimate relationships (Hattery & Smith, 2007).

Moreover, Black women, a group already systematically oppressed, are disproportionately burdened with caregiving tasks and are economically and emotionally taxed when a loved one is incarcerated. Black Feminist Criminology (BFC) highlights the unique challenges Black women face when attempting to navigate this type of state family violence, emphasizing how structural inequalities compound the personal and relational impacts of incarceration (Comfort, 2008).

Further, Black women often experience the effects of mass incarceration and the broader carceral system as a form of intimate partner violence via coercive carceral care, which refers to the emotional, logistical, and caretaking labor they perform in support of incarcerated or system-impacted partners (James, 2020; Monterrosa, 2023). While this care is often rooted in genuine love and concern, it unfolds within a context shaped by racialized carceral control and gendered expectations, where emotional manipulation, dependency and limited reciprocity transforms care into a form of coercion. A key feature of this dynamic is stonewalling where women are met with emotional withdrawal, shutdown, or silence from their partners (Monterrosa, 2021a, 2021b, 2023). This behavior functions in multiple ways: at times as a means of asserting control or withholding reciprocity, but also as a response to overwhelming fear, frustration, and trauma stemming from dehumanizing constraints of the carceral system.

This withdrawal is often a response to the emotional toll and psychological exhaustion of navigating constant surveillance, limited autonomy, and institutional barriers. In turn, women are forced to absorb and manage their partner's emotional distress by anticipating moods, de-escalating conflict, and regulating feelings, all of which fall under the unpaid and unacknowledged labor of intimate carceral care. For example, men who are deeply affected by incarceration often experience intense stress when navigating bureaucratic systems and state-imposed restrictions, leading them to withdraw or shut down emotionally (Clemmer, 1940; Martin, 2017). Their silence, while painful for partners, reflects internalized defeat and the psychological toll of prisonization (Conner & Denton, 2017; Clemmer, 1940), which women must then manage as part of their intimate labor (Monterrosa, 2021a, 2021b, 2023). In doing so, women often find themselves "walking on eggshells," trying to avoid triggering their partners' emotional collapse or despair in order to protect them from carceral consequences, what Monterrosa describes as intimate carceral labor (2023).

This labor operates within what Delerme (2025) defines as the carceral care economy, a system that exploits the labor, time, and emotional resources of families, particularly for women of color, to sustain the everyday functioning of the carceral state. Within this economy, the state shifts the burdens of incarceration onto families, extracting unpaid labor through care work, logistical coordination, and financial contributions such as commissary, phone calls, travel, and legal advocacy. Coercive carceral care, then, is not merely a personal sacrifice. It is structurally coerced, gendered labor that sustains both intimate relationships and state punishment (Delerme, 2025; James, 2021; Monterrosa, 2023). The emotional violence women endure marked by abandonment, surveillance, manipulation, and exhaustion is central to how the carceral system reproduces racialized and gendered control (Mercado, 2022). This entanglement of care and constraint reveals how the carceral system reshapes and imprisons intimacy, reproducing gendered subjugation and extending the reach of the state into the interpersonal violence into the romantic lives of women.

Practical Applications of Intersectionality and Black Feminist Criminology

The explanatory power of intersectionality and BFC cannot be overstated. This theoretical frame is particularly effective in addressing the ways victims of domestic violence are both victimized by intimate partners and disproportionately impacted by state systems like child welfare and the criminal legal system. The types of questions addressed by BFC include exploring how structural inequalities and systemic racism contribute to the unique experiences of Black women in abusive relationships, examining why Black women are disproportionately criminalized when defending themselves from domestic violence, and investigating how racial and gender stereotypes shape institutional responses to Black families experiencing violence. By highlighting the intersection of race, gender, and violence, BFC sheds light on the ways in which systemic oppression disproportionately affects Black women within the context of intimate partner violence, family violence, the child welfare system and the criminal legal system (Potter, 2006).

Moreover, it is important to emphasize that neither intersectionality nor BFC are limited to examining Black experiences. Racial-ethnic people, and other marginalized groups also benefit from a BFC framework, as it provides a lens through which the compounded effects of multiple forms of oppression, including race, class, gender, sexuality, and citizenship are addressed in the context of family violence, gender-based violence and criminalization.

Intersectionality and Black Feminist Criminology as Liberatory Praxis in Research

Intersectionality and Black Feminist Criminology (BFC) have been applied as a liberatory praxis in various research studies, offering both qualitative and quantitative insights into the intersectional oppression faced by Black women. In her article, "Trying to Get Free": A Theoretical Centering of Black Women's Post-Carceral Narratives of Systemic Unfreedom," Crawford Mondé (2021) employs BFC to examine how Black women's post-incarceration experiences reflect ongoing systemic violence, including racial profiling, economic disenfranchisement, and gendered violence. By centering Black women's lived experiences, Crawford Mondé critiques the carceral state's intersectional impacts and advocates for transformative justice aimed at dismantling systems of racial, gendered, and class-based oppression. Her work frames intersectionality and BFC as both a theoretical lens and a liberatory practice, calling for justice for Black women within and beyond prison walls.

Monterrosa's research explores how systemic factors such as economic instability, partner incarceration, and state surveillance shape the romantic relationships of Black women and other racial-ethnic marginalized groups and create conditions that render them vulnerable to intimate partner violence (2021a, 2021b). This research applies intersectionality and BFC as a liberatory theoretical and methodological praxis, highlighting the structural forces that influence personal and relational dynamics. Similarly, Gonzalez (2022) underscores the importance of centering Black feminist ethics in criminological research, arguing that BFC offers a necessary framework for addressing the complex, intersectional experiences of Black women and girls. Duhaney (2022) uses BFC to investigate the compounded criminalization and victimization experienced by Black women subjected to IPV, further illustrating the framework's utility in examining how multiple systems of oppression converge in shaping lived realities.

Moreover, Potter (2015) discusses how quantitative methodologies can be integrated within an intersectional criminological framework, emphasizing the need to use intersectionality as both a theoretical guide and a foundational principle for data collection, analysis, and interpretation. By incorporating race, gender, class, sexuality, citizenship and other marginalized variables into quantitative analyses, researchers can better interrogate the structural inequalities that drive domestic violence and justice outcomes. Potter's work demonstrates how Black feminist criminology can bridge qualitative insights with empirical rigor, fostering a holistic approach to understanding and addressing the systemic oppression faced by Black women.

Policy Development and Transformative Justice

Intersectionality and BFC can inform trauma-informed, culturally responsive prevention and intervention approaches that account for the intersection of systemic inequalities in addressing family violence. For example, policies should focus on reducing punitive responses and increasing access to economic support, housing stability, and counseling services tailored for Black women and other racial-ethnic marginalized women. Applying an intersectional lens could lead to more equitable treatment of women who act in self-defense in IPV situations, advocating for changes to self-defense laws that recognize cumulative trauma (Hattery et al., 2022).

Lastly, this chapter demonstrates the explanatory power of intersectionality and BFC by linking personal relationship outcomes to broader systemic injustices. It highlights the need for policy interventions that address structural barriers to healthy family dynamics for marginalized communities. Collins and Bilge (2020) argue that intersectional theory is more than a framework for understanding structural power, it also requires a call to action. By integrating structural, historical, and intersectional perspectives, Black Feminist Criminology remains one of the most robust frameworks for understanding and addressing family violence in ways that center Black women's lived experiences and advocate for transformative justice.

References

Baca Zinn, M., & Zambrana, R. (2019). Chicanas/Latinas advance intersectional thought and practice. *Gender & Society, 33*(5), 677–701. https://doi.org/10.1177/0891243219853753

Bierria, A., & Lenz, C. (2022). Defending self-defense: A call to action by Survived and Punished. https://survivedandpunished.org/2022/03/31/defending-self-defense-a-call-to-action-by-survived-punished/

Carbado, D. W., Crenshaw, K. W., Mays, V. M., & Tomlinson, B. (2013). INTERSECTIONALITY: Mapping the Movements of a Theory. *Du Bois Review: Social science Research On Race, 10*(2), 303–312. https://doi.org/10.1017/S1742058X13000349

Clear, T. (2009). Incarceration and communities: Todd Clear considers the impact of high rates of incarceration on crime prevalence in poor American neighbourhoods. *Criminal Justice Matters, 75*(1), 26–27. https://doi.org/10.1080/09627250802699749

Clemmer, D. (1940). *The prison community*. Holt, Rinehart & Winston.

Collins, P. H. (1990). Black feminist thought in the matrix of domination. In P. H. Collins (Ed.), *Black feminist thought: Knowledge, consciousness, and politics of empowerment* (pp. 221–238). Unwin Hyman.

Collins, P. H. (2005). *Black sexual politics: African Americans, gender, and the new racism*. Routledge.

Collins, P. H. (2015). Intersectionality's definitional dilemmas. *Annual Review of Sociology, 41*(1), 1–20. https://doi.org/10.1146/annurev-soc-073014-112142

Collins, P. H. (2019). *Intersectionality as critical social theory*. Duke University Press.

Collins, P. H., & Bilge, S. (2020). *Intersectionality* (2nd ed.). Polity Press.

Connor, D. P., & Denton, A. N. (2017). Clemmer, Donald. In K. R. Kerley (Ed.), The encyclopedia of corrections. Wiley. https://doi.org/10.1002/9781118845387

Collins, P. H. (1998). The tie that binds: race, gender and US violence. *Ethnic and Racial Studies, 21*(5), 917–938. https://doi.org/10.1080/014198798329720

Combahee River Collective. (1986). *The Combahee River Collective statement: Black feminist organizing in the seventies and eighties*. Women of Color Press.

Comfort, M. (2008). *Doing time together: Love and family in the shadow of the prison*. University of Chicago Press.

Crawford Mondé, G. (2021). "Trying to get free": A theoretical centering of Black Women's post-carceral narratives of systemic unfreedom. CrimRxiv. https://doi.org/10.21428/cb6ab371.e4c0db81

Crenshaw, K. (1989). Demarginalizing the intersection of race and sex: A Black feminist critique of antidiscrimination doctrine, feminist theory and antiracist politics. *University of Chicago Legal Forum, 1989*(1), 139–167.

Crenshaw, K. (1991). Mapping the margins: Intersectionality, identity politics, and violence against women of color. *Stanford Law Review, 43*(6), 1241–1299. https://www.jstor.org/stable/1229039

De Coster, S., & Heimer, K. (2021). Unifying theory and research on intimate partner violence: A feminist perspective. *Feminist Criminology, 16*(3), 286–303.

Delerme, R. (2025). "It's Heartbreaking. It's Expensive. It's Hard": How the Carceral Care Economy Harms Black and Latine Mothers. *Gender & Society, 39*(3), 349–374. https://doi.org/10.1177/08912432251331534 (Original work published 2025).

Dettlaff, A. J., & Boyd, R. (2020). Racial disproportionality and disparities in the child welfare system: Why do they exist, and what can be done to address them? *Annals of the American Academy of Political and Social Science, 692*(1), 253–274. https://doi.org/10.1177/0002716220980329

Duhaney, P. (2021). Criminalized Black Women's Experiences of Intimate Partner Violence in Canada. *Violence Against Women, 28*(11), 2765–2787. https://doi.org/10.1177/10778012211035791 (Original work published 2022)

Duthu, B. (2008, August 11). Broken justice in Indian country. *The New York Times*. https://www.nytimes.com/2008/08/11/opinion/11duthu.html

Gonzalez, C. M. F. (2022). A Call for a Black Feminist Liberatory Ethics in Criminological Research on Black Women and Girls' Offending and Victimization. Crime & Delinquency, 70(5), 1484–1504. https://doi.org/10.1177/00111287221131009

Geller, A., Garfinkel, I., Cooper, C. E., & Mincy, R. B. (2012). Parental incarceration and child well-being: Implications for urban families. *Social Science Quarterly, 93*(1), 304–327.

Goodmark, L. (2023). *Imperfect victims: Criminalized survivors and the promise of abolition feminism*. University of California Press.

Harp, K. L. H., & Bunting, A. M. (2020). The Racialized Nature of Child Welfare Policies and the Social Control of Black Bodies. *Social politics, 27*(2), 258–281. https://doi.org/10.1093/sp/jxz039

Human Rights Campaign Foundation. (2024, November 19). The epidemic of violence against the transgender and gender non-conforming community in the United States. https://reports.hrc.org/an-epidemic-of-violence-2024

Hamer, F. L. (1964, December 20). *I'm sick and tired of being sick and tired*. Speech delivered at the Williams Institutional CME Church. Retrieved from https://awpc.cattcenter.iastate.edu/2019/08/09/im-sick-and-tired-of-being-sick-and-tired-dec-20-1964/

Hattery, A. J. & Smith, E. (2007). *African American Families*. Sage.

Hattery, A. J., Kafonek, K., Monterrosa, A., Porter, E. F., & Smith, E. (2022). Theories of family violence: Implications for prevention and treatment. In P. Sturmey (Ed.), *Violence in families* (Advances in Preventing and Treating Violence and Aggression series). Springer.

James, J. (2020). Presidential powers and captive maternals: Sally, Michelle, and Deborah. https://blog.apaonline.org/2020/05/06/presidential-powers-and-captive-maternals-sally-michelle-and-deborah/

Johnson, M. P. (1995). Patriarchal terrorism and common couple violence: Two forms of violence against women. *Journal of Marriage and the Family, 57*(2), 283–294. https://doi.org/10.2307/353683

Leemis, R. W., Friar, N., Khatiwada, S., Chen, M. S., Kresnow, M. J., Smith, S.G., Caslin, S., & Basile, K.C. (2022). The National Intimate Partner and Sexual Violence Survey: 2016/2017 Report on Intimate Partner Violence. National Center for Injury Prevention and Control, Centers for Disease Control.

Martin, L. (2017). "Free but Still Walking the Yard": Prisonization and the Problems of Reentry. *Journal of Contemporary Ethnography, 47*(5), 671–694. https://doi.org/10.1177/0891241617737814

McKay, T. (2023). No escape: Mass incarceration and the social ecology of intimate partner violence against women. *Violence against Women.* https://doi.org/10.1177/10778012231158110

Mercado, M. (2022). Chicana/x Carework: Invisible Feminized Labor, Chicana/x Carceral Community, and the Variegated Nature of Feminist Agency in Carceral Contexts. UC Davis. ProQuest ID: Mercado_ucdavis_0029D_21307. Merritt ID: ark:/13030/m5r0159p. Retrieved from https://escholarship.org/uc/item/5k85k624

Monterrosa, A. E. (2021a). How race and gender stereotypes influence help-seeking for intimate partner violence. *Journal of Interpersonal Violence, 36*(17–18), NP9153–NP9174.

Monterrosa, A. E. (2021b). Romantic (in)justice: Criminal-legal system-impacted Black women's romantic relationship status and quality. *Feminist Criminology, 16*(4), 424–446.

Monterrosa, A. E. (2023). Imprisoning Intimacy: The Expanding Sites of Racialized-Gendered Carceral Violence. *Gender & Society, 37*(3), 447–467. https://doi.org/10.1177/08912432231171169

Monterrosa, A., & Hattery, A. J. (2023). Mapping coercive violence. *Violence against Women, 29*(9), 1743–1763. https://doi.org/10.1177/10778012221125499

Moraga, C., & Anzaldúa, G. (Eds.). (1981). *This bridge called my back: Writings by radical women of color.* Persephone Press.

Pager, D. (2007). *Marked: Race, crime, and finding work in an era of mass incarceration.* University of Chicago Press.

Potter, H. (2006). An argument for Black feminist criminology. *Feminist Criminology, 1*(2), 106–124. https://doi.org/10.1177/1557085106286547

Potter, H. (2007). Battered Black women's use of religious services and spirituality for assistance in leaving abusive relationships. *Violence against Women, 13*(3), 262–284.

Potter, H. (2015). Intersectionality and Criminology: Disrupting and revolutionizing studies of crime (1st ed.). Routledge. https://doi.org/10.4324/9780203094495.

Richie, B. E. (2012). *Arrested justice: Black women, violence, and America's prison nation.* NYU Press.

Richie, B., & Eife, E. (2021). Black bodies at the dangerous intersection of gender violence and mass criminalization. *Journal of Aggression, Maltreatment & Trauma, 30*(7), 877–888. https://doi.org/10.1080/10926771.2019.1703063

Roberts, D. (1997). *Killing the Black body: Race, reproduction, and the meaning of liberty.* Vintage Books.

Roberts, D. (2002). *Shattered bonds: The color of child welfare.* Basic Books.

Roberts, D. (2022). *Torn apart: How the child welfare system destroys Black families—and how abolition can build a safer world.* Basic Books.

Romero, M. (2008). The inclusion of citizenship status in intersectionality: What immigration raids tell us about mixed-status families, the state, and assimilation. *International Journal of Sociology of the Family, 34*(2), 131–152.

Salinas, M. D. (2023). Latinas as carceral collateral: Violence in the lives of Latinas across the carceral community. Latino Studies, 21(3), 477–501. https://doi.org/10.1057/s41276-023-00445-z

Stark, E. (2010). Do violent acts equal abuse? Resolving the gender parity/asymmetry dilemma. *Sex Roles, 62*(3–4), 201–211. https://doi.org/10.1007/s11199-009-9717-2

Sweet, P. (2021). *The politics of surviving: How women navigate domestic violence and its aftermath.* University of California Press.
Trozzo, A. M. (2022). Victim blaming: Failure to protect laws as a legislative attack on mothers. *Georgetown Journal of Gender and the Law, 23*(1).
Truth, S. (1851, May). *Ain't I a Woman?* Speech delivered at the Women's Convention, Akron, Ohio. Retrieved from https://www.nps.gov/articles/sojourner-truth.htm
Wells-Barnett, I. B. (1895). A red record: Tabulated statistics and alleged causes of lynchings in the United States, 1892–893–1894. [1528719166].
West, C. M. (2021). Widening the lens: Expanding the research on intimate partner violence in Black communities. *Journal of Aggression, Maltreatment & Trauma, 30*(6), 749–760. https://doi.org/10.1080/10926771.2021.1919811
Wildeman, C., & Emanuel, N. (2014). Cumulative risks of foster care placement by age 18 for U.S. children, 2000–2011. *PloS one, 9*(3), e92785. https://doi.org/10.1371/journal.pone.0092785
Wildeman, C., & Western, B. (2010). Incarceration in fragile families. *The Future of Children, 20*(2), 157–177. https://doi.org/10.1353/foc.2010.0006
Zuberi, T., & Bonilla-Silva, E. (2008). *White logic, white methods: Racism and methodology.*

Chapter 8
Family Functioning and Aggression and Violence: Radical Behavioral Analytic Approaches

Peter Sturmey

Name of the theory: Applied Behavior Analysis: which sometimes is incorporated under other learning theories such as Social Learning Theory, and referenced under learning processes such as modeling etc.

Proponents of the theory: Applied Behavior Analysis is associated with B. F. Skinner as the founding parent of behavior analysis, and other behavior analysts such as Wolf, Baer and, Risley and social learning theorist Gerald Patterson. It is also associated with behavioral marital therapy developed by Neil Jacobson.

What the theory says: Behavior includes observable overt behavior and covert behavior, which is observable only to the person behaving, and includes thoughts and feelings.

Behavior comes from three forms of evolution: Biological evolution, cultural evolution and evolution of operant behavior over the organism's lifespan. Aggression is functional or useful in obtaining consequences such as defending the organism or obtaining material or social benefits. Emphasis is placed on the current environment both as the cause of aggression and locus for intervention. Analysis identifies the antecedents and consequences of aggression both for understanding aggression and as the basis for intervention. Antecedents include both motivating operations, such as reinforcer deprivation or ongoing aversive stimulation, and discriminative stimuli, such as the

P. Sturmey (✉)
The Graduate Center and Queens College, City University of New York, New York, USA
e-mail: sturmeyaptva@gmail.com

Brock University, St. Catharines, Ontario, USA

Endicott University, Massachusetts, USA

A. Hattery and E. Smith (eds.), *Theories of Family Violence*, Advances in Preventing and Treating Violence and Aggression, https://doi.org/10.1007/978-3-032-17095-8_8

physical presence of a partner. Consequences may include positive reinforcement, such as obtaining tangible or social consequences, and removal of aversive stimuli, such as aversive social interaction with another family member's aversive behavior. Intervention should be based on a functional assessment or analysis of aggressive behavior to identify the important and manipulable independent variables that affect aggressive behavior and that can be modified to increase appropriate social behavior and decrease aggression. Emphasis is placed on increasing prosocial behavior, including skills training.

Understanding family aggression and violence and related prosocial behavior can be done from numerous theoretical perspectives (Sturmey, 2022, 2023). This chapter reviews one highly characteristic approach to the philosophy of science—radical behaviorism—an approach based on a particular philosophy of science associated with the work of B. F. Skinner and related researchers. This chapter begins by delineating what radical behaviorism is and then reviews two well known broadly based behavioral models of family aggression and violence—the coercive family processes model from Gerald Patterson and behavioral marital therapy associated with Neil Jacobson. The chapter then revisits these models from a more rigorous behavior analytic approach and delineates specific behavioral mechanisms by which aggression and violence can be learned within families and their implications for intervention. Finally, this chapter reviews some examples of functional assessments and analyses of aggression and violence within the context of families. The reader should note that this chapter does not make any fundamental distinction between aggression and violence other than perhaps differences in behavioral intensity (Sturmey, 2022, 2023).

What is Radical Behaviorism?

Radical behaviorism is philosophy of science, a way to proceed to understand and ask questions about all forms of behavior—human and non-human behavior, typical and atypical and includes both overt behavior that can be observed by two or more people and covert behavior, such as thinking and feeling, that can be observed by only one person (the person doing the thinking and feeling). The word "radical" is used in the sense of the word's etymology (Latin *radix* for root) meaning it is a fundamental or basic departure from other forms of behaviorism. There are other forms of behaviorism such as methodological behaviorism which, although they superficially appear similar to radical behaviorism at first sight because they share some common features such as a strong emphasis on learning and the environment, are quite different from radical behaviorism and hence should be clearly distinguished from one another.

Radical behaviorism is conceptually close to biological evolution in a number of ways. The conceptual framework of biological evolution is that the environment selects certain forms of physiology, morphology and behavior that contribute to the survival of genes that may be inherited to the next generation from among the many variations that currently exist. Over time, small steps in natural selection can result in highly differentiated forms of life that are well adapted to the environment and as the environment changes this process may further propel further evolution. For variations to be transmitted across generations there must be some mechanism for transmitting selected features of the organism. Natural selection gives humans and families important adaptations that promote survival of the genes we carry. These include reflexes, such as the rooting reflexes that promote survival of infants, aversive behavior such as infant crying that occasions interaction from others to terminate the aversive stimulation, and natural reinforcers such as sweet flavors that often promote survival by ensuring sufficient caloric consumption for the survival of the organism. But natural selection can only prepare organisms for relatively unchanging aspects of the environment such as gravity, painful and dangerous stimuli, such as intense stimulation that threatens the integrity of the organism (fires and extreme cold). But natural selection does not prepare human infants for baby bottles or the internet.

Fine tuning what is inherited through natural selection comes from two other sources: Cultural selection and selection of operant behavior and other learning mechanisms. Cultural differences in the behavior of families are readily apparent. For example, some cultures find toilet training at the age of 3 years to be cruel because it stresses children too much; Americans today toilet train their children much later than in the past perhaps due to the availability of disposable diapers and both parents working in many families. Other cultures find it cruel to toilet train infants at age 3 years because infants should be toilet trained from birth and should be dry by 6 months (DeVries & DeVries, 1977) and not to do so exposes the infant to unnecessary hardships indicating incompetent or neglectful parenting. How do such cultural differences arise?

Cultural evolution occurs when variations in cultural practices are selected by the environment and which ultimately contribute to the survival of the culture. The physical environment plays a part in selecting cultural practices. For example, the properties of fire select certain forms of cultural practices and behavior that prevent people from getting burned (handles, pot holders, good parenting that teaches members of the culture to teach their children to keep their distance from fire to prevent being burned). But much more prominent and important is the social transmission of cultural practices (eating three meals a day, using utensils instead of hands to eat, saying prayers during meals etc.)

Cultural practices are transmitted through two main mechanisms: Generalized imitation and rule governed behavior (RGB). Generalized imitation is behavior in which the learner's behavior matches the behavior of a model where the reinforcer maintaining imitation is the match between the behavior of the learner and the model (Kymissis& Poulson,1990). This definition is subtle. Merely reinforcing imitating someone else by itself would not produce much behavior change but learning to imitate novel models without a previous history of reinforcement for imitating that specific model is of paramount importance because of its potential to produce very broad behavior change. When a family caregiver reinforces many examples of imitating siblings when they play nice and say "thank you", for example, they may establish imitating sibling's behavior more generally without explicit reinforcement for doing so for better and for worse! Thus, behaving like other people in context is an important skill for cultural transmission of behavioral practices. Parents and other caregivers may learn good and bad parenting practices through imitation of other family members and caregivers behaving with offspring both through live modeling when observing other family members and parents in public, and through the media such as TV shows portraying idealized, humorous or fascinatingly awful family behavior. Additionally, many people learn *when* to imitate. Some forms of imitation are called being smart and socially sensitive and other forms of imitation are called cheating. Learning which fork to use when eating is an example of this process of discriminating when to imitate (Brown et al., 2008).

The generalized reinforcer of "behaving like other people in context" establishes and maintains culturally typical behavior. Deviation from conventional behavior may encounter contingencies of punishment, such as parents getting a side-eye on the train when they slap their child to control their children's aggressive behavior. Generalized imitation of family behavior may also in part account for aggressive behavior in families as when parents imitate their own parents' aggressive child rearing practices.

The second and most important mechanism of cultural transmission of behavioral practices is RGB. RGB is behavior which is under the stimulus control of a stated or implied rule. For example, if a neighbor says "Buy your kids' toys at Walmart, they are just fine" a parent or other caregiver might do so because of a long history of following instructions generally and/or specifically from their neighbor. Rules may be spoken or written (as in text message or magazine on parenting). A rule may also be explicit ("Your kids should be in bed by 9 pm, what are you doing?") or implied ("Your kids are still up? Wow!"). RGB also specifies or implies a contingency. For example, we may read "Park closes at 10 pm. Gates will be locked" which specifies a contingency for remaining in the park after hours. We might also read "Be kind to your friends" which implies but does not state a contingency.

Notice that the contingencies of reinforcement for RGB are not obvious. Disapproval for failure to buy your kids' toys from Walmart is a distant and uncertain consequence and as is the behavior of buying the toys which is also distant from the good advice. Something must bridge the gap between the statement of the rule and the subsequent behavior. So, in between the rule and its distant outcomes is other behavior and associated environmental changes. For example, one may look at the store web page to find out what toys are available and see attractive toys that you think your child might like, one may make a list of preferred toys, and check one's bank balance to see how much money is available to buy the toys etc. These behaviors all generate their own consequences (seeing the images of the toys on the web page etc.) and it is these consequences that may bridge the gap between the statement of the rule and its final outcome—your kids reinforcing the parents for giving them nice toys.

The notion of cultural evolution allows for the possibility of purposeful and planned cultural design (Skinner, 2001). Societies constantly engage in cultural design through mechanisms such as laws, taxation, education, psychotherapy and governmental policies. Such cultural practices often address a wide range of family issues including aggression within the family. Such attempts at cultural design are often haphazard and rarely evaluated as politicians' behavior is often responsive to short-term contingencies such as appearing in the media, receiving legal donations and bribes, and getting reelected. Further, when attempts are made in terms of explicit behavioral processes members of society often rebel, cheat or reject such ideas. (Consider, for example, the initial often negative response to congestion pricing in both London and New York as an example of cultural design to reduce excessive driving and pollution).

The most challenging problem with naturally occurring cultural evolution and planned cultural design is that although the immediate outcomes of promoting certain types of family behavior are potentially readily observable, the long-term outcomes in terms of future cultural survival are not observable and thus uncertain. For example, limiting children's exposure to certain foods may avoid illnesses and allergic reactions in some children, but the long-term outcomes of such practices are not yet known; today they are unknowable. Nevertheless, cultures are actively engaged in cultural design by promoting certain kinds of behavior in families through parenting classes, the media and the legal system. For example, we may attempt to prohibit or limit parents spanking their children through modeling and parenting classes, but we do not yet completely know if that promotes positive forms of parent behavior, its effects on child aggression, parent behavior or the long-term outcomes of such changes in norms for raising children in some countries.

As well as the philosophy of science that is radical behaviorism, there are also two aspects of practice. The first is the experimental analysis of behavior (EAB) which is the field of basic behavior analytic research. EAB investigates the basic science of learning and behavior to understand learning for its own sake, although such studies may uncover new ways of changing behavior that have implications for practice. In EAB studies the behavior studied and the context are relatively unimportant other than to allow a clear and unambiguous experiment to be conducted. Hence, EAB research often uses rats, pigeons and other non-human animals as participants in controlled environments such as Skinner boxes. EAB may also study basic learning in humans with no obvious immediate applicability. Applied behavior analysis (ABA) is the application of behavioral principles to socially significant problems. ABA emphasizes understanding the environmental variables that control behavior, including aggression, by conducting functional assessments and functional analyses to identify the controlling variables (antecedents and consequences) of behavior prior to intervention. Intervention is then based on changing the variables that control and predict relevant behavior. Although the role of natural selection and cultural evolution is acknowledged, the focus of ABA is on the current environment as this is what can be observed and modified. This approach includes operational definitions of behavior, identifying its antecedents (motivating operations and discriminative stimuli) and consequences as well as verbal behavior and rule governed behavior.

ABA addresses any socially significant problem from autism, to littering, to climate change and aggression within families.

EAB research on aggression is illustrated by work on pain-elicited aggression. Azrin and colleagues demonstrated that noncontingent pain to one animal elicits aggression by that animal to a nearby animal, an effect demonstrated in numerous species including humans (Hutchinson, et al., 1965; Ulrich, et al., 1965). This is an example of the EAB because aggression between pigeons is not a socially important problem—nobody was complaining about pigeons pecking each other. In contrast Derby et al. (1997) treated various forms of severe problem behavior in four children with developmental delays in their family settings by identifying the communicative function of the problem behavior and teaching an acceptable alternative form of communication. For example, Danny, a boy aged 2 1/2 years diagnosed with moderate to severe developmental and language delay, exhibited aggression in the form of throwing objects and non-compliance. A functional assessment and analysis identified that he often escaped work requests by demonstrating aggressive behavior. Thus, intervention involved teaching him to ask for a break. Teaching this functional communication skill resulted in reduced aggression, increased play and increased social behavior. This is an example of ABA because aggressive behavior was a limiting factor in his adaptive behavior at home and a distressing problem for him and his family members.

When one asks radical behaviorist, "why did Kai's sister hit him?", one can give three intersecting answers. The immediate environmental answer is that in the past Kai had given his sister his candies and toys when she hit him, reinforcing her aggressive behavior. The antecedent of her aggression was being close to Kai when he was holding a snack and his sister's favorite toy and the antecedent that she had had nothing else to do for 10 min and hence was deprived of snacks and toys as reinforcers. She does not hit him when she has those things. Her aggressive behavior was positively reinforced by obtaining toys and snacks quickly. An important additional consideration was that when she asked appropriately for the things she wanted she did not get them. Additionally, harmonious family relationships contribute to survival and success of family members in direct and indirect ways in the future. Finally, any genetic predisposition to aggression in this situation may have survival value for the organism, such as acquisition of food and abolishing hunger, a powerful negative reinforcer.

Learning in Families

The definition of a family is gradually evolving and multiple definitions and types of families exist. Families can be defined by historical and contemporary legislation relating to marriage, divorce and child protection; mandated reporting of child abuse and neglect; health and other insurance policies; and self- and other-identification (Settles, 2023). Families are a dynamic social learning environment where the behavior of each of the members affects one another in numerous ways.

When a family is formed, the new members arrive with a learning history from previous social relationships and other families. They bring with them skills and skill deficits, acquired reinforcers, and social behavior related to family behavior acquired through modeling, and RGB. As well as parents, other family members such as grandparents, other relatives, paid and other informal caregivers, and paid employees, may be part of the picture. Within that context family members behave and interact with the physical and social environment that we call a family.

Behavior analysts have investigated social behavior in many ways. How does behaviorism think about social behavior? An iconic paper in this area is the Jack and Jill study (Epstein et al., 1980), an example of EAB research into the processes that underlie social behavior. In this study the experimenters taught a simple sequence of social behavior using basic behavioral methods such as differential reinforcement and chaining. They taught Jack to ask Jill "What color?" by pressing an illuminated key. Jill learned to look behind a curtain, observe which of three colored disks was illuminated, return to Jack and report the color she observed by pressing a key corresponding to the color she saw while Jack observed her response. Jack then reinforced Jill's behavior with food by pecking an illuminated button that said "thank you". Jack then reported the color Jill had described to him by pressing his own key. Finally Jack's accurate reporting was also reinforced with food. Interestingly, Jack and Jill were pigeons. The way they learned these social behaviors with one another were clearly programmed by the experimenters using basic principles of learning such as reinforcement, prompting, and chaining. The authors concluded that the example of Jack and Jill was a model of social behavior (Epstein et al., 1980).

So what has this got to do with aggressive behavior in families? The Jack and Jill paper is a very simplified model of group interactions: There are only two participants, there is a limited number of schedules of reinforcement for each participant, the impact of the environment outside the Skinner box was not investigated the experiments did not investigate the participants' previous learning history or intergenerational effects on aggression. Nevertheless, this study demonstrated that social behavior can be modeled and understood through such EAB experiments.

Aggression and related social behavior are social behaviors which may be learned within families. There are numerous sources of such evidence, but one important one is the meaningful differences study from behaviorists Hart et al. (1997). These authors observed patterns of interaction one hour per week between 42 mothers and their children from ages 7 months to 3 years in their natural family settings. They observed everything the mother and child said to one another during each observation session. They counted the number of words the child uttered and heard; the rate of parental interactions; parental positive/praise statements; and parents' use of different types of *wh*-questions.

Hart et al. (1997) found very large differences in the learning environments of these children. Some families were characterized as having very few interactions and little parental models of language. Other families interacted frequently and presented a rich variety of language models to their children. Additionally, some families were very directive with their children and others were more conversational and stimulating. Family learning environments at 7 months predicted adaptive behavior, such as language and social behavior, as well as intelligence at age 3 years. These results suggest that children's early language environment is crucial to the acquisition of language and social behavior that may be central to the development of aggression or alternative behavior in children.

Studies of the development of severe problem behavior—even self-injury—suggest that the development of severe problem behavior involves contingencies of reinforcement between family members such as mutual shaping of behavior between caregivers and children (Oliver et al., 2005). These results parallel experimental studies of the development of self-injury in non-human primates through explicit learning mechanisms such as shaping and intermittent reinforcement (Schaefer, 1970).

Patterson and Coercive Family Processes

One of the earliest formal statements of a behavioral model of the development of aggression throughout the lifespan which addresses family aggression and violence comes from an extensive body of empirical and conceptual work from Patterson (1982). Patterson et al. (2017) outlined a developmental model of aggression in which early family life plays a key role in the development of aggression. According to this model, the origins of childhood aggression lie within the child's early family learning history and reflect poor parental discipline and monitoring of their child. Poor parental discipline reflects failure to instruct, model and positively reinforce a wide range of prosocial behavior including social skills, language, including functional communication skills, problem solving, tolerance for delays to reinforcement, and tolerance of aversive stimulation. It may also include discouragement of prosocial behavior, including positive punishment for appropriate social behavior, such as instructing the child to be quiet and not move and punishing their behavior when they do so. Poor parental discipline can be characterized by low rates of parental interaction with the child, thereby presenting few opportunities to learn prosocial behavior, and/or high rates of aversive control such as parental threats, yelling and explosive parental behavior. The idea that learning environments vary substantially between families was confirmed by the Hart et al. (1997) study above. The second facet of the early family history in this model is parental neglect, referring to low frequency observation and monitoring of the child again resulting in the loss of many opportunities for the child to learn and remain safe. Patterson refers to this learning environment as one in which (a) both parties escape and avoid one another and provocative situations, (b) which trains child antisocial behavior, (c) fails to teach child social skills and (d) promotes parental aversive control of the child. Over time through mutual shaping, the child acquires more precursors to aggression and actual aggressive behavior and the parent acquires more aversive behavior to control the child. Risk factors for early aggression in the family, such as poverty, can also be interpreted from this perspective as factors that limit learning and appropriate parenting behavior.

When these at-risk children arrive in preschool nurseries or first grade, they are likely to be socially rejected by peers and teaching staff as they have poor social and other important skills and use aggression rather than prosocial behavior to obtain their needs. Thus, these children may be at risk for early social isolation and academic failure. This in turn may result in membership of deviant groups which, through modeling and reinforcement of deviant behavior and punishment of prosocial behavior, train up early deviant behavior and its precursors. As this process elaborates, the children become adolescents at risk for dropping out of school, gang membership, poor work skills and unemployment, poor adult relationships, divorce, substance abuse, incarceration and institutionalization.

Patterson's model of family aggression is full of implications for prevention and treatment including training parents in relevant skills that they do not possess, motivating parents to use the skills they have, increasing monitoring of their children, and teaching a wide range of prosocial skills to their children. There is an enormous literature on parent training related to aggression. For example, Patterson et al. (1982) reported a randomized control trial in which 19 adolescents living with their families received either parental training or wait list control. The parents training was a standard skills training package which was supplemented with training to manage child resistance to change and support for improved therapist implementation of the training package. The initial response to treatment was good. The average reduction in the rate of aggression in the experimental group was 0.92 per min in baseline and 0.32 per min at the end of treatment. There was minimal change in the rate of aggression in the control group. These differences were statistically significant. Additionally, social validity was high as parents reported high satisfaction with the intervention and considered it to be highly effective.

Subsequently, there has been a very large body of research on parent training to reduce child and adolescent aggression at home based on Patterson's model. Meta-analyses have confirmed that this general approach is often quite effective. For example, Piquero et al. (2016) identified 78 outcome studies published between 2008 and 2015 that addressed the effects of parent training on delinquency and antisocial behavior. The overall Cohen's *d* effect size was 0.37. Programs that consisted of home visits and educating parents had a somewhat smaller effect size ($d = 0.28$) than programs using direct parent training ($d = 0.39$). There were also differences between three most commonly used parent training packages with parent–child interaction therapy being the most effective ($d = 0.98$, $p < 0.01$), Triple P Parenting Program being the next most effective ($d = 0.56$, $p < 0.001$), and the Incredible Years Parenting Program being the least effective of these three programs ($d = 0.31$, $p < 0.001$).

Couples Violence as Learned Behavior

The effects of parental behavior on child behavior is but just one example of learning approaches to understanding and treating aggression and violence within families. Adults within families influence one another's behavior considerably. For example,

Babcock et al. (1993) studied marital violence in straight couples where there was a power discrepancy between the husband and wife in terms of economic power, decision making and communication skills. They found that in couples where the husband was less empowered than his wife, domestic violence was more likely than in couples where this was not the case. Babcock et al. suggested that "violence may be compensatory behavior to make up for husbands' lack of power in other arenas of marriage" (p. 40). Put another way, these results can be interpreted as an example of concurrent schedules of reinforcement (simultaneous schedules of reinforcement for non-violent and violent behavior). When reinforcement is weak or absent for non-violent behavior, such as problem solving, this potentiates the reinforcing value of violence for the husband to obtain his goals. Conceptually, such findings are analogous to Patterson's work with children and adolescents in that skill deficits may be important risk factors for family violence that can be remedied by skills training interventions.

Perhaps some of the best known behavioral work on violence in families between couples is that of Jacobson and colleagues (1992). This group collected both observational and self-report data on pleasing and displeasing events, affectionate and instrumental behaviors such as sharing feelings and yelling at the children. Studies of distressed and non-distressed couples indicated that pleasant and unpleasant events and actions were independent of one another and displeasing events were most predictive of daily satisfaction with the relationship.

This model provides rationales for intervention to improve the quality of relationships and reduce marital violence. One such approach to improving relationships using behavioral marital therapy is to teach problem solving and increase mutually pleasant activities. Jacobson (1979) reported that this improved the quality of relationships in six spouses using single subject experimental designs. Several studies have also found that behavioral marital therapy can decrease aggression and violence (e. g., Fals-Stewart et al., 2002). At least three meta-analyses have demonstrated that Behavioral Marital Therapy is superior to no treatment control groups and has over 30 randomized controlled trials to support its effectiveness (Shadish & Baldwin, 2005). Subsequent meta-analyses have replicated this finding but have additionally found that these initial effects may not maintain over time and that other forms of marital therapy may be as or more effective than Behavioral Marital Therapy (Dunn & Schwebel, 1995; Rathgeber et al., 2019).

Additionally, these studies tend to report change in broad measures of marital functioning rather than specifically aggression. The findings of these meta-analyses support the notion that intervention based on behavioral models of marital relationships may be one approach worth considering.

Learning and Unlearning Aggressive and Violent Behavior in Families

The preceding section on coercive family processes and behavioral marital therapy are best characterized as broadly behavioral approaches to understanding, preventing and treating family aggression and violence. Several of the studies incorporate non-behavioral concepts such as beliefs and feelings as causal agents, but not are rigorously behavior analytic in a number of ways. For example, they often do not use the concepts of behaviorism consistently, use self-report rather than observational data as the primary outcomes data and for treatment integrity and do not use pre-intervention functional assessment and analysis as an integrated component of intervention. Let us look more carefully at the possible explicit behavioral mechanisms by which families teach one another to engage in either prosocial or violent behavior.

Families can teach non-aggressive or aggressive behavior in a number of ways. It should be noted that they may be unaware of doing so in some circumstances, but in other circumstances that may explicitly teach aggression to one another. The first way in which family members might teach is that they may reinforce aggressive behavior either inadvertently or explicitly. A reinforcer is a consequence which strengthens the behavior in the future.

Reinforcers include positive reinforcers, when a stimulus is presented after the response, and negative reinforcers, when a stimulus is removed following a response which strengthens that behavior in the future. Both positive and negative reinforcers strengthen future behavior and are defined by their effects on behavior rather than by subjective experience or topography of the consequence. An example of positive reinforcement of aggression might be a parent who gives their child a videogame to "calm down" when their child hits their sibling. An example of negative reinforcement of aggression might be a family member asks an elderly family member to go take a shower, the senior pushes them away and the first family member says "OK, maybe later" and defers the non-preferred activity.

A second mechanism based on consequences that may teach aggression is the weakening of adaptive behavior that competes with aggression, for example, through punishment of adaptive behavior. A punisher is a stimulus that occurs after the response that weakens that behavior in the future. A positive punisher is a stimulus that is presented after the behavior that weakens the behavior in the future. For example, if a significant other meekly asks "Would you mind doing the dishes, honey" and the other spouse raises their voice saying "You are obsessed with your kitchen!" and the first spouse stops asking nicely in the future, then this might be an example of punishment for prosocial behavior. A negative punisher is the removal of a stimulus following a response that weakens the behavior in the future. For example, suppose a parent has repeatedly asked a child to do their chores and the child eventually says "Ok, I'll tidy up my room" but the parent now comes back immediately and yells "I said do it right now!" and the child scurries to tidy up their room. The removal of the requests is a negative reinforcer because in the future the child may no longer comply nicely but instead throw toys at their parents as they approach.

A second consequence-based mechanism that may weaken appropriate behavior is extinction. Extinction is the removal of the contingency between a reinforcer and the behavior it maintains. Extinction has four effects: weakening the behavior in the future, increasing behavioral variability, emotional side effects (including aggression) and sometimes a temporary increase in behavior called an extinction burst. In addition, behavior that has been previously extinguished may spontaneously reemerge, which may be one mechanism for treatment relapse. Extinction may occur naturally or may be programmed to occur during behavioral treatment. An example of extinction might be when a partner used to comply with quiet polite requests in the past. Over time, they may become careless and no longer follow the request. Extinction may underlie several aggression-related phenomena. For example, extinguishing adaptive behavior related to aggression such as communication may make aggression more likely. Second, if during extinction of adaptive behavior more intense problematic behavior such as precursors to aggression or actual aggressive behavior occur, then aggression may be reinforced and shaped (See below).

Sometimes new forms of aggressive behavior occur. Since the behavior is new it cannot have a history of reinforcement. How might new forms of aggression be learned? One mechanism is called shaping. Shaping consists of reinforcement of successive approximations toward a final behavior and extinction of previously reinforced behavior. For example, a child might have a learning history of reaching and picking up a desired object. Perhaps sometimes their sibling is in the way and the first child learns to wave their hand to remove them and access a desired object. Reaching is not reinforced and hand waving is reinforced. If subsequently, the child's sibling does not move out of the way, then waving is extinguished and some new behavior such as pushing them out of the way can be reinforced. In this way, novel aggressive behavior can be inadvertently shaped.

As well as consequences affecting aggression antecedent stimuli can also come to affect aggression. Stimuli that predict reinforcement and punishment often affect subsequent behavior (Think of the effects of red and green traffic lights for instance). For example, if one parent has consistently punished aggression children may refrain from aggressive behavior in their presence and only engage in aggression in their absence. Likewise, if the children have a history of positive reinforcement for prosocial behavior with another adult, they may tend to show adaptive behavior and no aggression only in their presence. One example of an antecedent stimulus is instructions. Instructions come to influence our behavior through a history of reinforcement. For example, in a fight between two siblings a third sibling might encourage aggression when they say "hit her!" and after aggression occurs, the third sibling might reinforce aggression by saying "Yeh! That showed her!". Direct instruction of aggressive behavior can occur when some parents in effect train their children in aggressive behavior by signing them up for violent sports or when parents directly instruct their children to fight one another.

One of the most established learning mechanisms for acquisition of aggression is modeling in which the model's behavior is an antecedent for aggression. In modeling the behavior of another person, or in some cases a puppet, cartoon or video, is paired with reinforcement for emitting the model promptly. In some cases it is necessary to also include prompting such as additional instructions or physical prompts to ensure the model influences subsequent behavior. Modeling may occur both naturally and as a programmed intervention and has been applied to teach an almost never ending list of behavior in numerous contexts to many populations. The classic studies of modeling and aggression come from Albert Bandura's Bobo doll experiments in which adult models either played nicely with toys or aggressed toward a large doll. When the model aggressed toward the doll, the children were much more likely to aggress against the doll subsequently, especially if the model's aggressive behavior was reinforced (Bandura, 1965; Bandura et al., 1961, 1963). The role of modeling in family violence is often raised with respect to parental modeling of aggression to their own children and intergenerational transmission of aggression and also the effects of TV and other media violence on violence in the home.

Another antecedent mechanism that may affect aggression is RGB. RGB is behavior in which a contingency of reinforcement is stated such as "Slow down. Roadworks ahead". We learn to follow rules, including new rules, generally through repeated exposure to instructions and contingencies of reinforcement and punishment during our lifetime. RGB is one of the most important ways in which cultural practices are transmitted between members of a culture and across generations. For example, a parent may say to a teenage family member "Just ignore grandma. She lost her mind a long time ago". This statement may function as an example of RGB in that the teenager may no longer talk to his grandma often. This might affect subsequent attention-aggression if his grandma receives little attention for a long period of time, she emits aggressive behavior to a family member and everyone rushed over to protect the family member and calm grandma down thereby inadvertently reinforcing aggression and extinguishing other forms of appropriate behavior. As a generalization, RGB is less sensitive to its consequences than other behavior. That is we may tend to follow rules whether or not we come into contact with the alleged consequences immediately. For example, if someone says "Don't insult your Dad, he will get mad" we might refrain from insulting one's father, but never experience his father's anger when someone insults him. Thus, the reinforcer for RGB is not obvious, but probably comes from the reactions of others who might state "Thanks. It's better to keep on Dad's right side". Another important property of RGB is that, unlike discriminative stimuli, it influences behavior over longer periods of time. For example, if a parent instructs a child "Always be nice to people and good things will happen" the child may engage in prosocial behavior at a much later time.

One of the most well researched behavioral paradigms for aggression is pain-elicited aggression. This is a respondent or classically conditioned mechanism in which an unconditioned stimulus (pain) elicits an unconditioned response (aggression toward the source of the pain). In a typical experiment two conspecifics are kept close to each other, one receives an electric shock which elicits aggression from the shocked organism to the second organism. Pain can elicit aggression to both conspecifics and objects and organisms will engage in operant behavior such as pulling on a chain, to obtain access to engage in aggression suggesting that access to aggression is now a positive reinforcer. One sometimes observes something that looks like pain-elicited aggression when caregivers engage in assisting a family member with a self-help task and hurt the other caregiver, for example, if they have a painful medical condition such as arthritis. Other examples are also possible.

Numerous studies since the 1930s have demonstrated pain-elicited aggression in both humans and non-human species (e. g., Hutchinson et al., 1965; Ulrich et al., 1965). Within the context of families one can imagine situations where one family member experiences pain, such as dropping a stove on their foot, and lashes out at a second nearby family member or a family caregiver helping a second family member with arthritis and inadvertently hurts their family member who then lashes out at their family member caregiver. This phenomenon has obvious biological significance in that it maintains the integrity of the organism through termination of high intensity stimulation that may result in damage to the organism. In some circumstances repeated trials of pain elicited aggression may establish certain situations as discriminative stimuli for aggression. For example, if the elderly family member routinely experiences pain when being taken to be showered they may become agitated and aggression generally in situations leading up to and during the shower.

If aggression within families has a significant learning component we have a cause for optimism. Perhaps early intervention can focus on teaching better parenting and life skills to parents before they have children and/or when they already have children to buffer them against the vicissitudes of parenting. If children acquire aggressive behavior or its precursors, perhaps intervention can reverse this problematic behavior through learning-based interventions.

However, families are more complicated than the Jack and Jill experiment discussed above. There are multiple participants, multiple contingencies, multiple schedules of reinforcement, verbal behavior, community rules for parents that affect aggressive behavior and a long history of learning and living together.

Functional Assessment of Family Aggression and Violence

Although applied behavior analysis has made extensive contributions to understanding and treating aggression in children, adolescents and to some extent adults with intellectual disabilities and/or autism mostly, but not exclusively, in contexts outside the family such as schools and residential settings (Brosnan & Healy, 2011; Im, 2021; Matson et al., 2005). These studies show that aggression in these children is sensitive to its consequences and identification of the antecedents and consequences maintaining aggression in these children can be used to predict effective behavioral treatments within families, reduce aggression and increase a wide range of prosocial behavior. But what about the most common forms of family violence?

Outside of neurodevelopmental disabilities, ABA has mostly focussed on developing behavioral models of family aggression and behavioral interpretations of other, non-behavior analytic approaches to understanding and treatment aggression including domestic violence. For example, Myers (1995) noted that women in heterosexual domestic situations were at great risk for violence from their male partners including physical violence, severe injury, rape, and murder. Myers casts this in the context of broad societal suppression of women, through mechanisms such as low pay, modeling and other legitimization of male violence toward women, including RGB and training of boys to be aggressive. Myers noted that the traditional behavioral model of antecedent—behavior—consequences can be applied to domestic violence. For example, he suggested that escape and avoidance of male verbal and physical abuse can negatively reinforce women's compliance with domestic chores and sexual compliance. He also suggested that men's aggressive behavior can be reinforced by meal preparation, quiet children, and increased leisure time. Men who engage in domestic violence may also have this behavior reinforced by peers and other family members through avoidance of ridicule. Additionally, Myers suggested that there is a lack of effective policing and other societal contingencies to control domestic violence, such as those from other family members and neighbors, to control male violence. Thus, there are few immediate and effective punitive consequences for male aggression in the home. Yet, for women who attempt to avoid male aggression by engaging in assertive behavior or leaving the home there are many punitive consequences in terms of effort required to establish an independent and safe life, and loss of money and home etc. Despite these potential contingencies the consequences probably occur intermittently. It is unlikely that observing violent media immediately triggers a man to strike his female partner. If that is the case, what is going on?

Myers arguesd that the historical and contemporary contexts involve overarching, contingency specifying conditions that promote male battering of women in the home. The culture is full of events, such as media modeling of stereotypical women's roles as homemakers and working in clerical positions, rather than as breadwinners and industry leaders. Meyers went on to suggest that these events function as contingency-specifying rules, i.e., RGB. These contingency specifying rules when combined with the mere presence of a woman are the relevant variables that can occasion male domestic violence toward women. The implications for prevention and treatment are diffuse and broad. Whereas function-based communication training is the prototypical intervention for aggression in children and adolescents with neurodevelopmental disabilities, behavior analytic intervention for domestic violence, according to Myers, should be much broader. The four kinds of interventions he recommended include "assistance for battered women, behavior-reducing legal and judicial consequences for batterers, programs to teach batterers nonabusive behavior, and changing of community mores".

In a subsequent commentary on and elaboration of Myers' article, Peterson and Calhoun (1995) expanded this analysis in a number of ways. They proposed that a comprehensive account of domestic violence should also incorporate factors such as poverty, unemployment, history of experience with violence, intrafamily control and substance abuse. They also noted that Myers emphasized the effect of the behavior of the male abuser on the female victim both in terms of analysis and treatment. They proposed that it would be better to include acknowledgement of the two-way interaction to include the effects of the woman's behavior on the man's behavior. For example, they suggested that some of the woman's behavior such as talking back or flirting with other men, may elicit aggression from the man in a manner similar to respondent, classically conditioned aggression and that the woman may not always discriminate (notice) her own behavior that elicits aggression. This naturally occurring phenomenon should not be taken as justification for victim blaming, but should be considered as part of the understanding of the learning mechanisms that may underlie domestic violence and which may be useful in crafting function-based interventions for domestic violence. In addition, they suggested that intervention should not focus on changing the man's behavior which is unlikely to change because the reinforcement for aggression is immediate and consistent and any punitive consequences, should there be any, are distant and uncertain. Thus, male aggression is an example of impulsivity—choosing the immediate small reinforcer over the more distant and less certain larger reinforcer. In this bidirectional model, the authors proposed that where the woman attempts to or leaves home, the focus should be on massive skills training to support an independent, safe and productive life including work, social and problem-solving skills. They noted the dearth of well conducted research on marital therapy that has included women victims of violence and the lack of available shelters for women. They proposed that as well as individual interventions, society can begin to combat gender stereotypes and implicit permission for male on female aggression through the inclusion of models of men as nurturing, performing domestic chores and reporting domestic violence.

Behavior analysis' approach to domestic violence, especially in its approach to treatment, may not seem unique, indeed, both Myers' (1995) and Peterson and Calhoun's (1995) treatment recommendations overlap considerably with non-behavioral approaches to preventing and treating domestic violence. Behavior analytic approaches are distinct in at least two ways. First, these behavior analytic models understand domestic violence in terms of current environmental influences on behavior including both immediate antecedents, behavior and consequences and broader RGB. Second, behavior analytic approaches emphasize direct skills training using modeling, rehearsal feedback, both for the family members and professionals and others.

Summary

This chapter shows that behavior analytic ideas have been extensively applied to several forms of family aggression. Empirical work has focussed mostly on children and adolescents with neurodevelopmental disabilities but theoretical models of aggression within the family have also been developed which have important implications for prevention and treatment. Behavioral approaches to the understanding, prevention and treatment of family aggression continue to show promise for both theory and practice in the realm of family violence.

References

Babcock, J. C., Waltz, J., Jacobson, N. S., & Gottman, J. M. (1993). Power and violence: The relation between communication patterns, power discrepancies, and domestic violence. *Journal of Consulting and Clinical Psychology, 61*(1), 40.

Bandura, A. (1965). Influence of models' reinforcement contingencies on the acquisition of imitative responses. *Journal of Personality and Social Psychology, 1*(6), 589.

Bandura, A., Ross, D., & Ross, S. A. (1961). Transmission of aggression through imitation of aggressive models. *The Journal of Abnormal and Social Psychology, 63*(3), 575–595.

Bandura, A., Ross, D., & Ross, S. A. (1963). Imitation of film-mediated aggressive models. *The Journal of Abnormal and Social Psychology, 66*(1), 3–11.

Brosnan, J., & Healy, O. (2011). A review of behavioral interventions for the treatment of aggression in individuals with developmental disabilities. *Research in Developmental Disabilities, 32*(2), 437–446.

Brown, A. K., Brown, J. L., & Poulson, C. L. (2008). Discriminating which fork to use: Teaching selective imitation to people with autism. *Research in Autism Spectrum Disorders, 2*(2), 199–208.

Derby, K. M., Wacker, D. P., Berg, W., Deraad, A., Ulrich, S., Asmus, J., et al. (1997). The long-term effects of functional communication training in home settings. *Journal of Applied Behavior Analysis, 30*(3), 507–531.

DeVries, M. W., & DeVries, M. R. (1977). Cultural relativity of toilet training readiness: A perspective from East Africa. *Pediatrics, 60*(2), 170–177.

Dunn, R. L., & Schwebel, A. I. (1995). Meta-analytic review of marital therapy outcome research. *Journal of Family Psychology, 9*(1), 58–68.

Epstein, R., Lanza, R. P., & Skinner, B. F. (1980). Symbolic communication between two pigeons, (*Columba livia domestica*). *Science, 207*(4430), 543–545.

Fals-Stewart, W., Kashdan, T. B., O'Farrell, T. J., & Birchler, G. R. (2002). Behavioral couples therapy for drug-abusing patients: Effects on partner violence. *Journal of Substance Abuse Treatment, 22*, 87–96.

Hart, B., Risley, T. R., & Kirby, J. R. (1997). Meaningful differences in the everyday experience of young American children. *Canadian Journal of Education, 22*(3), 323.

Hutchinson, R. R., Ulrich, R. E., & Azrin, N. H. (1965). Effects of age and related factors on the pain-aggression reaction. *Journal of Comparative and Physiological Psychology, 59*(3), 365–369.

Im, D. S. (2021). Treatment of aggression in adults with autism spectrum disorder: A review. *Harvard Review of Psychiatry, 29*(1), 35–80.

Jacobson, N. S. (1979). Increasing positive behavior in severely distressed marital relationships: The effects of problem-solving training. *Behavior Therapy, 10*(3), 311–326.

Jacobson, N. S. (1992). Behavioral couple therapy: A new beginning. *Behavior Therapy, 23*(4), 493–506.

Kymissis, E., & Poulson, C. L. (1990). The history of imitation in learning theory: The language acquisition process. *Journal of the Experimental Analysis of Behavior, 54*, 113–127.

Matson, J. L., Dixon, D. R., & Matson, M. L. (2005). Assessing and treating aggression in children and adolescents with developmental disabilities: A 20-year overview. *Educational Psychology, 25*(2–3), 151–181.

Myers, D. L. (1995). Eliminating the battering of women by men: Some considerations for behavior analysis. *Journal of Applied Behavior Analysis, 28*(4), 493–507.

Oliver, C., Hall, S., & Murphy, G. (2005). The early development of self-injurious behaviour: Evaluating the role of social reinforcement. *Journal of Intellectual Disability Research, 49*(8), 591–599.

Patterson, G. R. (1982). *Coercive family process*. Castalia.

Patterson, G. R., Chamberlain, P., & Reid, J. B. (1982). A comparative evaluation of a parent-training program. *Behavior Therapy, 13*(5), 638–650.

Patterson, G. R., DeBaryshe, B. D., & Ramsey, E. (2017). A developmental perspective on antisocial behavior. In T. R. McGee, & P. Mazerolle, P. (Eds.), *Developmental and life-course criminological theories* (pp. 29–35). Routledge.

Peterson, L., & Calhoun, K. (1995). On advancing behavior analysis in the treatment and prevention of battering: Commentary on Myers. *Journal of Applied Behavior Analysis, 28*(4), 509–514.

Piquero, A. R., Jennings, W. G., Diamond, B., Farrington, D. P., Tremblay, R. E., Welsh, B. C., & Gonzalez, J. M. R. (2016). A meta-analysis update on the effects of early family/parent training programs on antisocial behavior and delinquency. *Journal of Experimental Criminology, 12*, 229–248.

Rathgeber, M., Bürkner, P. C., Schiller, E. M., & Holling, H. (2019). The efficacy of emotionally focused couples therapy and behavioral couples therapy: A meta-analysis. *Journal of Marital and Family Therapy, 45*(3), 447–463.

Schaefer, H. H. (1970). Self-injurious behavior: Shaping “head-banging” in monkeys. *Journal of Applied Behavior Analysis, 3*(2), 111–116.

Settles, B. H. (2023). What is a family? Issues in defining family. In *Violence in Families: Integrating Research into Practice* (pp. 3–30). Springer International Publishing.

Shadish, W. R., & Baldwin, S. A. (2005). Effects of behavioral marital therapy: A meta-analysis of randomized controlled trials. *Journal of Consulting and Clinical Psychology, 73*(1), 6.

Skinner, B. F. (2001). The design of cultures. *Behavior and Social Issues, 11*(1), 4.

Sturmey, P. (2022). *Violence and aggression*. Springer.

Sturmey, P. (2023). *Violence in families*. Springer.

Ulrich, R. E., Hutchinson, R. R., & Azrin, N. H. (1965). Pain-elicited aggression. *The Psychological Record, 15*(1), 111.

Chapter 9
Male Peer Support Theory

Walter S. DeKeseredy

Name of the theory: Male Peer Support Theory.
Proponents of the theory: **Walter DeKeseredy** and **Martin D. Schwartz**.
What the theory says: male peer support theory argues that many men experience various types of stress in intimate heterosexual relationships, ranging from sexual problems to challenges to their perceived patriarchal authority. Some men try to deal with these problems themselves, while others turn to their male friends for advice, guidance, and other kinds of social support. The resources provided by these peers may encourage and justify woman abuse under certain conditions. Further, male peer support can influence men to abuse their current or former partners regardless of stress.

Introduction

Some scholars state that sociological insights no longer dominate criminological study generally (Cullen, 2009; Posick et al., 2022), but this trend is not evident in the study of the abuse of women. Most of the theoretical work on this topic continues to be resolutely sociological (Brubaker, 2019). One key example is male peer support theory. Originally developed nearly 40 yearsago (see DeKeseredy, 1988a), the concept of male peer support refers to the attachments to male peers and the resources that these men provide that encourage and legitimate face-to-face and technologically-facilitated types of woman abuse. This chapter chronicles how male peer support theory was created and expanded over the past four decades to remain a vitally alive theory.

W. S. DeKeseredy (✉)
West Virginia University, Morgantown, WV, USA
e-mail: walter.dekeseredy@mail.wvu.edu

A. Hattery and E. Smith (eds.), *Theories of Family Violence*, Advances in Preventing and Treating Violence and Aggression, https://doi.org/10.1007/978-3-032-17095-8_9

History of Male Peer Support Theory

The 11 types of male peer support theory developed so far grew out of intellectual seeds planted at York University, in Toronto, Canada and at the 1987 American Society of Criminology conference in Montreal Canada, where Walter DeKeseredy first met his long-time collaborator Martin D. Schwartz. DeKeseredy crafted the first rendition of male peer support theory in 1988, and it was strongly influenced by social support theory (DeKeseredy, 1988a), which social psychologists use to explain the role of social support in health maintenance and disease prevention. However, it cannot be emphasized enough that the male peer support models developed by DeKeseredy and his colleagues would not have emerged without the guidance, advice, and inspiration of colleagues affiliated with the LaMarsh Research Center on Violence and Conflict Resolution that was based at York University. The Center now has a new name, and its research programs focus primarily on youth problems. Nevertheless, its empirical and theoretical contributions to an interdisciplinary understanding of violence are still felt around the world today.

The LaMarsh Center was established in 1980 under the leadership of sociologist Desmond Ellis. Walter DeKeseredy completed three degrees in sociology under Ellis' supervision, and he became heavily involved in LaMarsh Center scholarly activities in 1985 as a doctoral student. At that time, the Center's Executive Board included psychologists David Weisenthal, Richard Goranson, James Check, and sociologists Michael D. Smith and Alice Propper. All these colleagues were engaged in vibrant and timely academic projects, including research on women's abuse. That said, Ellis and Smith had the greatest impact on DeKeseredy's early work on male peer support.

In 1985, the study of woman abuse in dating had a "short history" (Riggs & O'leary, 1989). There were a few studies of sexual assault in dating conducted in the late 1950s and late 1960s (e.g., Kirkpatrick & Kanin, 1957), but physical violence in this intimate context received limited, if any, social scientific attention until James Makepeace (1981) published the first study of *courtship violence* among U.S. college students. This survey opened the door to several other scholars in the 1980s who challenged the *marriage license is a hitting license thesis* (Straus et al., 1981). This thesis includes two main contentions. First, marriage is a special institution that places women at high risk for abuse. Second, married women are more likely to be beaten than unmarried women (Gelles, 1982). Yet, in the mid-1980s, no comparable Canadian data contradicted this claim made by Murray Straus and his colleagues. Thus, this research gap helped launch DeKeseredy's Ph.D. thesis in sociology and all his subsequent male peer support theories.

In 1985, Michael D. Smith was in the process of developing a representative sample survey of woman abuse in Toronto, and Desmond Ellis was doing pioneering research on post-separation male violence against women. DeKeseredy decided to conduct a study of woman abuse in university/community college dating and wanted to administer a self-report survey of potential male offenders. His major challenge at that time was finding a sound theoretical framework to inform his empirical work, and from November 1985 to the early part of 1986, DeKeseredy toiled in York

University's library looking for theoretical guidance, and his frustration grew with each passing day. Then, in the fall of 1986, while in York University's *Cock and Bull Pub,* drinking his morning coffee and preparing for an undergraduate tutorial, he was shortly to lead, one of the most important events in his life transpired. At a nearby table was a group of undergraduates, and DeKeseredy overheard them offering "solutions" to one group member's dating problems. The recipient of advice was very upset because he took a woman out for dinner, and she refused to have sex with him at the end of the evening. Some of his peers suggested that he stop seeing her, while others stated that he should have physically forced her to have sex with him.

At that moment, DeKeseredy remembered Kanin's (1967) *reference group theory*. He was the first North American sociologist to answer this important question: How do all-male groups make sexual abuse in courtship legitimate? Furthermore, how do they perpetuate this problem over time? DeKeseredy, then, with an improved outlook on the future, went to his tutorial and shortly after told Smith about his experience. Smith was keenly interested in the *violent subculture hypothesis* derived from Wolfgang and Ferracuti's (1967) work and tested it using interview data from over 700 ice hockey players (see Smith, 1979, 1983). Smith was also familiar with the literature on what was then referred to as *wife beating*, and he advised DeKeseredy to read Bowker's (1983) book *Beating Wife-Beating*, which included, for its time, one of the more developed male peer support theories of wife abuse. Smith's recommendation is one of the best that DeKeseredy ever received, and he continues to cite Bowker's book throughout his work. Note that Bowker's claim that the male patriarchal subculture of violence is "spread through all parts of society" still has much international empirical support and will be addressed in greater detail further down in this chapter (p. 136).

After reading Bowker's work and revisiting Kanin's (1967) theory, DeKeseredy developed his theoretical framework and soon published it in a journal and in a book (DeKeseredy, 1988a, 1988b). He also broadened his analysis of woman abuse to include sexual and psychological abuse and to examine how male groupings contribute to the multidimensional nature of "the dark side of the ivory tower" (Sloan & Fisher, 2011).

Key Tenets of Male Peer Support Theory

Male peer support data collected over the years support a basic sociological argument promoted by *differential association theorists* (e.g., Sutherland, 1939) and *social learning theorists* (e.g., Akers, 1977): that the abuse of women is behavior that is socially learned from interactions with others. Greatly influenced by Bowker (1983), DeKeseredy's (1988a) first male peer support theory is designed to explain how social interactions with male peers are associated with various forms of female victimization in postsecondary school dating relationships. He contends that many men experience various types of stress in intimate heterosexual relationships, ranging from female sexual rejection to other kinds of threats to the kinds of authority that patriarchal culture had led them to expect to be their rights by being male. Some men try to deal with these problems themselves, while others turn to their male friends for advice, guidance, and other kinds of social support. The resources provided by these peers often encourage and justify woman abuse under certain conditions. Further, male peer support can influence men to victimize their dating partners regardless of stress.

Like Bowker (1983), DeKeseredy argued that male peer support also encourages men to resist attempting to end their abusive behavior. There is a literature (see DeKeseredy & Schwartz, 2013) showing that after beating female intimates, some men display contriteness and offer pleas for forgiveness. However, peers alleviate such post-abuse-related stress by assuring the man that what he did was correct. They can encourage post-abuse men to continue asserting their authority through harmful means.

There is empirical support for this theory. Based on analyses of self-report survey data gathered from a convenience sample of 333 Canadian male undergraduates, DeKeseredy (1988b) found that social ties with physically, sexually, and/or psychologically abusive peers are strongly related to abuse among men who experience high-levels of dating life-events stress. Simply put, among those men suffering from stress caused by their relations with women, the ones who chose to abuse women were friends with other men whom they knew also abused women.

In sum, DeKeseredy's original model and statistics gleaned from a test of it challenge traditional social support theory, which emphasizes only the beneficial features of social support (Heller & Swindle, 1981). Data gathered by DeKeseredy and his colleagues over the past 40 years confirm Vaux's (1985) argument that "social support may facilitate the resolution of problems or the management of distress, but there are no guarantees that such a resolution is free of cost" (p. 102). Even so, DeKeseredy's original model has some pitfalls, one of which is that it does not account for other explanatory variables. Therefore, five years later, DeKeseredy and Schwartz (1993) developed the modified male peer support model of woman abuse in postsecondary school dating.

In addition to addressing the importance of the factors included in DeKeseredy's (1988a) model, DeKeseredy and Schwartz's offering focuses on the contribution of the *ideology of familial patriarchy* (a discourse that supports the abuse of women who violate the ideals of male power and control over women in intimate relationships), alcohol consumption, membership in formal groups (e.g., fraternities), and the *absence of deterrence* (e.g., no punishments for abusing women). Using national Canadian self-report survey data from 1,307 male university and community college students (see DeKeseredy & Schwartz, 1998a), DeKeseredy and Schwartz obtained some empirical support for their theory. For example, their findings show that males who report abusing their dating partners are more likely to espouse the ideology of familial patriarchy than those who do not report abusive behavior. These men are even more likely to abuse their partners when supported by their male peers. Male peer support, then, does contribute to the relationship between patriarchal ideology and female victimization in university/college courtship.

DeKeseredy and Schwartz's (1998a) Canadian national data show that not only is woman abuse in postsecondary school dating multidimensional in nature but so is male peer support.

This finding is corroborated by studies of male peer support outside the limited realm of college dating (see DeKeseredy, 2019). Thus far, research, like that done by DeKeseredy and Schwartz, consistently identifies these five variants of male peer support:

- *routine activities with other men*, such as playing sports or going to bars or nightclubs;
- *informational support*, which refers to the guidance and advice that influence men to assault their current or former female partners;
- *attachments to male peers who have abused their current or former female partners*;
- *peers' patriarchal attitudes and beliefs*; and
- *male peer pressure to have sex.*

Until recently, the research method most often associated with male peer support theory is the self-report survey of men. Hypotheses, though, derived from the above two male peer support theories of women abuse in institutions of higher learning have since been tested using victimization surveys (e.g., DeKeseredy et al., 2018). Newer theories of male peer support have been tested using rich in-depth interviews with separated/divorced women, abused women in rural places and sport-related contexts, and with a victimization survey administered in Canadian socially and economically public housing communities (see DeKeseredy et al., 2003; DeKeseredy & Schwartz, 2013).

It is now time to revisit the self-report technology used by DeKeseredy (1988b) and DeKeseredy and Schwartz (1998a) because it yields better answers to some fundamental questions, such as "Why Does He Do That?" (Bancroft, 2002). As Scully (1990) observes, there are problems in entirely depending on females to report the behaviors of male abusers because "Women cannot reveal the motivations and justifications of the men who [abuse] them because they don't share the reality of… violent men. Such insight is acquired through invading and critically examining the social constructions of… men" (p. 4). Interviews with men, as Scully uncovered, also provide this insight.

Assessment of Male Peer Support Theory

Quantitative and qualitative data show that male peer support theory can explain woman abuse in different social contexts and intimate relationships. Ten years after DeKeseredy crafted his first male peer support model and tested it, he and Schwartz (see DeKeseredy & Schwartz, 1998b) seriously doubted that male peer support was a universal risk factor, in that all men receive this support regardless of their place on the socioeconomic ladder. Now, they are firmly convinced that what Bowker (1983) stated 42 years ago about all-male, patriarchal subcultures of violence is correct:

> This is not a subculture that is confined to a single class, religion, occupational grouping or race. It is spread throughout all parts of society. Men are socialized by other subculture members to accept definitions of the situation, norms, values, and beliefs about male dominance and the necessity of keeping their women in line. These violence-supporting relations may occur at any given time and in any place (pp. 135–136).

Male peer pressure that legitimates the sexual objectification of women and the sexual, physical, and/or psychological abuse of them is found in sport-related contexts (DeKeseredy et al., 2023), among African American men in Chicago (Wilson, 1996), among Puerto Rican drug dealers in East Harlem and poor African American boys in parts of St. Louis (Bourgois, 1995; Miller, 2008), on North American college campuses and their immediate surroundings (DeKeseredy & Schwartz, 2013), in rural Ohio and Kentucky (DeKeseredy, 2021; Websdale, 1998), in rural New Zealand and South Africa (Cambell, 2000; Jewkes et al., 2006), in Canadian public housing communities (DeKeseredy et al., 2003), and in natural resource extraction communities around the world (DeKeseredy & Donnermeyer, 2023). There is also evidence of the emergence of pro-abuse male peer support groups in cyberspace (DeKeseredy, 2025), and many men who abuse women consume electronic forms of pornography with their male friends (DeKeseredy, 2020; DeKeseredy & Corsianos, 2016; DeKeseredy & Schwartz, 2016).

Male peer support theories provide helpful answers to this question: Why do so many men beat, sexually assault, psychologically abuse, and otherwise harm their current and former intimate female partners in ways that few people can imagine? The world is, of course, multivariate, and it is impossible to pick out one sociological factor and announce that it covers all cases of woman abuse on every occasion. Nevertheless, all the research into variants of male peer support theory covered in the extant literature supports the central tenets, showing that it is a powerful explanation of the mechanism that contributes to much of North America's woman abuse.

Practical Applications of Male Peer Support Theory

Some examples of research informed by male peer support theory are provided in previous sections of this chapter and therefore this section briefly covers how this perspective informs policy and practice. Directly relevant here is the work done by those referred to in some academic and activist circles as *feminist, pro-feminist,* or *anti-sexist men* (DeKeseredy, 2025; Messner et al., 2015). Such men are involved in the ongoing practice of changing themselves, self-examination, and self-discovery (DeKeseredy et al., 2017a), with the goal of shedding their "patriarchal baggage" (Thorne-Finch, 1992). Though constituting a relatively small but growing group, these men work individually and collectively to change other men. Depending on their time and energy, some feminist men work on the dual-level of changing individual people and social institutions. Others have limited goals. Most limited of all are those who privately support the principles of feminism and restrict their efforts to create and maintain egalitarian relationships. This separation of private and public attempts to eliminate patriarchy continues to be one of the most central challenges for feminist men (DeKeseredy, 2025).

Male peer support theorists and other types of feminist scholars who study sexist all-male peer groups (e.g., Bates, 2020) recommend that feminist men's work be incorporated into mainstream education to prevent boys from becoming woman abusers. For them, it is time for more male teachers, administrators, and athletic coaches to "step up to the plate" and demonstrate some progressive leadership by offering programs on gender issues in their schools. They can also do things personally (Katz, 2006), such as talking to male students and faculty in assemblies, classes, sporting events, faculty and school training, and in private conversations (DeKeseredy & Corsianos, 2016). It would also, according to male peer support theorists (e.g., DeKeseredy, 2025; Schwartz & DeKeseredy, 1997), be useful for school staff to employ the following strategies informed by the work of Bates (2020), Messerschmidt (2012), Thorne-Finch (1992, pp. 236–237), and Warshaw (1988, pp. 161–164):

- Confront students, teachers, and athletic staff who speak about violence against women and misogynistic social media and pornography in an approving manner.
- Confront students and staff who perpetuate and legitimate rape myths.
- Take every opportunity to speak out against misogynistic social media and other symptoms of gender inequality.
- Create social media forums about the harms of misogyny and how men and boys can work together to curb patriarchal discourses and practices.
- Develop school curricula that make gender, healthy relationships, and sexuality core subjects.

Many other strategies advanced by male peer support theorists could easily be discussed in this chapter. And, it is likely that more new approaches will be required as we encounter both new technologies and various societal changes that will affect and shape gender relations.

Indeed, 35 years ago, who would have ever thought of "sexting" becoming an integral part of youth peer culture? What is next? Many progressive scholars, practitioners, and activists are afraid to hear the answer, given the potential for significant patriarchal harm to women that is mixed in with the tremendous changes for good provided by the internet, smartphones, and other modern technology.

Critique of Male Peer Support Theory

To the best of my knowledge, so far, only two male peer support theories center on online all-male patriarchal social exchanges and how they influence men to abuse women (see DeKeseredy, 2025; DeKeseredy & Schwartz, 2016). This emphasis on mainly theorizing face-to-face abuse is likely to change soon because of studies revealing that some men assault women in a variety of ways but do not directly interact with abusive or sexist peers on an in-person basis. This is not to say, though, that they are not influenced to victimize women by male peers. Indeed, we are now seeing the rapid development of patriarchal online communities (e.g., incels) with members who never come into face-to-face contact with each other but frequently exchange misogynistic written, audio, and visual communication with their peers (Huber, 2023; Thornburn et al., 2023; Tranchese & Sugiura, 2021).

To date, there are no answers to these important questions because of the conspicuous absence of longitudinal male peer support research:

- Do some members drop out of sexist male peer groups and rely on other means of social support to help "keep their women in line"?
- Do some members of a particular patriarchal male peer support group move on to join another group with similar values, beliefs, and practices?
- Do some all-male group members mature out of them as they get older and become employed?
- Are current or former members of sexist peer groups who get married or end up in cohabiting relationships more or less likely to be physically, sexually, and psychologically abusive?
- Do some men who join male peer groups eventually quit and then join again?

There are also no conclusive answers to these questions: Is male peer support a constant or a variable? Are White men more or less likely than Black, Indigenous, or Hispanic males to join and be influenced by sexist all-male collectives? Are working-class men more or less likely than their more affluent counterparts to receive male peer support?

DeKeseredy and other male peer support theorists recognize that what is especially necessary is a male peer support perspective that focuses on adolescent males because peers play an integral role in the lives of these boys and many of them are at very high risk of abusing girls (DeKeseredy et al., 2023). Perhaps, too, male peer support theory can help explain male intimate violence against older women. Estimates of lifetime prevalence range from 16.5 to 54.5% (Pathak et al., 2019), and many perpetrators likely receive support from their friends. Still, a study designed to discern whether peer influence is a significant determinant is required before attempting to chart such a new theoretical terrain.

In the last few years, DeKeseredy and some of his colleagues recognized that it was time to move peer support research beyond the realm of studying only the relationship between pro-abuse peer group dynamics and violence against heterosexual women. Using representative sample survey data from large-scale campus climate survey conducted at a large residential college in a South Atlantic part of the U.S., DeKeseredy et al. (2017b, 2019) found that LGBTQ students' peers play a key role in the physical, sexual, and stalking victimization experiences.

They termed the more open support that offenders might receive from LGBTQ friends as *negative peer support*. Based on their findings, they rightfully state that another important step to take is to develop and test theories of negative peer support and violence against LGBTQ students.

Unquestionably, other topics can be included in a list of new theoretical directions, such as the bullying of girls in school. Since the late 1990s, a small cadre of sociologists have modified DeKeseredy's (1988a) first male peer support theory and we are likely to see more new versions in the coming years.

Conclusions

Dragiewicz (2011) concluded in her brief review of the scholarly evidence of patriarchal support for violence against women that "Studies have documented the influence of patriarchal peer support for men's violence against women at the mesosystem level in a variety of contexts, including studies of battered wives, dating violence, batterer narratives, campus sexual assault, separation assault, and woman abuse in representative random samples" (p. 113). Unfortunately, male peer support seems to be ubiquitous and has a long history. The data gathered and the theories produced to date tell us much, but there are still many unanswered questions and new avenues to explore. Chief among the problems in the state of male peer support theory and research is the question of how male peer support groups form or come together. Regardless of what the future brings, sociological work on male peer support will stay the course of avoiding falling into the trap of what the late Mills (1959) referred to as *abstracted empiricism* (e.g., research divorced from theory) and continue to prioritize a gendered analysis of rape, beatings, coercive control, and the like.

References

Akers, R. L. (1977). *Deviant behavior: A social learning approach* (2nd ed.). Wadsworth.

Bancroft, L. (2002). *Why does he do that?* Penguin.

Bates, L. (2020). *Men who hate women: The extremism nobody is talking about*. Simon & Schuster.

Bourgois, P. (1995). *In search of respect: Selling crack in el barrio*. Cambridge University Press.

Bowker, L. H. (1983). *Beating wife-beating*. Lexington Books.

Brubaker, S. J. (2019). *Theorizing gender violence*. Cognella.

Campbell, H. (2000). The glass phallus: Pub(lic) masculinity and drinking in rural New Zealand. *Rural Sociology, 65*(4), 562–581. https://doi.org/10.1111/j.1549-0831.2000.tb00044.x

Cullen, F. T. (2009). Preface. In A. Walsh & K. M. Beaver (Eds.), *Biosocial criminology: New directions in research and theory* (pp. xv–xvii). Routledge.

DeKeseredy, W. S., & Schwartz, M. D. (1993). Male peer support and woman abuse: An expansion of DeKeseredy's model. *Sociological Spectrum, 13*(4), 393–413. https://doi.org/10.1080/02732173.1993.9982041

DeKeseredy, W. S. (1988a). Woman abuse in dating relationships: The relevance of social support theory. *Journal of Family Violence, 3*(1), 1–13. https://doi.org/10.1007/bf00994662

DeKeseredy, W. S. (1988b). *Woman abuse in dating relationships: The role of male peer support*. Canadian Scholars' Press.

DeKeseredy, W. S., & Schwartz, M. D. (1998a). *Woman abuse on campus: Results from the Canadian national survey*. Sage.
DeKeseredy, W. S., & Schwartz, M. D. (1998b). Male peer support and woman abuse in postsecondary school courtship: Suggestions for new directions in sociological research. In R. Kennedy Bergen (Ed.), *Issues in intimate violence* (pp. 83–96). Sage.
DeKeseredy, W. S. (2019). Some reflections on male peer support theory. In S. J. Brubaker (Ed.), *Theorizing gender violence* (pp. 45–49). Cognella.
DeKeseredy, W. S. (2020). *Understanding the harms of pornography: The contributions of social scientific knowledge*. Culture Reframed.
DeKeseredy, W. S. (2021). *Woman abuse in rural places*. Routledge.
DeKeseredy, W. S., Alvi, S., Schwartz, M. D., & Tomaszewski, E. A. (2003). *Under siege: Poverty and crime in a public housing community*. Lexington Books.
DeKeseredy, W. S., & Schwartz, M. D. (2013). *Male peer support & violence against women: The history & verification of a theory*. Northeastern University Press.
DeKeseredy, W. S., & Corsianos, M. (2016). *Violence against women in pornography*. Routledge.
DeKeseredy, W. S., & Schwartz, M. D. (2016). Thinking sociologically about image-based sexual abuse: The contribution of male peer support theory. *Sexualization, Media, & Society*. https://doi.org/10.177/2374623816684692
DeKeseredy, W. S., Dragiewicz, M., & Schwartz, M. D. (2017a). *Abusive endings: Separation and divorce violence against women*. University of California Press.
DeKeseredy, W. S., Hall-Sanchez, A., Nolan, J., & Schwartz, M. D. (2017b). A campus LGBTQ community's sexual violence and stalking experiences: The contribution of pro-abuse peer support. *Journal of Gender-Based Violence, 1*(2), 169–186. https://doi.org/10.1332/239868017x15099845241783
DeKeseredy, W. S., Hall-Sanchez, A., & Nolan, J. (2018). College campus sexual assault: The contribution of peers' proabuse informational support and attachments to abusive peers. *Violence against Women, 24*(8), 922–935. https://doi.org/10.1177/1077801217724920
DeKeseredy, W. S., Nolan, J., Hall-Sanchez, A., & Messinger, A. M. (2019). Intimate partner violence victimization among heterosexual, gay, lesbian and bisexual students: The role of pro-abuse peer support. *Journal of Aggression, Maltreatment & Trauma, 28*(9), 1057–1068. https://doi.org/10.1080/10926771.2018.1551820
DeKeseredy, W. S., & Donnermeyer, J. F. (2023). A new theory of globablization, natural resource extraction and violence against women: Toward solving the linkage problem. *Critical Criminology*. https://doi.org/10.1007/s10612-022-09668-3
DeKeseredy, W. S., Cowan, S., & Schwartz, M. D. (2023). *Skating on thin ice: Professional hockey, rape culture, & violence against women*. Aevo University of Toronto Press.
DeKeseredy, W. S. (2025). Misogyny and woman abuse in the incelosphere: The role of online male peer support. In J. B. Walther & R. E. Rice (Eds.), *Social processes of online hate* (pp. 73–92). Routledge.
Dragiewicz, M. (2011). *Equality with a vengeance: Men's rights groups, battered women, and antifeminist backlash*. Northeastern University Press.
Gelles, R. J. (1982). Domestic criminal violence. In M. E. Wolfgang & N. E. Weiner (Eds.), *Criminal violence* (pp. 201–229). Sage.
Heller, K., & Swindle, R. W. (1981). Social networks, perceived social support and coping with stress. In R. E. Feiner, L. A. Jason, J. N. Moritsugu, & S. S. Farber (Eds.), *Preventive psychology: Theory, research and practice* (pp. 87–103). Pergamon.
Huber, A. R. (2023). Image-based sexual abuse: Online communities and the broader misogynistic landscape. *The British Journal of Criminology, 63*(4), 967–983. https://doi.org/10.1093/bjc/azac067
Jewkes, R., Dunkle, K., Koss, M. P., et al. (2006). Rape perpetration by young rural South African men: Prevalence, patterns, and risk factors. *Social Science and Medicine, 63*(11), 2949–2961. https://doi.org/10.1016/j.socscimed.2006.07.027

Kanin, E. J. (1967). An examination of sexual aggression as a response to sexual frustration. *Journal of Marriage the Family, 29*(3), 428–433. https://doi.org/10.2307/349577
Katz, J. (2006). *The macho paradox: Why some men hurt women and how all men can.* Sourcebooks, Inc.
Kirkpatrick, C., & Kanin, E. J. (1957). Male sex aggression on a university campus. *American Sociological Review, 22*(1), 52–58. https://doi.org/10.2307/2088765
Makepeace, J. M. (1981). Courtship violence among college students. *Family Relations, 30*(1), 97–102. https://doi.org/10.2307/584242
Messerschmidt, J. W. (2012). *Gender, heterosexuality, and youth violence: The struggle for recognition.* Rowman & Littlefield.
Messner, M. A., Greenberg, M. A., & Peretz, T. (2015). *Some men: Feminist allies & the movement to end violence against women.* Oxford University Press.
Miller, J. (2008). *Getting played: African-American girls, urban inequality, and gendered violence.* Oxford University Press.
Mills, C. W. (1959). *The sociological imagination.* Oxford University Press.
Pathak, N., Dhairyawan, R., & Tariq, S. (2019). The experience of intimate partner violence among older women: A narrative review. *Maturitas, 121*, 63–75. https://doi.org/10.1016/j.maturitas.2018.12.011
Posick, C., Roque, M., & Barnes, J. C. (2022). *Fitting the facts of crime: An invitation to biopsychosocial criminology.* Temple University Press.
Riggs, D. S., & O'Leary, K. D. (1989). A theoretical model of courtship aggression. In M. A. Pirog-Good & J. E. Stets (Eds.), *Violence in dating relationships: Emerging social issues* (pp. 53–71). Praeger.
Schwartz, M. D., & DeKeseredy, W. S. (1997). *Sexual assault on the college campus: The role of male peer support.* Sage.
Scully, D. (1990). *Understanding sexual violence.* Unwin Hyman.
Sloan, J. J., & Fisher, B. S. (2011). *The dark side of the ivory tower: Campus crime as a social problem.* Cambridge University Press.
Smith, M. D. (1979). Hockey violence: A test of the violent subculture hypothesis. *Social Problems, 27*(1), 235–247. https://doi.org/10.2307/800371
Smith, M. D. (1983). *Violence and sport.* Butterworths.
Straus, M. A., Gelles, R. J., & Steinmetz, S. K. (1981). *Behind closed doors: Violence in the American family.* Anchor.
Sutherland, E. H. (1939). *Principles of criminology* (3rd ed.). Lippincott.
Thorburn, J., Powell, A., & Chambers, P. (2023). A world alone: Masculinities, humiliation, and aggrieved entitlement on an in cel forum. *The British Journal of Criminology, 63*(1), 238–254. https://doi.org/10.1093/bjc/azac020
Thorne-Finch, R. (1992). *Ending the silence: The origins and treatment of violence against women.* University of Toronto Press.
Tranchese, A., & Sugiura, L. (2021). "I don't hate all women, just those stuck-up bitches": How in cels and mainstream pornography speak the same extreme language of misogyny. *Violence against Women, 27*(14), 2709–2734. https://doi.org/10.1177/1077801221996453
Vaux, A. (1985). Variations in social support associated with gender, ethnicity, and age. *Journal of Social Issues, 41*(1), 89–110. https://doi.org/10.1111/j.1540-4560.1985.tb01118.x
Warshaw, R. (1988). *I never called it rape.* Harper & Row.
Websdale, N. (1998). *Rural woman battering and the justice system: An ethnography.* Sage
Wilson, W. J. (1996). *When work disappears: The world of the new urban poor.* Knopf.
Wolfgang, M. E., & Ferracuti, F. (1967). *The subculture of violence: Toward an integrated theory in criminology.* Tavistock.

Chapter 10
Theories of Elder Abuse

Pamela B. Teaster, Karen A. Roberto, and Ruthann Froberg

Name of the theory: Socio-Ecological Systems Theory, Life Course Theory, and the Contextual Theory of Elder Abuse.
Proponents of the theory: Urie Bronfenbrenner, Glen Elder, Karen Roberto, and Pamela Teaster.
What the theory says: Elder abuse has received scant attention in the family violence literature. The phenomena can occur in community settings, facility settings, or both. According to the World Health Organization, in one year, one in six adults 60 years of age and older experiences some kind of abuse. The Socio-Ecological Systems Theory (SEST) includes five systems that help explain how and why people experience elder abuse. Frequently paired with SEST, Life Course Theory extends SEST by considering the influence of association js and experiences across time. The newest theory, the Contextual Theory of Elder Abuse, is conceived specifically for the topic and recognizes micro through macro contexts occurring across time.

P. B. Teaster (✉) · R. Froberg
Center for Gerontology, Virginia Tech, Blacksburg, VA, USA
e-mail: pteaster@vt.edu

R. Froberg
e-mail: rfroberg@vt.edu

K. A. Roberto
Institute for Society, Culture, and Environment, Blacksburg, VA, USA
e-mail: kroberto@vt.edu

A. Hattery and E. Smith (eds.), *Theories of Family Violence*, Advances in Preventing and Treating Violence and Aggression, https://doi.org/10.1007/978-3-032-17095-8_10

Theories of Elder Abuse

Elder abuse is a global term that refers to any "knowing, intentional, or negligent act by a caregiver or any other person that causes harm or a serious risk of harm to a vulnerable adult" (ACL, 2019). Frequently excluded from the family violence literature, violence harming older adults, or elder abuse, can take many forms (i.e., physical, financial, psychological, neglect, sexual), and may occur multiple times by a single or multiple harmers or in combination, which is referred to as polyvictimization (Teaster, 2017).

Abuse occurs in community settings, facility settings, or both. In community settings, each year, one in six adults 60 years of age and older experiences some kind of abuse (World Health Organization [WHO], 2024). A meta-analysis by Yon et al. (2019) revealed a high self-reported prevalence rate of abuse in facilities but was unable to determine an overall prevalence estimate. Yon et al. (2019) went on to assert that prevalence estimates for abuse types as reported by older residents were the highest for psychological abuse (33.4%), followed by physical abuse (14.1%), financial abuse (13.8%), neglect (11.6%), with the lowest for sexual abuse (1.9%).

During the early years of research on elder abuse, there was little use of theory because no theory attributed solely to elder abuse existed and because academicians and practitioners were skeptical of the value of theory for understanding the problem. However, from the early 2000s, as scholarship on elder abuse became more widespread, rigorous, and externally funded, researchers typically borrowed theories from other disciplines to guide their research (Biggs & Goergen, 2010; Jackson & Hafemeister, 2013). As elder abuse scholars began to consistently use theories to inform their research, theory helped inform professional practices and policy.

In this chapter, we discuss three highly relevant theories that have reliably guided and informed the study of elder abuse: the Socio-Ecological Systems Model, the Life Course Perspective, and the Contextual Theory of Elder Abuse. Throughout the chapter, we use the term "theory" to acknowledge concepts that some may regard as models, frameworks, or perspectives.

The Socio-Ecological Systems Theory

Perhaps the earliest and most versatile theory for the study of elder abuse is Urie Bronfenbrenner's (1986) *Ecological Model*. Also referred to as the Socio-Ecological Systems Theory (SEST), it suggests that a person is situated within a series of nested environmental systems that interact with one another and that influence development and life experiences.

Disciplines in Which the Socio-Ecological Systems Theory is Used

Many disciplines have made extensive use of this theory, which enjoys wide applicability because of the wide array of systems it embraces. These include human development, family science, psychology, sociology, family therapy, education, public health, and social work.

History of Socio-ecological Systems Theory

The author of SEST, Urie Bronfenbrenner (1917–2005), earned his doctorate in developmental psychology. Across his life experiences and his scholarship, Bronfenbrenner recognized that, rather than simply individual processes, human development was shaped by interactions between and among a person and their environment (Bronfenbrenner, 1979). Bronfenbrenner realized that tenets of developmental psychology alone proved inadequate when confronting individual experience. Rather, human development was shaped by a multiplicity of influences or systems from those closest to an individual to those from the societal level, including a person's position within the life cycle. He recognized that a theory of human development involved influences on many levels or systems (Bronfenbrenner, 1986).

Key Tenets of Socio-Ecological Systems Theory

The SEST involves five nested rings representing diverse yet intertwined systems (Bronfenbrenner, 1979) (Fig. 10.1). The innermost system, or the *micro-system*, involves an individual's immediate surroundings and relationships.

Surrounding the microsystem is the *mesosystem*, which has connections and interactions between and among different aspects of a person's environment (e.g., family, friends, community groups, healthcare providers). The third system, the *exosystem* encompass proximal agencies, family, and acquaintances. The fourth layer is the *macrosystem,* which includes an individual's culture, belief systems, legal frameworks, the media, the economy, and public policy, all of which influence interactions with each of the other systems. The final and outermost system is the *chronosystem,* which entails time, including but is not limited to life transitions (e.g., marriage, chronic illness) and societal experiences (e.g., wars, pandemics, natural disasters).

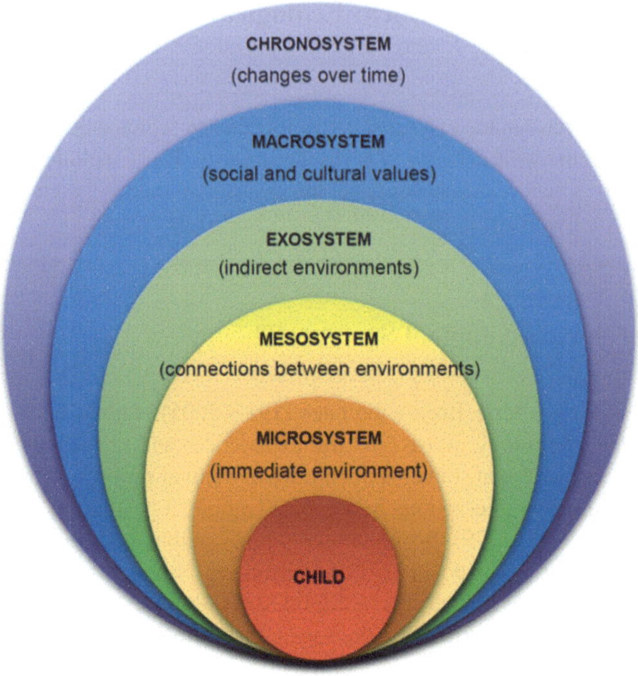

Fig. 10.1 Socio-ecological systems model. *Note* From Whole Child (n.d.)

Contributions to the Study of Elder Abuse

One of the earliest references to Bronfenbrenner's theory in the elder abuse literature was made by Schiamberg and Gans (1999), who were building upon research by Kosberg and Nahmaish (1996) that highlighted the necessity of scholars situating their research within broader frameworks of elder abuse. Schiamberg and Gans (1999) combined ecological theory and the life course perspective (see below) to examine contextual risk factors for elder abuse by adult child caregivers. They proposed a model that focused on the adult child and the aging parent (Schiamberg & Gans, 1999, 2000), assigning equal importance to the context in which their relationship occurred and suggesting six risk factors for abuse within each system: (1) *aging parent microsystem* (e.g., gender, marital status, chronological age, health, dementia, provocative/disruptive behavior, substance abuse, psychological factors, and social isolation); (2) *adult child microsystem* (e.g., substance abuse, mental/emotional conditions, dementia, lack of caregiving experience, reluctance, stress and burden, personality traits, and lack of social support); (3) *family microsystem* (e.g., dependency, living arrangements, history of abuse in the family, intergenerational transmission of violent behavior, and multigenerational demands); (4) *adult child mesosystem/older adult exosystem* (e.g., employment status and financial resources, social isolation, and lack of formal support); (5) *older parent mesosystem/adult child exosystem* (e.g., social isolation and lack of formal support); and (6) *macrosystem* (e.g., cultural norms and public policy).

Later, Parrra-Cardona and colleagues (2007) expanded on variables in the theory and identified factors and dynamics associated with elder abuse in Latino families. They found that, although many of the risk factors identified in the ecological model were relevant, additional factors could come into play in systems, including country of origin, language, cultural identity, and barriers to health care.

Applicable Methodological Approaches

It is not necessary to apply a multitude of variables within the layers of the SEST or incorporate all systems identified to study elder abuse. For example, researchers have come to understand elder abuse through an examination of individual experiences (microsystem; Awuviry-Newton et al., 2020) and how life experiences promote elder abuse or protect older adults against it (chronosystem; Fettig et al., 2024).

Assessment of the Theory as It Relates to Elder Abuse

The SEST helps to explain the occurrence of elder abuse on systemic levels. In particular, the theory helps parse out why elder abuse occurs and why policies, programs, and funding are still inadequate to address the problem. Recently, the theory has helped explain how systemic ageism (e.g., inadequate healthcare, insecurities, poverty) can affect all types of abuse (Pillemer et al., 2021).

Application of Socio-Ecological Systems Theory

One of the only studies to address each of the ecological systems, Teaster et al. (2006) organized and interpreted data from their qualitative study of the intimate partner violence experienced by rural older women and community service professionals. Findings revealed multiple interacting influences that perpetuated violence in the lives of the rural older women: individual and family contexts (microsystem); relationships between the women and their extended family, church, and others (mesosystem); community support or its absence (exosystem), and the culture of rurality (macrosystem).

Critique of the Theory

The SEST enjoys wide applicability, particularly when exploring questions of elder abuse and addressing the problem through systemic intervention (e.g., community supports; access to healthcare; policies/programs). It has less utility when exploring individual relationships between and among older adults and their family and friends, where theories concerning behaviors and relationships may prove more appropriate.

Conclusion

The applicability and influence of Bronfenbrenner's SEST is vast, particularly among social scientists. His theory widened thinking about what factors influence relationships for individuals of all ages—that they do not exist in a social vacuum but rather have lives embedded within structures of relationships, community, society, economics and politics, as well as the time in which these occur. The SEST helped push developmental research beyond interpersonal relationships to use various qualitative and quantitative methodologies to explore the impact of environmental factors on human development and activity.

Life Course Theory

Often used in conjunction with or alongside SEST, Life Course Theory (LCT) focuses on individual lives within the context of relationships and sociohistorical events. Developed by sociologists in the 1970s, LCT posits that throughout the life course, individuals are influenced by social and historical events as well as by people whose lives intersect (Elder, 1974). Research applying LCT traces trajectories of life events and decisions across time and recognizes the interconnectedness of these influences throughout the lifespan. When utilized to understand elder abuse, LCT can support research about historical, societal, and interpersonal factors that increase risk or serve as protective factors for older adults and their caregivers.

History of Life Course Theory

LTC was conceived by Glen Elder in the 1970s while he was following the life paths of a cohort of individuals who grew up during the Great Depression (Elder, 1998). Elder traced the impact of economic hardship on his participants and their families, careers, and life trajectories. As a sociologist, Elder used LCT to explore the complex interrelationship between individuals (i.e., linked lives); social structures;

and the impact of time, place, and history on individuals' lives. Other scholars have contributed to the refinement of LCT through the addition of concepts such as cumulative dis/advantage (Dannefer, 2003) and application to the complexities of aging (Settersten, 2003).

Key Tenets of Life Course Theory

LCT focuses on the sociohistorical context of individual lives and its impact on human development across the lifespan. Central tenets include the bilateral influence between individual lives and the era in which they live, with individual agency (i.e., choices/actions) and linked lives (i.e., relationships) being central to understanding human development (Elder, 1998). Both the sociohistorical context and individual decision-making shape a person's social pathway, which is composed of a series of trajectories and transitions that determine a person's role and identity at different times of their life (Elder, 1998). Another critical concept of LCT is the significance of time–the timing, order, and length of life events can drastically change trajectories and development in positive or negative ways (Bengtson & Allen, 1993).

LCT is often paired with other theories to highlight certain relationships, social pathways, or cumulative advantages/disadvantages that uniquely affect individuals as they move through the life course. For example, it has been paired with SEST to examine life course victimization (Turanovic, 2023, with feminist theory to examine later in life mother-child relationships (Turanovic, 2023) and critical race theory to examine the lifelong impact of racism (DiAquoi, 2018).

Life Course Theory and Elder Abuse

LCT underlies the study of several types of elder abuse including physical (Band-Winterstein et al., 2016), emotional (Simmons & Swahnberg, 2021), and financial abuse (Podnieks, 2017). Its key tenets provide framing for an individual's meaning-making and actions that contextualize it within their experience with family, significant others, social institutions, and systems of oppression. The longitudinal lens of the theory helps reveal dynamics adapted in response to individual and family development that potentially heightens risk for abuse.

Applicable Methodological Approaches

Researchers have utilized longitudinal data sets such as the Lehigh Longitudinal Study (Herrenkohl et al., 2021) and the Wisconsin Longitudinal Study (Kong & Easton, 2019) to address life course influences on violence and abuse. Qualitative research employs LCT and its approaches (e.g., life history interview) to examine connections between early life experiences of abuse and elder abuse (Asyraf et al., 2021; Chen & Fu, 2022). However, data collection using LCT can prove challenging because time and participant investment are required to build longitudinal data, extensive interviewing to conduct retrospective qualitative interviews, and access required for multiple data sources to conduct cross-sectional data analyses.

Application of Life Course Theory

Using LCT, researchers have examined the phenomenon of lifetime victimization. For example, Easton and Kong (2021) analyzed how adverse childhood experiences influence individuals throughout the life course to discern patterns of later in life abuse, shedding light on the importance of understanding cumulative advantage/disadvantage in the abuse experiences of older adults. Others have examined how lifelong intimate partner violence is experienced in old age (Roberto & McCann, 2021), and the interaction of age and violence across the life course (Band-Winterstein & Eisikovits, 2009).

Critique of the Theory

Critics of LCT point out that it confounds different variables, such as social change for social forces, and utilizes overly broad terms such as time and change. Other critiques stress that it overemphasizes a person's ability to freely exercise agency to determine life trajectories and that it does not sufficiently acknowledge variability within a cohort's experience of the same time era (Allen & Henderson, 2016).

Conclusion

LCT contextualizes risk and protective factors around elder abuse, providing insights for developing intervention strategies. Its limitations include the challenges of operationalizing the theory and gathering longitudinal data to fully assess its utility.

The Contextual Theory of Elder Abuse

Recognizing the challenges of theorizing, Roberto and Teaster (2017) proposed the Contextual Theory of Elder Abuse (CTEA) to undergird research specifically on elder abuse and emphasized its relevance for scholars and practitioners alike (Fig. 10.2).

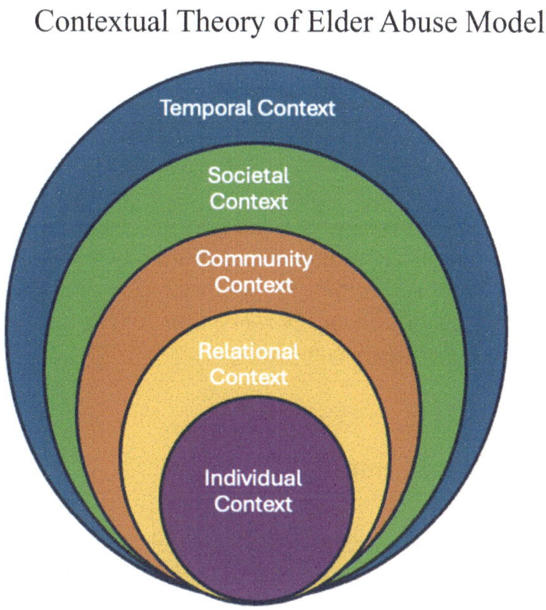

Fig. 10.2 Contextual Theory of Elder Abuse

Karen Roberto earned her doctorate in human development, and Pamela Teaster earned her doctorate in public administration and public affairs. They struggled with the inadequacies of borrowing theories from other disciplines in their collective research, and thus, proposed the first theory specifically for elder abuse while writing a chapter covering theories used for elder abuse research (Fig. 10.2; Roberto & Teaster, 2017). The CTEA considers the highly complex nature of elder abuse, including the legal standing of most adults, their long lives (as compared to that of children), and, for many, their lives linked with their abusers.

Abuse Model Disciplines in Which the Contextual Theory of Elder Abuse Has Been Used

The CTEA theory has been used in the disciplines of public health and human development (Steinshem et al., 2023; Teaster et al., 2023).

Key Tenets of the Contextual Theory of Elder Abuse

Acknowledging the important contribution of Bronfenbrenner's (1986) ecological model and the Social-Ecological Model promulgated by the Centers for Disease Control (2015) applied to violence in general, the CTEA has at its center the victim, representing the first context considered in any examination of elder abuse. Placing the victim of abuse at the center of the theory resonates with "person-centered" or "person-directed" approaches (Burnes et al., 2023; Mosqueda et al., 2016). The theory originally included four contexts, but in this chapter, the authors evolve the theory to include the *temporal context*. Within each of the five contexts, principles of life course theory come into play.

Individual Context

The *individual context* includes biological and personal factors that influence how a person behaves, how risk factors increase the likelihood of becoming a victim or perpetrator, and how factors, such as poor health or dementia, affect individuals during and after abuse occurs. Within the individual context, variables of interest may be individual (e.g., age, sex, gender, race/ethnicity; Acierno et al., 2010; Laumann et al., 2008), education, habilitation, location (e.g., community or long-term care setting; rural or urban area), income level, physical health, mental health, and cognitive capacity (Lachs et al., 1997).

Relational Context

Relationships occur on multiple levels. They are dynamic, and can develop quickly, over time, and may end in the same manner. The *relational context* emphasizes interactions with older adults and individuals they encounter to identify relationships between victims and perpetrators (Mosqueda et al., 2016) and to understand the role social networks play in preventing and facilitating abuse (Burnes et al., 2019).

Community Context

The *community context* sheds light on an older adult's location and how members relate to one another within the space in which they live. The structure and culture of communities may shield older adults from abuse; however, they may also enable it. Within this context, questions raised about elder abuse include characteristics of settings (rural or urban), the community's responses and support for older people who experience abuse, and the community response to perpetrators.

Community programs and networks can exert a strong influence over interactions with and treatment of older adults that are accepted. Most communities have formal programs and services intended to enhance individual and social well-being, assist day to day functioning, and provide rehabilitation and long-term care (e.g., case management, home care, hospice).

Participation in community-based services and programs designed to enhance individual and social well-being can help moderate vulnerability and risks associated with elder abuse (Burnes et al., 2023). Support services can include obligatory relationships, such as those charged with addressing the problem of elder abuse. In the United States, Adult Protective Services (APS) is the principal public agency responsible for investigating abuse in the community and many facilities. Others, including criminal justice, social work, mental health, and healthcare systems that work individually or in concert with APS to prevent or intervene when elder abuse is alleged.

Societal Context

The *societal context* comprises factors that create or enable a climate in which abuse is accepted or discouraged. Within the context are significant changes in power and control-age-related changes in social positions and financial resources that may increase later life abuse (Brossoie et al., 2012) or the tendency of persons or systems to abuse (Straka & Montminy, 2006). In the United States and globally, ageism perpetuates prejudice and marginalization. Tolerance of elder abuse is a direct consequence of ageism (Pillemer et al., 2021).

Within the societal context are large scale actions of government and systems. Enactment of the Elder Justice Act in 2010 and the Elder Protection Act of 2021 was a societal acknowledgement that the welfare and safety of older adults is important and worthy of national action. Part of the larger Patient Protection and Affordable Care Act, the Elder Justice Act includes provisions for federal resources to address elder abuse, neglect, and exploitation. Shared by the Administration for Community Living and the Department of Justice (United States Government Printing Office, 2010). The Elder Protection Act established within the Department of Justice a national elder fraud hotline, affords civil legal aid to elder abuse victims, and includes resources in English and Spanish (Elder Abuse Protection Act, 2021).

Temporal Context

Here the authors update their CTEA by adding a *temporal context*. This context acknowledges that many older adults have lived long lives and have had many varied experiences. Many have grown up during such seismic events as the Great Depression and World Wars. They also have been touched by changing attitudes towards race and gender, the invention and proliferation of the computer, and the ability to travel around the world. Recently, people around the globe were affected by COVID-19, with older adults especially vulnerable to the disease.

Contributions of the Contextual Theory of Elder Abuse to the Study of Elder Abuse

Like most theories, the CTEA continues to evolve. Its strength is that it is specific to elder abuse. As such, it makes a distinct contribution to family violence by specifically addressing the abuse of older people. While the underlying assumption of the CTEA is that each context influences elder abuse, like the SEST, it is not necessary for a study to investigate each context. The strength of CTEA is its breadth for explaining elder abuse on multiple levels and for suggesting invention and prevention efforts. As a new theory, its limitation is the lack of rigorous testing.

Applicable Methodological Approaches. The CTEA is suitable for quantitative and qualitative approaches as well as research using mixed methods. The theory is most useful in explaining and suggesting comprehensive implications of and solutions for elder abuse.

Assessment of the Theory as It Relates to Family Violence

The CTEA is most salient when exploring elder abuse on systemic levels. In particular, the theory helps demystify why elder abuse occurs and how policies, programs, and funding can help mitigate the problem. Because it focuses on elder abuse, the theory can help explain the various subtypes of abuses (e.g., elder mistreatment, financial exploitation, and self-neglect).

Application of the Contextual Theory of Elder Abuse

Two studies, both of which include the authors of the theory, have used the CTEA (Roberto & Teaster, 2025; Teaster et al., 2023). In both, they concentrated on the relational, community, and societal contexts.

Critique of the Theory

The power of the application of this relatively new theory lies in its specificity on the problem of elder abuse and how it may be used in both individual and societal situations. The application of the temporal context has yet to be critiqued.

Conclusion

The CTEA emphasizes that elder abuse is not "just a family problem." Its five contexts suggest that abuse occurs against a backdrop and the interplay of contextual issues. Regardless of the type of abuse, the perpetrator, location of the abuse, or the population of older adults under study, without an awareness of context, the understanding of elder abuse is incomplete.

Summary

The three strong theories discussed above paint an important backdrop and underpinning for examining elder abuse. The theories are specific enough to explain relational aspects of the issue, the mainstay of early research on the topic. Relational theories alone, however, prove inadequate when incidence and prevalence studies reveal that the problem occurs on a large and global scale and is escalating. The theories discussed in this chapter help scholars and practitioners explain the scope of the problem as well as reasons for its continued existence and increasing occurrence. With the consistent application and testing of these theories, research, practice, and policy will become more exact and potent in reducing the significant harms that elder abuse creates-to present individuals and to societies.

References

Administration for Community Living. (2019). What is elder abuse?. https://acl.gov/programs/elder-justice/what-elder-abuse#:~:text=In%20general%2C%20elder%20abuse%20is,of%20elder%20abuse%20prevention%20laws

Acierno, R., Hernandez, M. A., Amstadter, A. B., Resnick, H. S., Steve, K., Muzzy, W., & Kilpatrick, D. G. (2010). Prevalence and correlates of emotional, physical, sexual, and financial abuse and potential neglect in the United States: The national elder mistreatment study. *American Journal of Public Health, 100*, 292–297. https://doi.org/10.2105/ajph.2009.163089

Allen, K. R., & Henderson, A. C. (2016). *Family theories: Foundations and applications*. Wiley.

Asyraf, M., Dunne, M. P., Hairi, N. N., Mohd Hairi, F., Radzali, N., & Wan Yuen, C. (2021). The association between elder abuse and childhood adversity: A study of older adults in Malaysia. *PLoS One, 16*(7), e0254717.

Awuviry-Newton, K., Nkansah, J. O., & Ofori-Dua, K. (2020). Attributions of elder neglect: A phenomenological study of older people in Ghana. *Health & Social Care in the Community, 28*(6), 2172–2178. https://doi.org/10.1111/hsc.13028

Band-Winterstein, T., & Eisikovits, Z. (2009). "Aging out" of violence: The multiple faces of intimate violence over the life span. *Qualitative Health Research, 19*(2), 164–180.

Band-Winterstein, T., Avieli, H., & Smeloy, Y. (2016). Harmed? Harmful? Experiencing abusive adult children with mental disorder over the life course. *Journal of Interpersonal Violence, 31*(15), 2598–2621. https://doi.org/10.1177/0886260515579505

Bengtson, V., & Allen, K. (1993). The life course perspective applied to families over time. In P. Boss, W. Doherty, R. LaRossa, W. Schumm, & S. Tenmetz (Eds.), *Sourcebook of family theories and methods* (pp. 469–504). Plenum. https://doi.org/10.1007/978-0-387-85764-0_19

Biggs, S., & Goergen, T. (2010). Theoretical development in elder abuse and neglect. *Ageing International, 35*(3), 167–170. https://doi.org/10.1007/s12126-010-9066-z

Bronfenbrenner, U. (1979). *The ecology of human development*. Harvard University Press.

Bronfenbrenner, U. (1986). Ecology of the family as a context for human development: Research perspectives. *Developmental Psychology, 22*(6), 723–742. https://doi.org/10.1037/0012-1649.22.6.723

Brossoie, N., Roberto, K. A., & Barrow, K. M. (2012). Making sense of intimate partner violence in late life: Comments from online news readers. *The Gerontologist, 52*(6), 792–801. https://doi.org/10.1093/geront/gns046

Burnes, D., Breckman, R., Henderson, C. R., Lachs, M. S., & Pillemer, K. (2019). Utilization of formal support services for elder abuse: Do informal supporters make a difference? *The Gerontologist, 59*(4), 619–624. https://doi.org/10.1093/geront/gny074

Burnes, D., Connolly, M.-T., Salvo, E., Kimball, P. F., Rogers, G., & Lewis, S. (2023). RISE: A conceptual model of integrated and restorative elder abuse intervention. *The Gerontologist, 63*(6), 966–973. https://doi.org/10.1093/geront/gnac083

Centers for Disease Control and Prevention. (2015). The social-ecological model: A framework for prevention. http://www.cdc.gov/violenceprevention/overview/social-ecologicalmodel.html

Chen, M., & Fu, Y. (2022). Adverse childhood experiences: Are they associated with greater risk of elder abuse victimization? *Journal of Interpersonal Violence, 37*(19–20), NP17662–NP17687. https://doi.org/10.1177/08862605211028328

Dannefer, D. (2003). Cumulative advantage/disadvantage and the life course: Cross-fertilizing age and social science theory. *The Journals of Gerontology: Series B, 58*(6), S327–S337. https://doi.org/10.1093/geronb/58.6.S327

DiAquoi, R. C. (2018). Critical race life course perspective theory: A framework for understanding racism over the life course. *International Journal of Qualitative Studies in Education, 31*(1), 36–54. https://doi.org/10.1080/09518398.2017.1379622

Elder, G. H. (1974). *Children of the great depression*. W. W. Norton & Company.

Elder, G. H. (1998). The life course and human development. In R. M. Lerner (Ed.), *Handbook of child psychology: Vol. 1. Theoretical models of human development* (5th ed., pp. 939–991). Wiley.

Elder Abuse Protection Act of 2021, H. R. 2922, 117th Cong. (2021). https://www.congress.gov/bill/117th-congress/house-bill/2922

Fettig, N., Mitchell, H., Gassoumis, Z., Nizam, Z., Whittier Eliason, S., & Cory, S. (2024). Adult maltreatment risk factors: Adding community-level factors to an individual-level field. *Trauma, Violence, & Abuse, 25*(1), 5–21. https://doi.org/10.1177/15248380221137659

Herrenkohl, T. I., Roberto, K. A., Fedina, L., Hong, S., & Love, J. (2021). A prospective study on child abuse and elder mistreatment: Assessing direct effects and associations with depression and substance use problems during adolescence and middle adulthood. *Innovation in Aging, 5*(3), igab028–igab028. https://doi.org/10.1093/geroni/igab028

Jackson, S. L., & Hafemeister, T. L. (2013). *Understanding elder abuse: New directions for developing theories of elder abuse occurring in domestic settings*. https://www.ncjrs.gov/pdffiles1/nij/241731.pdf

Easton, S. D., & Kong, J. (2021). Childhood adversities, midlife health, and elder abuse victimization: A longitudinal analysis based on cumulative disadvantage theory. *The Journals of Gerontology. Series B, Psychological Sciences and Social Sciences, 76*(10), 2086–2097. https://doi.org/10.1093/geronb/gbaa095

Kong, J., & Easton, S. D. (2019). Re-experiencing violence across the life course: Histories of childhood maltreatment and elder abuse victimization. *The Journals of Gerontology: Series B, 74*(5), 853–857.

Kosberg, J. I., & Nahmiash, D. (1996). Characteristics of victims and perpetrators and milieus of abuse and neglect. In L. A. Baumhover & S. C. Ball (Eds.), *Abuse, neglect and exploitation of older persons: Strategies for assessment and intervention* (pp. 31–50). Jessica Kingsley.

Lachs, M. S., Williams, C., O'Brien, S., Hurst, L., & Horwitz, R. (1997). Risk factors for reported elder abuse and neglect: A nine-year observational cohort study. *The Gerontologist, 37*(4), 469–474. https://doi.org/10.1093/geront/37.4.469

Laumann, E. O., Leitsch, S. A., & Waite, L. J. (2008). Elder mistreatment in the United States: Prevalence estimates from a nationally representative study. *The Journals of Gerontology: Series B, 63*(4), S248–S254. https://doi.org/10.1093/geronb/63.4.s248

Mosqueda, L., Burnight, K., Gironda, M. W., Moore, A. A., Robinson, J., & Olsen, B. (2016). The abuse intervention model: A pragmatic approach to intervention for elder mistreatment. *Journal of the American Geriatrics Society, 64*(9), 1879–1883. https://doi.org/10.1111/jgs.14266

Parra-Cardona, J. R., Meyer, E., Schiamberg, L., & Post, L. (2007). Elder abuse and neglect in Latino families: An ecological and culturally relevant theoretical framework for clinical practice. *Family Process, 46*(4), 451–470. https://doi.org/10.1111/j.1545-5300.2007.00225.x

Pillemer, K., Burnes, D., & MacNeil, A. (2021). Investigating the connection between ageism and elder mistreatment. *Nature Aging, 1*(2), 159–164. https://doi.org/10.1038/s43587-021-00032-8

Podnieks, E. (2017). Elder abuse in Canada: A growing dilemma in an aging society. *Innovation in Aging, 1*(suppl_1), 106–106. https://doi.org/10.1093/geroni/igx004.445

Roberto, K. A., & McCann, B. R. (2021). Violence and abuse in rural older women's lives: A life course perspective. *Journal of Interpersonal Violence, 36*(3–4), NP2205–2227NP. https://doi.org/10.1177/0886260518755490

Roberto, K. A., & Teaster, P. B. (2017). Theorizing elder abuse. In *Elder abuse* (pp. 21–41). Springer International Publishing AG. https://doi.org/10.1007/978-3-319-47504-2_2

Roberto, K. A., & Teaster, P. B. (2025, accepted). Family ties and opioid lies: Pathways to elder abuse in rural Appalachia. *Innovation in Aging.*

Schiamberg, L. B., & Gans, D. (1999). An ecological framework for contextual risk factors in elder abuse by adult children. *Journal of Elder Abuse & Neglect, 11*(1), 79–103. https://doi.org/10.1300/J084v11n01_05

Schiamberg, L. B., & Gans, D. (2000). Elder abuse by adult children: An applied ecological framework for understanding contextual risk factors and the intergenerational character of quality of life. *International Journal of Aging and Human Development, 50*(4), 329–359. https://doi.org/10.2190/DXAX-8TJ9-RG5K-MPU5

Settersten, R. A. (2003). *Invitation to the life course: Toward new understandings of later life.* Baywood.

Simmons, J., & Swahnberg, K. (2021). Lifetime prevalence of polyvictimization among older adults in Sweden, associations with ill-heath, and the mediating effect of sense of coherence. *BMC Geriatrics, 21*(1), 129–129. https://doi.org/10.1186/s12877-021-02074-4

Steinsheim, G., Malmedal, W., Follestad, T., Olsen, B., & Saga, S. (2023). Contextual factors associated with abuse of home-dwelling persons with dementia: A cross-sectional exploratory study of informal caregivers. *International Journal of Environmental Research and Public Health, 20*(4), 2823. https://doi.org/10.3390/ijerph20042823

Straka, S. M., & Montminy, L. (2006). Responding to the needs of older women experiencing domestic violence. *Violence against Women, 12*(3), 251–267. https://doi.org/10.1177/1077801206286221

Teaster, P. B., Roberto, K. A., & Dugar, T. A. (2006). Intimate partner violence of rural aging women. *Family Relations, 55*(5), 636–648. https://doi.org/10.1111/j.1741-3729.2006.00432.x

Teaster, P. B. (2017). A framework for polyvictimization in later life. *Journal of Elder Abuse & Neglect, 29*(5), 289–298.

Teaster, P. B., Roberto, K. A., Savla, J., Du, C., Du, Z., Atkinson, E., Shealy, E. C., Beach, S., Charness, N., & Lichtenberg, P. A. (2023). Financial fraud of older adults during the early months of the COVID-19 pandemic. *The Gerontologist, 63*(6), 984–992. https://doi.org/10.1093/geront/gnac188

Turanovic, J. J. (2023). Victimization and its consequences over the life course. *Crime and Justice (Chicago, Ill.), 52*(1), 265–342. https://doi.org/10.1086/727029

United States Government Printing Office. (2010). Public law 111-148-MAR. http://www.gpo.gov/fdsys/pkg/PLAW-111publ148/pdf/PLAW-111publ148.pdf

Whole Child. (n.d.). Ecological theory [Figure]. In *Whole child*. https://rotel.pressbooks.pub/whole-child/chapter/ecological-theory-2/

World Health Organization. (2024). Abuse of older people. https://www.who.int/news-room/fact-sheets/detail/abuse-of-older-people

Yon, Y., Ramiro-Gonzalez, M., Mikton, C. R., Huber, M., & Sethi, D. (2019). The prevalence of elder abuse in institutional settings: A systematic review and meta-analysis. *European Journal of Public Health, 29*(1), 58–67. https://doi.org/10.1093/eurpub/cky093

Chapter 11
Theories of Sibling Abuse

John Caffaro

- **Name of the theory**: Systems Theory, Social Learning Theory, Trauma Theory
- **Proponents of the theory**: Urie Brofenbrenner, Albert Bandura, Bessel van der Kolk
- **What the theory says**: Family relations, and interpersonal relationships in general, exist within larger social structures, such as community and societal influence where each person's behavior affects the others, highlighting their interdependence. The interactive patterns of parents, teachers, siblings, and other socializing agents have a potent influence on children's behavior. Trauma can disrupt normal attachment and impair one's ability to regulate their emotions, complicating the formation of healthy relationships and increasing the potential for interpersonal conflict and abuse.

Introduction

Siblings—those persons who are defined as biological brothers and sisters, step-siblings, half-siblings, adoptive siblings, foster siblings and social siblings—children not biologically or legally related but who have been brought up together and share an enduring bond, occupy a unique position in family dynamics and have been largely overlooked in social science research (Conger & Kramer, 2010; Kim et al., 2006). This neglect has led to a minimization of the impact of sibling relationships on personal development, psychological health, and family dynamics over time. While siblings frequently serve as primary caregivers and companions, instances

J. Caffaro (✉)
Alliant University, San Diego, CA, USA
e-mail: jcaffaro@alliant.edu

A. Hattery and E. Smith (eds.), *Theories of Family Violence*, Advances in Preventing and Treating Violence and Aggression, https://doi.org/10.1007/978-3-032-17095-8_11

of sibling abuse often go unnoticed, dismissed by parents and researchers alike. In contrast, other forms of familial violence, such as parent–child abuse and intimate partner violence, have received significant attention. Notably, research indicates that more children experience abuse from siblings than from peers (Finkelhor et al., 2015), highlighting a critical gap in the existing literature, child welfare policy, and professional intervention (Morrill et al., 2018; Caffaro & Conn-Caffaro, 2005; Desir & Karatekin, 2021).

Amy Dye was a nine-year-old girl from Kentucky who was tragically killed by her older adopted brother in 2011. She had suffered from ongoing abuse before her death. Her case gained national attention due to failures in the child welfare system; Amy's death was not included in the state's child protection records because its regulations stated it could investigate abuse only by a parent or caregiver, not by a sibling. The case led to increased scrutiny of Kentucky's child protection services and highlighted systemic issues in handling abuse reports.

Researchers have investigated several types of sibling abuse. Each type is described below:

1. *Sibling physical abuse* is an ongoing pattern of aggression by a sibling with more power that causes evident harm or a strong likelihood of harm, but a serious one-time event can also be abuse (Sibling Aggression and Abuse Research and Advocacy Initiative, 2024).
2. *Sibling emotional abuse* includes comments by one sibling toward another aimed at ridiculing, insulting, threatening, terrorizing, and belittling a child; rejecting, degrading, and exploiting a sibling; destroying a brother or sister's personal property; and behavior that includes neglect of a sibling as well as exposing a sibling to violence by peers or other siblings (Caffaro, 2014).
3. *Sibling sexual abuse* consists of sexual acts initiated by one sibling toward another without the other's consent or ability to provide consent, by use of force or coercion, or where there is a power differential between the siblings (Caffaro, 2021).
4. *Sibling financial abuse* is the misappropriation of financial resources for the self-interest of the sibling rather than the care of a brother or sister (adapted from Spira et al., 2020)

This chapter examines the primary theories that inform our understanding of sibling abuse including Systems, Social Learning, and Trauma theory. It covers the fundamental concepts of each theory, their contributions to sibling abuse research, associated research methods, and practical examples. Each chapter concludes with a critique, addressing unresolved questions in the field.

Systems Theory and Sibling Abuse

Systems theory offers a vital lens for understanding sibling abuse, focusing on the interplay between individual children, sibling relationships, and the family unit. It emphasizes how changes in one element of the family system can influence others. Family members interact within a network where each person's behavior affects the others, highlighting the interdependence of family dynamics. This perspective also incorporates contextual influences, including the broader community and cultural factors. Key to systems theory is the idea that parents often replicate unresolved conflicts from their own childhoods within their families.

Studies consistently demonstrate that children of extremely stressed or traumatized parents are at higher risk for mental and physical adverse outcomes (Bowers & Yehuda, 2016; Narayan et al., 2021) Similarly, research on the integrational transmission of violence indicates that many parents of siblings who engage in violence were themselves victims of abuse and that victims of sibling violence may be more likely to abuse their own parents (Perkins et al., 2018). However, professionals often overlook the dynamics of intergenerational sibling relationships in families, focusing instead on parent–child patterns. Bronfenbrenner's (1979) bioecological theory significantly influenced the study of child and family psychology.

His model posits that all interpersonal relationships exist within larger social structures, such as community and societal influences.

This theory acknowledged the complex interactions between individual development and environmental factors, including behavioral genetics (Bronfenbrenner & Ceci, 1994). Minuchin (1985) applied these concepts to family systems therapy, shifting the focus from individual symptoms to the family system's role in a child's behavior. He noted that negative patterns, such as child abuse and harsh parenting, often recur across generations.

Others (Caffaro & Conn-Caffaro, 2005; Caffaro, 2014; Yates & Allardyce, 2021) have made important contributions to our understanding of sibling abuse through the systems theory lens. Caffaro (2020) argues that sibling maltreatment arises from interactions among multiple systems rather than a single factor. Developmental stages, sibling dynamics, and family context all influence the potential for abuse. Individual approaches fail to capture the complexities of these relationships, making a systemic understanding essential. Understanding the family environment is crucial in addressing child abuse and in reaching out to affected children (Alink et al., 2019; Beckerman et al., 2018; de Maat et al., 2021).

Key familial relational factors linked to sibling abuse include parental unavailability, power imbalances among siblings, and high levels of familial conflict. Caffaro and Conn-Caffaro (2005) conducted an early qualitative study of adult survivors of sibling abuse, utilizing the structural family therapy model (Minuchin, 1985) to analyze thematic results. They identified three distinct family risk factors for sibling abuse (1) parental emotional unavailability and neglect, (2) parentified older sibling in charge and, (3) presence of an older stepsibling. These systemic risk factors, coupled with a lack of protective factors, indicated a heightened vulnerability to sibling abuse. Findings also highlighted the relational trauma experienced by adult survivors, revealing estranged connections with family members. Similar studies (McCartan et al., 2023; Simons et al., 2024) have confirmed that many adult survivors of sibling abuse have not disclosed their abuse and cut off contact with family members. While barriers to the disclosure of sibling sexual abuse have been examined (Adams, 2024; Bertele & Talmon, 2021; Tidefors et al., 2010), further research is needed to explore what encourages children and adult survivors to disclose abuse and how family and cultural contexts influence this process.

A recent qualitative study by McCartan et al. (2023) examined characteristics of family systems where sibling sexual abuse occurred. Researchers interviewed predominantly female adult survivors and identified ten markers reflecting family structure, systems, processes, and functionalities that contributed to conditions fostering sibling sexual abuse. Findings suggested that sibling sexual abuse is often intertwined with other forms of abuse and stressful family environments, potentially exacerbated by factors such as a lack of supervision, parental emotional unavailability, patriarchal culture, and harmful sexualization.

Critique of the Theory

The family systems perspective can sometimes neglect individual psychological factors and personal histories that may also contribute to sibling abuse. While systems theory provides insights into patterns and roles within families, it may inadequately address the complexities of evolving power dynamics. Feminist critiques (Hoffman & Edwards, 2004) highlight the dynamics of power and control in families where sibling abuse occurs, often linked to high levels of stress, parental conflict, and domestic violence. Despite this, connections between family factors and sibling abuse remain underexplored. Understanding parental backgrounds and stress management strategies is crucial for greater understanding of the etiology of sibling abuse.

Additionally, insight into why some children engage in sibling abuse without prior victimization histories warrants further investigation.

Social Learning Theory and Sibling Abuse

Social learning theory emphasizes the influence of interactive patterns on children's behavior, suggesting that children learn behaviors from their parents and other socializing agents, such as teachers, siblings, and peers. These learned behaviors become part of a child's repertoire, guiding their actions throughout life. For instance, children who observe conflict resolution through aggression or physical punishment are more likely to adopt similar strategies in their own interactions, especially when they become caregivers themselves. This theory highlights the significant impact of early learning, indicating that negative interaction patterns can extend beyond the family context into other relationships (Stauffacher & DeHart, 2006).

Within this framework, sibling abuse is understood as a learned behavior, influenced by modeling and reinforcement in the family environment (Bandura, 1973). Research indicates that sibling victimization is more likely to occur in households where other forms of family violence exist (Goodlin & Dunn, 2010; Tucker et al., 2015). Sibling abuse may also arise from competition between siblings for limited parental resources. Social learning theory investigates how various family relationships contribute to the development of sibling abuse, with father-to-child violence identified as a significant predictor of sibling aggression (Noland et al., 2004). Boys tend to exhibit higher levels of sibling violence, likely due to their identification with and imitation of male parental figures.

Studies have also explored how the dynamics of conflict-laden couples affect sibling relationships. Children exposed to parental violence often model aggressive behavior in both overt and subtle manners. Margolin and Gordis (2000) note that children learn not only aggressive behaviors but also the contexts in which aggression is deemed acceptable in intimate relationships. Evidence suggests that children in families with intimate partner violence and physical abuse are more likely to engage in physical aggression toward their siblings (Katz, 2014; Meyers, 2014). Recent findings by Tucker et al. (2019) identified inconsistent and harsh parenting, family adversity, witnessing family violence, and child maltreatment as predictors of sibling victimization. In some cases, parents attempt to curb sibling aggression through corporal punishment, inadvertently perpetuating a cycle of violence (Meyers, 2014; Petri et al., 2012). This reinforces the idea that aggressive behaviors and poor relationship skills displayed within the family can lead to similar behaviors among siblings and peers, further demonstrating principles of social learning theory (Espelage et al., 2012; Underwood et al., 2008; Van Berkel et al., 2018).

The concept of "parents as gatekeepers" has been examined to understand sibling violence, with studies indicating that different types of maltreatment correlate with specific sibling relationship patterns. For instance, Witte et al. (2020) explored sibling relationship dynamics within the context of family abuse and neglect, revealing a significant correlation between types of maltreatment and sibling relationship patterns. They found that heightened parental emotional neglect was predictive of either a distanced or hostile sibling relationship, while parental emotional abuse correlated with hostile or emotionally intense sibling interaction. This aligns with social learning theory, which posits that siblings often imitate the behaviors exhibited by their parents.

In her memoir, Mariah Carey discloses abuse she suffered as a child at the hands of an older sister. Her older sister and brother had been emotionally and physically abused by their father, complicating Carey's own relationship with her siblings. According to Carey, the sibling abuse took a violent turn when at age, 12, her sister threw boiling hot tea on Mariah during a tense encounter. Mariah suffered third degree burns so intense that she temporarily blacked out.

Cycle of Abuse

Children who experience sibling sexual victimization are often also targets of emotional, sexual, or physical abuse from parents or other relatives (Carlson et al., 2006; McDonald & Martinez, 2019). This suggests a potential pattern of generalized learning within the family structure.

Salazar et al. (2005) highlighted cases where daughters abused by their fathers later became victims of sibling abuse. Moreover, early childhood sexual experiences have been linked to the development of subsequent sibling sexual offenses (Latzman et al., 2011; Tidefors et al., 2010; Grant et al., 2009; Thornton et al., 2008). Studies consistently report that male sibling sexual abusers often have a background of physical abuse in childhood (Worling, 1995; Boyd et al., 2000; Veneziano & Veneziano, 2002). Children who suffer sexual abuse from siblings may therefore often be categorized as poly-victims, while those who inflict harm may embody a dual status of 'harmed-harmer.'

Social learning theory may also be used to understand instances of sibling financial abuse such as stealing or misusing money, inheritance manipulation, or financially exploiting a vulnerable brother or sister. If a sibling witnessed financial exploitation within the family, they may learn through modeling to repeat these behaviors with a brother or sister. Similarly, if a sibling successfully takes financial advantage of a brother or sister without consequences, their behavior may be reinforced and continue, believing it is acceptable. Birth order and family roles may also create power imbalances in the family, making sibling financial abuse more likely.

Siblings, concerned about the potential loss of relationship with their brother or sister, may minimize the financially exploitative experience and dismiss any allegations of abuse. The reporting and detection of sibling financial abuse may be distorted by family loyalties and a reluctance to disclose as well as cultural taboos against sharing family secrets.

Feminist Theory

Hoffman et al. (2005) and Hoffman and Edwards (2004) leveraged feminist and social learning theories to explain sibling violence. Feminist theory links violence against women and girls to societal patriarchy, suggesting that men utilize violence as a means of control, particularly when feeling powerless. This dynamic creates a power imbalance in families, making younger and female siblings more vulnerable to victimization. Additionally, studies indicate that differential parental treatment can contribute to sibling abuse, particularly if such treatment reflects distorted gender roles. For instance, parents who grew up in misogynistic environments may inadvertently model abusive behavior toward daughters, increasing the risk of violence from brothers. Gender also plays a critical role in sibling sexual abuse dynamics, with societal norms portraying girls as submissive and boys as dominant as reflected in studies by King-Hill et al. (2023). A clinical example from an adult survivor of sibling sexual abuse illustrates this dysfunctional dynamic:

My brother was the hero of the family. He was the firstborn, and there was a great deal of importance placed on him being a male. My father tended to talk to him about the family business and ignore us girls. My mother would hang on every word he said. If my brother ever messed up or did something wrong, my parents would soon forgive and forget. When I finally disclosed that Josh had sexually abused me as a young girl at first, they didn't believe me. Later, they suggested I just get over it.

Critique of the Theory

While social learning theory effectively explains individual behavior acquisition through observation, it falls short of addressing the systemic factors influencing sibling abuse. This theory can unintentionally frame abusers as "bad," neglecting the broader family context that shapes their actions. Family structure, including status and dynamics, significantly influences who becomes a sibling perpetrator or victim, emphasizing the need for systemic analysis beyond individual behavior. Moreover, cultural influences related to sibling abuse are under-explored, highlighting the necessity for further research in this area to understand its etiology and impact.

Trauma Theory and Sibling Abuse

Trauma theory provides a crucial lens for comprehending the dynamics of sibling abuse by emphasizing how adverse experiences shape individual behaviors and family relationships. At its core, trauma theory posits that exposure to traumatic events—such as physical, emotional, or sexual abuse—can profoundly affect a person's psychological development and interpersonal relationships. Consider a scenario where two children grow up in a family environment marked by domestic violence. The older sibling, having witnessed their mother being abused, internalizes feelings of fear, helplessness, and rage. This sibling, grappling with their own trauma, may direct their unresolved emotions toward their younger brother or sister, perpetuating a cycle of abuse. The younger sibling, on the other hand, becomes both a victim and a witness to familial violence, leading to their own trauma responses, such as anxiety, depression, or an increased risk of becoming a future perpetrator. Witnessing violence directed at one's siblings can also inflict trauma. Research by Teicher and Vitaliano (2011) revealed that witnessing violence towards siblings in families occurred nearly as frequently as observing violence against mothers.

This exposure can lead to heightened psychiatric symptomatology, suggesting that the impact of witnessing violence towards siblings warrants attention in both research and clinical settings. Trauma theory also underscores the significance of resilience. While some individuals develop coping mechanisms that enable them to overcome their traumatic experiences, others may find themselves trapped in patterns of behavior that replicate the abuse they endured.

The traumatic impact of sibling abuse can be particularly insidious. Survivors often struggle with feelings of betrayal, shame, and confusion, as the abuser is typically a family member with whom they share a deep emotional bond (Caffaro, 2014). Trauma theory highlights how relational trauma stemming from abuse can impair one's ability to connect with others and regulate emotions (Van der Kolk, 2005). Adult survivors of sibling abuse may recount experiences of feeling isolated and stigmatized, grappling with the duality of love and fear in their relationships (Meyers, 2014). They may often face challenges in forming healthy attachments in adulthood, as their early experiences have disrupted their ability to trust others (Caffaro, 2016).

Researchers have also documented the trauma specifically associated with sibling emotional abuse, one of the most prevalent but overlooked forms of sibling maltreatment. Between 30 and 80% of siblings experience some form of psychological maltreatment by a brother or sister (Skinner & Kowalski, 2013; Kiselica & Morrill-Richards, 2007). This type of abuse can be difficult to detect as it often masquerades as "teasing". Many parents mistakenly accept emotional abuse as a normative aspect of sibling interactions, which complicates its detection (Caffaro, 2020).

A remarried family came to counseling after their eleven-year-old son, Eddie, set a fire in the garage following an argument with his mother about an unsupervised visit to his friend's house. Eddie reacted angrily, shutting himself in his room after his mother called him and his biological father "losers." In the counseling session, his younger brother, Trevor, accused Eddie of avoiding chores, prompting Eddie to kick the leg of Trevor's chair and glare directly at him—Trevor stopped in the middle of his sentence.

Notably, the negative effects of peer and sibling emotional abuse do not significantly differ from those of parental emotional abuse. Teicher et al., (2010) found that childhood exposure to peer emotional abuse correlated with increased substance use and elevated psychiatric symptoms in adulthood, including significant increases in depression, anxiety, and dissociation. Their findings underscored sibling emotional abuse as a potent childhood stressor. Evidence (Finkelhor et al., 2015) that more children are physically assaulted by a sibling than by a parent, sibling sexual abuse may be up to three times more prevalent than parent–child sexual abuse (Krienert & Walsh, 2024), and that children who experience sibling abuse, whether physical, sexual, or emotional, report short- and long-term psychological distress (Dantchev et al., 2019; van Berkel et al., 2018; Yates et al., 2024) mirroring outcomes observed in cases of parental maltreatment, suggest that sibling abuse should be considered an adverse childhood experience (ACES). Due to stigma and familial loyalty, sibling abuse is too often underreported, and many adult survivors of sibling abuse remain silent about their experiences, complicating the understanding of its prevalence and effects (Caffaro & Conn-Caffaro, 2005; McCartan et al., 2023). Trauma theory suggests that understanding the roots of this abuse and its impacts is crucial for developing effective interventions and support systems for affected families. By promoting awareness of sibling abuse and its connection to trauma, we can foster healthier family dynamics and support the healing of those impacted.

Critique of the Theory

Trauma theory is a valuable framework for understanding the effects of trauma, but it has limitations in addressing sibling abuse. It primarily focuses on individual trauma experiences, often overlooking the intricate family dynamics and relationships that contribute to sibling abuse. This may result in a perspective that neglects factors like power imbalances, jealousy, and competition among siblings. Additionally, trauma theory does not adequately consider the cultural, social, and economic contexts influencing family interactions. While it highlights the impact of past experiences, it may miss the ongoing behaviors that perpetuate sibling abuse. Power dynamics, such as older siblings dominating younger ones, play a significant role, as do feelings of jealousy and rivalry over parental attention. Cultural norms regarding discipline and family hierarchy shape perceptions of sibling abuse, with collectivist cultures fostering supportive relationships and individualistic cultures potentially promoting conflict. Furthermore, cultural attitudes towards discipline can normalize aggressive behaviors among siblings, complicating the understanding of sibling interactions.

Conclusion

The exploration of sibling abuse through various theoretical lenses reveals the complexity and multifaceted nature of these dynamics within family systems. Sibling relationships, often overshadowed in discussions of familial violence, merit significant attention due to their profound implications for individual development and psychological well-being. The existing literature underscores the prevalence of sibling abuse, with alarming statistics indicating that many children face maltreatment from siblings rather than parents.

Systems theory emphasizes the interconnectedness of family members and the impact of environmental factors, suggesting that sibling abuse arises not from individual pathology but from broader familial dynamics. This perspective is crucial in understanding how unresolved parental conflicts and childhood experiences can perpetuate cycles of abuse. Social learning theory further elucidates how children model behaviors observed within their familial context, indicating that aggression and violence can be learned rather than innate. The implications of this theory highlight the necessity of addressing parental behaviors and relational patterns to mitigate the risk of sibling abuse. Trauma theory adds another layer of understanding by illustrating how exposure to violence and neglect can disrupt attachment and emotional regulation, leading to a cycle of victimization and perpetration among siblings. The psychological ramifications of sibling abuse are profound, often resulting in long-lasting effects that extend well into adulthood.

However, critiques of these theories reveal gaps in addressing the individual psychological factors, power dynamics, and cultural contexts that contribute to sibling abuse. Future research must prioritize the exploration of these dimensions to develop a comprehensive understanding of the etiology of sibling abuse. Furthermore, a more nuanced approach that integrates these theoretical frameworks can inform effective interventions and prevention strategies. Ultimately, recognizing and addressing sibling abuse is vital not only for the well-being of the affected children but also for fostering healthier family environments. By illuminating the complexities of sibling relationships and their potential for both harm and healing, we can better advocate for the support and resources necessary to protect vulnerable children and promote healthier familial bonds.

References

Adams, A. (2024). Family characteristics, responses, and dynamics associated with sibling sexual abuse: A scoping review. *Child Abuse & Neglect*. https://doi.org/10.1016/j.chiabu.2024.106795

Alink, L. R. A., Cyr, C., & Madigan, S. (2019). The effect of maltreatment experiences on maltreating and dysfunctional parenting: A search for mechanisms. *Development and Psychopathology, 31*(1), 1–7. https://doi.org/10.1017/S0954579418001517

Bandura, A. (1973). *Aggression: A social learning theory analysis*. Prentice.

Beckerman, M., van Berkel, S. R., Mesman, J., & Alink, L. R. A. (2018). Negative parental attributions mediate associations between risk factors and dysfunctional parenting: A replication and extension. *Child Abuse & Neglect, 81*, 249–258. https://doi.org/10.1016/j.chiabu.2018.05.001

Bertele, N., & Talmon, A. (2021). Sibling sexual abuse: A review of empirical studies in the field. *Trauma, Violence, & Abuse, 24*, 2, Sage. https://doi.org/10.1177/15248380211030244

Bowers, M., & Yehuda, R. (2016). Intergenerational transmission of stress in humans. *NeuropsycHopharmacology Reviews, 41*, 232–244.

Boyd, N., Hagan, M., & Cho, M. E. (2000). Characteristics of adolescent sex offenders: A review of the research. *Aggression and Violent Behavior, 5*(2), 137–146.

Bronfenbrenner, U. (1979). Contexts of child rearing: Problems and prospects. *American Psychologist, 34*(10), 844–850. https://doi.org/10.1037/0003-066X.34.10.844

Bronfenbrenner, U., & Ceci, S. J. (1994). Nature-nurture reconceptualized in developmental perspective: A bioecological model. *Psychological Review, 101*(4), 568.

Caffaro, J. V., & Conn-Caffaro, A. (2005). Treating sibling abuse families. *Aggression and Violent Behavior., 10*, 604–623.

Caffaro, J. V. (2014). *Sibling abuse trauma* (2nd ed.). Routledge.

Caffaro, J.V. (2016). Treating adult survivors of sibling sexual abuse: A relational strengths-based approach. *Journal of Family Violence*. Springer, New York. https://doi.org/10.1007/s10896-016-9877-0

Caffaro, J. (2020). Sibling abuse of other children. In R. Geffner, V. Vieth, V. Vaughan-Eden, A. Rosenbaum, L. Hamberger, & J. White (Eds.), *Handbook of interpersonal violence across the lifespan*. Springer, Cham.

Caffaro, J. V. (2021). Sexual abuse of siblings. In T. K. Shackelford (Ed.) *Handbook of domestic violence*. Sage.

Carlson, B. E., Maciol, K., & Schneider, J. (2006). Sibling incest: Reports from forty-one survivors. *Journal of Child Sexual Abuse, 15*(4), 19–34. https://doi.org/10.1300/J070v15n04_02

Conger, K. J., & Kramer, L. (2010). Introduction to the special section: Perspectives on sibling relationships: Advancing child development research. *Child Development Perspectives, 4*(2), 69–71. https://doi.org/10.1111/j.1750-8606.2010.00120.x

Dantchev, S., Hickman, M., Heron, J., Zammit, S., & Wolke, D. (2019). The independent and cumulative effects of sibling and peer bullying in childhood on depression, anxiety, suicide ideation, and self-harm in adulthood. *Frontiers in Psychiatry, 10*, 651. https://doi.org/10.3389/fpsyt.2019.00651

de Maat, D. A., Jansen, P. W., Prinzie, P., Kizer, R., Franken, I. H. A., & Lucassen, N. (2021). Examining longitudinal relations between mothers' and fathers' parenting stress, parenting behaviors, and adolescents' behavior problems. *Journal of Child and Family Studies, 30*(3), 771–783. https://doi.org/10.1007/s10826-020-01885-0

Desir, M. P., & Karatekin, C. (2021). Characteristics of disclosing childhood victimization and risk of revictimization in young adulthood. *Journal of Interpersonal Violence, 36*(21–22), NP12225-NP12251.

Espelage, D. L., Basile, K. C., & Hamburger, M. E. (2012). Bullying perpetration and subsequent sexual violence perpetration among middle school students. *Journal of Adolescent Health, 50*(1), 60–65.

Finkelhor, D., Turner, H. A., Shattuck, A., & Hamby, S. (2015). Prevalence of childhood exposure to violence, crime and abuse: Results from the national survey children's exposure to violence. *Pediatrics, 169*, 746–754. https://doi.org/10.1001/jamapediatrics.2015.0676

Goodlin, W., & Dunn, C. S. (2010). Three patterns of domestic violence in households: Single victimization, repeat victimization, and co-occurring victimization. *Journal of Family Violence, 25*, 107–122. https://doi.org/10.1007/s10896-009-9274-z

Grant, J., Indermaur, D., Thornton, J., Stevens, G., Chamarette, C., & Halse, A. (2009). Intrafamilial adolescent sex offenders: Psychological profile and treatment. *Trends and Issues in Crime and Criminal Justice*. Report to the Australian Institute of Criminology.

Hoffman, K. L., & Edwards, J. N. (2004). An integrated theoretical model of sibling violence and abuse. *Journal of Family Violence, 19*(3), 185–200.

Hoffman, K. L., Kiecolt, K. J., & Edwards, J. N. (2005). Physical violence between siblings: A theoretical and empirical analysis. *Journal of Family Issues, 26*(8), 1103–1130.

Katz, C. (2014). The dead end of domestic violence: Spotlight on children's narratives during forensic investigations following domestic homicide. *Child Abuse & Neglect, 38*(12), 1976–1984. https://doi.org/10.1016/j.chiabu.2014.05.016

Kim, J. Y., McHale, S. M., Crouter, A. C., & Osgood, D. W. (2006). Longitudinal course and family correlates of sibling relationships from childhood through adolescence. *Child Development, 77*, 1387–1402.

King-Hill, S., Gilsenan, A., & McCartan, K. (2023). Professional responses to sibling sexual abuse. *Journal of Sexual Aggression, 29*(3), 359–373. https://doi.org/10.1080/13552600.2023.2241482

Kiselica, M. S., & Morrill-Richards, M. (2007). Sibling maltreatment: The forgotten abuse. *Journal of Counseling & Development, 85*, 148–161.

Krienert, J., Walsh, J., & Ingold, K. (2024). An empirical analysis of sibling sexual abuse: Examining offender, victim, and event characteristics in National Incident-Based Reporting System (NIBRS) data, 2018–2022. *Child Abuse & Neglect*. https://doi.org/10.1016/j.chiabu.2024.106871

Latzman, N. E., Viljoen, J. L., Scalora, M. J., & Ullman, D. (2011). Sexual offending in adolescence: A comparison of sibling offenders and nonsibling offenders across domains of risk and treatment need. *Journal of Child Sexual Abuse: Research, Treatment, & Program Innovations for Victims, Survivors, & Offenders, 20*(3), 245–263. https://doi.org/10.1080/10538712.2011.571233

Margolin, G., & Gordis, E. B. (2000). The effects of family and community violence on children. *Annual Review of Psychology, 51*, 445–479.

McCartan, K., Anning, A., & Qureshi, E. (2023). The impact of sibling sexual abuse on adults who were harmed as children. https://uwe-repository.worktribe.com/index.php/output/9458109/the-impact-of-sibling-sexual-abuse-on-adults-who-were-harmed-as-children

McDonald, C., & Martinez, K. (2019). Victim narratives of sibling emotional abuse. *Child Welfare, 97*(2), 1–21.

Meyers, A. (2014). A call to child welfare: Protect children from sibling abuse. *Qualitative Social Work: Research and Practice, 13*(5), 654–670. https://doi.org/10.1177/1473325014527332

Minuchin, P. (1985). Families and individual development: Provocations from the field of family therapy. *Child Development*, 289–302.
Morrill, M., Bachman, C., Polisuk, B., Kostelyk, K., & Wilson, S. (2018). An exploration of the relationship between experiences with sibling abuse and peer bullying: A pilot study. *Journal of Child and Adolescent Trauma., 11*(1), 113–120. https://doi.org/10.1007/s40653-017-0156-x
Narayan, A. J., Lieberman, A. F., & Masten, A. S. (2021). Intergenerational transmission and prevention of adverse childhood experiences (ACEs). *Clinical Psychology Review, 85*, Article 101997.
Noland, V. J., Liller, K. D., McDermott, R. J., Coulter, M. L., & Seraphine, A. E. (2004). Is adolescent sibling violence a precursor to college dating violence? *American Journal of Health Behavior, 28*, S13–S23.
Perkins, N. H., Spira, M., & Key, J. E. (2018). Intergenerational transmission of physical and emotional sibling violence: A potential connection to elder abuse. *Families in Society, 99*(3), 256–268. https://doi.org/10.1177/1044389418782429
Petri, C., Radix, K., & Wolf, K. (2012). Ressourcen, Belastungen und pädagogisches Handeln in der stationären Betreuung von Geschwisterkindern. Sozialpädagogisches Institutim SOS-Kinderdorf e.V: Geschwister in der stationären Erziehungshilfe. SOS-Kinderdorf e.V.
Salazar, L. F., Camp, C. M., DiClemente, R. J., & Wingood, G. M. (2005). Sibling incest offenders. In T. P. Gullotta & G. R. Adams (Eds.), *Handbook of adolescent behavioral problems: Evidence-based approaches to prevention and treatment* (pp. 503–518). Springer Science and Business Media.
Sibling Aggression and Abuse Research and Advocacy Initiative. (2024). Crimes Against Children Research Center. https://www.unh.edu/ccrc/saara/learn-more
Simons, A., Noordegraaf, M., & van Regenmortel, T. (2024). We can be a family again, but different than before. A single-case study on therapeutic interventions that initiated a recovery process in a family after the disclosure of sibling sexual behavior. *Child Abuse & Neglect*. https://doi.org/10.1016/j.chiabu.2024.106920
Skinner, J. A., & Kowalski, R. M. (2013). Profiles of sibling bullying. *Journal of Interpersonal Violence, 28*(8), 1726–1736.
Spira, M., Perkins, N., & Gilman, A. (2020). Trauma from physical and emotional sibling violence as a potential risk factor for elder abuse. *Journal of Gerontological Social Work, 63*(3), 162–173. https://doi.org/10.1080/01634372.2020.1733728
Stauffacher, K., & DeHart, G. B. (2006). Crossing social contexts: Relational aggression between siblings and friends during early and middle childhood. *Applied Developmental Psychology, 27*, 228–240.
Teicher, M. H., Samson, J. A., Sheu, Y. S., Polcari, A., & McGreenery, C. E. (2010). Hurtful words: Association of exposure to peer verbal abuse with elevated psychiatric symptom scores and corpus callosum abnormalities. *American Journal of Psychiatry, 167*, 1464–1471.
Teicher, M., & Vitaliano, G. (2011). Witnessing violence toward siblings: An understudied but potent form of early adversity. *PLoS ONE, 6*(12), Article e28852. https://doi.org/10.1371/journal.pone.0028852
Thornton, J., Stevens, G., Grant, J., Indermaur, D., Chamarette, C., & Halse, A. (2008). Intrafamilial adolescent sex offenders: Family functioning and treatment. *Journal of Family Studies, 14*(2–3), 362–375.
Tidefors, I., Arvidsson, H., Ingevaldson, S., & Larsson, M. (2010). Sibling incest: A literature review and a clinical study. *Journal of Sexual Aggression, 16*(3), 347–360. https://doi.org/10.1080/13552600903511667
Tucker, C. J., Finkelhor, D., Turner, H., & Shattuck, A. (2015). Family dynamics and young children's sibling victimization. *Journal of Family Psychology, 28*, 625–633. https://doi.org/10.1037/fam0000016
Tucker, C., Finkelhor, D., & Turner, H. (2019). Patterns of sibling victimization as predictors of peer victimization in childhood and adolescence. *Journal of Family Violence, 34*, 745–755.

Underwood, M. K., Beron, K. J., Gentsch, J. K., Galperin, M. B., & Risser, S. (2008). Family correlates of children's social and physical aggression with peers: Negative interparental conflict strategies and parenting styles. *International Journal of Behavioral Development, 32*, 549–562. https://doi.org/10.1177/0165025408097134

van Berkel, S. R., Tucker, C. J., & Finkelhor, D. (2018). The combination of sibling victimization and parental child maltreatment on mental health problems and delinquency. *Child Maltreatment, 23*(3), 244–253. https://doi.org/10.1177/1077559517751670

van der Kolk, B. (2005). Developmental trauma disorder: Towards a rational diagnosis for children with complex trauma histories. *Psychiatric Annals, 35*, 401–408.

Veneziano, C., & Veneziano, L. (2002). Adolescent sex offenders: A review of the literature. *Trauma, Violence, and Abuse, 3*(4), 247–260.

Worling, J. R. (1995). Adolescent sibling-incest offenders: Differences in family and individual functioning when compared to adolescent nonsibling offenders. *Child Abuse & Neglect, 19*(5), 633–643. https://doi.org/10.1016/0145-2134(95)00021-Y

Yates, P., & Allardyce, S. (2021). Sibling sexual abuse: A knowledge and practice overview. Centre of expertise on child sexual abuse. Barnardo House, Tanners Lane, Barkingside, Ilford, Essex IG6 1QG.

Yates, P., Mullins, E., Adams, A., & Kewley, S. (2024). Sibling sexual abuse: What do we know? Stage 1 analysis of a 2-stage scoping review. *Child Abuse & Neglect*. https://doi.org/10.1016/j.chiabu.2024.107076

Chapter 12
Theories of Child Maltreatment

Monica L. McCoy

- **Name of the theory**: Ecological/Transactional model.
- **Proponent(s) of the theory**: Dante Cicchetti, Michael P. Lynch, Jay Belsky, Ross Rizley and Urie Bronfenbrenner.
- **What the theory says:** In order to understand the causes and consequences of child maltreatment, it is imperative to consider multiple levels of explanation ad interactions across those levels. The four levels are: ontogenic, microsystem, exosystem, and macrosystem. Each level may contain risk factors and/or protective factors and these may be enduring or transient. The influences within the systems are bidirection and occur within a developmental context.

Introduction

Child maltreatment is a broad term that encompasses a wide range of behaviors. Child maltreatment includes both acts of commission (abuse) and acts of omission (neglect) on the part of caretakers. Charges of child maltreatment occur when caregivers fail to provide at least minimally adequate care for their children. The incidence of the different types of maltreatment varies considerably and many children experience more than one form of maltreatment.

According to the most recent data published by the U.S. Department of Health and Human Services (2025), the most common form of child maltreatment in 2023 was child neglect (64.1%). Neglect was followed by physical abuse (10.6%), sexual abuse (7.5%), psychological maltreatment (3.5%), medical neglect (0.8%), and sex

M. L. McCoy (✉)
Converse University, Spartanburg, SC, USA
e-mail: monica.mccoy@converse.edu

A. Hattery and E. Smith (eds.), *Theories of Family Violence*, Advances in Preventing and Treating Violence and Aggression, https://doi.org/10.1007/978-3-032-17095-8_12

trafficking (0.1%). In addition, 11.1% of child victims suffered from multiple forms of maltreatment. Given the broad range of experiences covered by the term child maltreatment, a complex theory is required to explain the origins and consequences of these behaviors.

The ecological/transactional model of child maltreatment was proposed by David Cicchetti and Michael Lynch (1993) to explain the etiology and consequences of child maltreatment. Building on the work of earlier theorists and the results of previous research studies, Cicchetti and Lynch stressed that child maltreatment cannot be fully understood in isolation. It is not sufficient to look at just the child or the just the parent. In fact, the determinates and sequelae of child maltreatment are most likely caused by the interplay of many factors across the many different systems within which the child exists. Furthermore, both risk factors and outcomes will vary according to the developmental level of the child. In other words, what constitutes maltreatment for an infant is quite different from what would be labeled as abusive for an adolescent.

Likewise, the impact that maltreatment has on the child's subsequent development will be, in part, determined by their age or developmental level at the time that the maltreatment occurs.

Key Terms

The ecological/transactional theory makes use of many terms that may be unfamiliar to anyone who has not studied developmental theory. As an aid to comprehending this theory, I included a alphabetical list of some of the key terms below along with a brief definition.

*Chronosystem*The chronosystem involves sociohistorical events that impact development.

*Ecological theory*Ecological theory stresses the environmental factors that impact development.

Exosystem—The exosystem contains settings that the child does not directly interact with, but that still have an impact on their experiences.

Longitudinal Study—In a longitudinal study, researchers collect data from the same group of participants over a long period of time which allows them to track changes across development. These studies are typically observational (i.e., no variables are manipulated).

Macrosystem—The macrosystem is the culture in which the child develops.

Mesosystem—The mesosystem is made up of the connections amongst the various microsystems.

Microsystem—The system in which the individual lives is their microsystem. Most of a child's interactions occur within microsystems including their family, daycare, and school.

*Ontogenic*The ontogenic system includes all aspects of development (physical, cognitive, and emotional) that are the result of the experiences a person has during their lifetime.
Transactional model of development—Transactional models emphasize the reciprocal nature of the relationship between children and their environments. Not only do parents influence their children, but children also influence their parents.

Disciplines in Which It is Primarily Used

The ecological/transactional theory is used most often in the fields of psychology, sociology, psychiatry, medicine, and social work.

History of the Theory

The first theories that were proposed to explain the origin of child maltreatment focused on a single cause. The earliest theorists hypothesized that the explanation for abuse was parental psychopathology. In other words, mental illness caused parents to maltreat their children.

However, researchers then demonstrated that the vast majority of maltreating parents did NOT meet the *DSM* (*Diagnostic and Statistical Manual of Mental Disorders*) criteria for diagnosis with mental illness and that many parents with mental illness did not maltreat their children.

Other early researchers looked to singular sociological factors such as poverty, lack of social support, a violent society, or social status to explain maltreatment. However, once again, none of these factors proved to be either necessary nor sufficient causal explanations for child maltreatment. In other words, focusing on poverty, many maltreated children were not poor and being poor did not lead to abuse in most cases. So, while single risk factors can be identified, none of them presents a full explanation for why one child is maltreated and another, in similar circumstances, is not.

The shift to a more complex explanation for child maltreatment began with the work of Bronfenbrenner (1979). Bronfenbrenner proposed an ecological theory of development. He suggested that we can not fully understand development if we study children in isolation. If we wish to comprehend development, we need to consider all of the systems that may impact a child—ranging from their immediate surroundings (e.g., their family) to the culture they live in. In 1980, Belsky applied Bronfenbrenner's theory to child maltreatment and added another level to contemplate—the ontogenic level. This level examines the parents' childhood experiences and factors within the individual that increase their risk for maltreating. In 1981, Cicchetti and Rizley proposed a transactional model of child maltreatment. In transactional models, different characteristics and forces are expected to influence each other and to contribute to developmental outcomes.

Researchers need to consider caregiver and child factors along with environmental forces. Within each area there will be both potentiating factors (risk factors that increase the chances that maltreatment will occur) and compensatory factors (protective factors that will decrease the likelihood of maltreatment). These factors may be transient (e.g., fluctuating or short-term) or enduring (e.g., more permanent or chronic). Maltreatment occurs when the potentiating factors outweigh or overwhelm the compensatory factors. Finally, in 1993, Cicchetti and Lynch integrated Belsky's ecological model with Cicchetti and Rizley's transactional model to develop the ecological/transactional model of child maltreatment. This model was developed to address both the causes and consequences of child maltreatment.

Key Tenants of the Theory

Bronfenbrenner (1979) was one of the first theorists to formally propose that a complete understanding of child maltreatment required the examination of multiple systems within which a child develops rather than merely studying a child in isolation. Bronfenbrenner urged researchers to consider microsystems, exosystems, mesosystems, chronosystems, and macrosystems. Microsystems are the contexts in which the child lives including their family, their school, and their neighborhood. Microsystems have the most direct impact on a child's development, but they are not the only thing that influences development. Bronfenbrenner argued that even systems that the child does not experience directly (what he termed exosystems) can influence their development. For example, a child may not visit their parent's workplace, but what happens in that setting can still have a significant impact on the child's development.

Parents who have stressful or demanding jobs may have less patience with their children or less time to spend interacting with them. If a parent's job requires extensive travel or deployment, they may not be around consistently to parent their children. It is also important to study the links between the systems in which a child develops, the mesosystem. How are experiences congruent or incongruent across settings ranging from the family to school to place of worship? How do events in one microsystem affect events in another system? Bronfenbrenner also said that researchers need to consider the broader context in which a child develops, the macrosystem, or the culture in which they are being raised. Researchers should consider how the beliefs, attitudes, and behaviors of the community that surrounds the child affect the child's development.

Finally, Bronfenbrenner noted that researchers should be attentive to the chronosystem (time in life and sociohistorical context). The child's age at the time an event occurs (e.g., death of a parent, exposure to trauma, birth of a sibling) will influence how that event impacts their development. The timing of major historical events is also likely to impact the development of children in different ways. For example, researchers might consider the impact of the Covid-19 pandemic on development and find that it had one effect on infants who were just learning to talk when faced with isolation versus young teenagers who were just beginning to date at that time.

When Belsky (1980) applied Bronfenbrenner's theory specifically to child maltreatment, he focused on three of the ecological systems proposed by Bronfenbrenner (microsystem, exosystem, and macrosystem) and added one additional system (ontogenic). Belsky drew on the work of Tinbergen (1951) when he noted that the understanding of behavior requires the comprehension of a persons' ontogenic development. As applied to child maltreatment, researchers focusing on ontogenic factors examine the childhood histories of parents (both maltreating and not) to determine if certain experiences are related to subsequent child maltreatment. Belsky suggested that Bronfenbrenner's model failed to account for the individual differences that parents brought to their role that might impact their ability to parent effectively. Focusing on ontogenic factors, researchers identify individual characteristics or experiences that are associated with an increased risk of being a perpetrator of child maltreatment (Cicchetti & Lynch, 1993). For instance, much attention has been paid to the cycle of violence or the integrational transmission of abuse. Researchers have noted that parents with a history of being maltreated are at an increased risk for maltreating their children. One explanation for this link comes from social learning theory as proposed by Bandura (1977). Bandura postulated that learning occurs by observing and modeling the behavior of others. In order for learning to occur the following four conditions must be met: attention, retention, reproduction, and motivation.

People learn by watching what others do and observing the consequences of those actions. For most people, the main models they have for parenting behavior are their own parents, so they may learn from abusive models how to treat children. In related findings, researchers have noted that parents with limited experience in caring for children are at increased risk for maltreating their children. Lack of experience with children means they did not have time to practice for their parenting role. Minimal experience with children prior to parenting also means that an adult may not know how children typically behave. Being uninformed about developmental norms might lead to parents having unrealistic expectations for their children and becoming frustrated when those expectations are not met (Belsky, 1980).

An ontogenic factor that has garnered a great deal of attention in this area is attachment style. According to Bowlby (1973) humans form strong affectional ties by the time they are just 6 months old. Typically, this first attachment is to the primary caregiver who is most often the mother. Based on how the caregiver responds to the infant's needs and desires, the infant learns the basis of relationships. Researchers have noted that child maltreatment is linked to insecure attachment, especially anxious attachment. This poor attachment is, in turn, associated with negative social and emotional outcomes across the child's lifespan. If a child victim does not learn to form secure attachments, they may be less likely to form a positive attachment with their own child (Bacon & Richardson, 2001). In this way, insecure attachment is both an ontogenic risk factor for child maltreatment and a possible negative outcome.

There are many more ontogenic factors that have been identified as potential risk factors for maltreatment. Cicchetti and Lynch (1993) reported that caregivers who are depressed, socially isolated, have poor impulse control, are unable to resolve conflict peacefully, and who are less satisfied with their children are all more likely to maltreat their children. While all of these are chronic, potentiating factors, none of them, on their own, causes maltreatment. In order to understand the etiology of child maltreatment, we must look at other systems and how they interact with ontogenic factors to increase or decrease the risk for abuse.

Even though Bronfenbrenner considered neighborhoods to be part of the microsystem, Belsky (1980) chose to focus on the family when he addressed the microsystem, so he shifted neighborhoods to the exosystem. Within the microsystem, Belsky encouraged researchers to consider the parents as well as the child(ren). While maltreatment is never blamed on the child, it is also the case that children can influence their parents' behavior. The relationship between parents and children is a reciprocal one. Child factors ranging from a difficult temperament to a lack of social responsiveness have been associated with a higher risk for maltreatment. However, Belsky pointed out that challenging child behavior is unlikely to lead to maltreatment if it is the only risk factor present. For example, it has been noted that child abuse is more likely in homes (microsystems) that involve marital conflict, or that include large numbers of children (that may stress the family resources). One might imagine that a child with a difficult temperament who is part of a microsystem that also involves marital conflict and a large number of children is at greater risk for maltreatment than the same child in a small family with a loving, stable parental bond. The first child would be at even greater risk if their parent's history included maltreatment and poor attachment (ontogenic factors).

Belsky (1980) defined the exosystem as the larger social units that encompass the family but in which the child does not participate directly. These units can be either formal or informal. Belsky focused specifically on the parents' workplaces and the neighborhood the family lived in. The strongest research findings linking parental work environment and child maltreatment focus on unemployment. Numerous researchers have found strong links between child abuse, and family violence more broadly, and unemployment. Various explanations have been proposed to explain this link. Unemployment is associated with a sense of powerlessness and a lack of resources as well as with increases in the time that a parent spends in close contact with their child. Other lines of research related to parental employment have dealt with associations between the type of work a parent does and their disciplinary style. Specifically, researchers have noted that parents who are dissatisfied with their jobs are more likely to use severe punishments with their children (Gershoff, 2002; Sampasa-Kanyinga et al., 2018).

With regard to neighborhoods, Belsky (1980) noted that families in which child maltreatment occurs tend to be isolated from both formal (e.g., social services, therapists) and informal (e.g., friends, neighbors, extended family members, role models) networks that could offer support. Formal networks involve professional, trained employees who are usually paid for their work while the informal networks develop over time, typically do not involve money or payment, and are based on emotional bonds. Social supports in the neighborhood can act as protective factors that may ameliorate the negative effects of stressors within the microsystem. However, parents who lack the ability to develop healthy relationships (ontogenic factor) may not have the social skills to reach out to formal networks or to develop informal ones. If a family is isolated they will have few opportunities for people to observe their parenting and offer feedback or support in cases where it is needed.

Looking at the big picture, Belsky (1980) encouraged researchers to acknowledge that the macrosystem also affects the likelihood that child maltreatment will occur. The culture in which a child is raised makes a difference in their experience. Most of the research at this level is focused on the impact of living within a violent culture; specifically, one that endorses the corporal (physical) punishment of children. The violent nature of the culture in the United States is evident when one examines crime rates, media programming, and the general acceptance of corporal punishment. Researchers who conducted cross-cultural studies, found that increased acceptance of physical punishment was associated with higher levels of child physical abuse.

Another cultural phenomenon that may impact child maltreatment is the view of children as the property of their parents. If one thinks of children in this way, it follows that children have fewer rights than other people. If a family lives in a violent culture while also facing other stressors, having limited support, and viewing children as property, they may engage in abusive behavior.

As theories of child maltreatment continued to evolve, Cicchetti and Rizley (1981) proposed a transactional model of child maltreatment that built upon Belsky's work. They argued that it is necessary to consider multiple systems in order to comprehend, predict, or treat child maltreatment. They further stressed that research on child maltreatment needs to be longitudinal because the effects of maltreatment may not be immediately obvious or they may change over time. In addition, a developmental perspective must be adopted in order to recognize that causes and consequences for children at one age may well differ from those in play at a different age.

Only when we know how children of different ages are likely to respond can we put together developmentally appropriate interventions. Finally, Cicchetti and Rizley (1981) recommended that researchers look not only at physical or cognitive outcomes, but that attention be paid to the socioemotional sequalae associated with maltreatment.

Within each system, Cicchetti and Rizley (1981) advised identifying both potentiating and compensatory factors and noting whether those factors were enduring or transient. Within each ecological system, there can be vulnerability factors (enduring/potentiating), challengers (transient/potentiating), protective factors (enduring/compensatory) and buffers (transient/compensatory). For example, vulnerability factors might include a child with a difficult temperament, a parent with a history of maltreatment or poor frustration tolerance, or living in poverty; challenges could include a brief period of unemployment or a short jail sentence; protective factors might include a strong social support network or living in a community with access to safe housing; buffers might include a long visit by a supportive family member, or a parenting class that offers free childcare (see Fig. 12.1).

Finally, in 1993, Cicchetti and Lynch integrated Belsky's ecological model with Cicchetti and Rizley's (1981) transactional model to develop the ecological/transactional model of child maltreatment. Cicchetti and Lynch were particularly

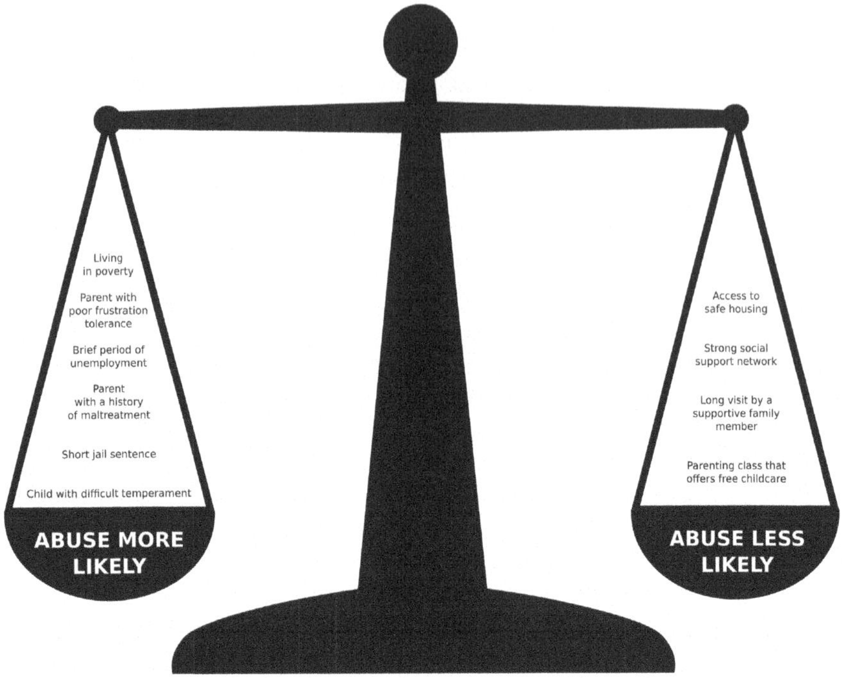

Fig. 12.1 Evaluating the likelihood that child maltreatment might occur

interested in how community violence interacted with other risk factors to contribute to the etiology and the consequences of child maltreatment. Their work grew from the literature that established a link between exposure to extreme violence and subsequent posttraumatic stress symptoms in children. Cicchetti and Lynch suggested that researchers explore the negative effects of both child maltreatment and exposure to community violence to see how each acts alone and how they may interact to impact child development.

A transactional model is one that recognizes that forces make reciprocal contributions to developmental outcomes. In other words, researchers need to consider two-way interactions between people and or systems. In this view, child development is a dynamic process in which not only do caregivers influence children, but children influence their caregivers. The people and the subsystems they exist in impact each other as they adapt over time. It is the interaction of the risk and protective factors within and between the various individuals and systems that ultimately determines outcome. Cicchetti and Lynch (1993) stated that "The presence of enduring protective factors and transient buffers at any level of the ecology may help to explain why some children display successful adaptation in the face of violence either within their communities of within families" (p. 99). For instance, Richters and Martinez (1993) found that witnessing violence led to fewer distress symptoms for children whose mothers had higher levels of education. In this case, mothers' education level (a chronic compensatory factor in the microsystem) was able to act as a protective factor that prevented negative symptoms following violence exposure (exosystem/marcosystem).

Key Contributions the Theory Makes to the Study of Family Violence

These theorists attempt to explain how community violence influences family violence in general and child maltreatment more specifically. In particular, Cicchetti and Lynch (1993) were interested in how community violence and family violence interacted to produce negative child outcomes. For instance, how does living in a culture with a high acceptance of violence influence violence within families? As an example, consider the enduring potentiating factor of the use of physical punishment to discipline children. While corporal punishment is illegal in some countries (e.g., Finland, Iceland, Germany, Italy, Sweden, Norway), it is legal and commonly accepted across the U.S. The vast majority of children in the United States (94%) report having been spanked by the age of 14. Furthermore, the use of physical punishment is associated with an increase in the likelihood of physical abuse (Gershoff, 2002). With regard to family violence, Fulu et al. (2017) noted that men who had a history of being harshly disciplined as children were more likely to be abusive toward women during their adulthood.

The family makes up the microsystem in this theory and it is considered the system that is most likely to impact the child's development. A good deal of research exists that establishes a link between partner violence and child maltreatment. In the language of ecological/transactional theory, partner violence is a potentiating factor within the microsystem and it should be considered in any theory of child maltreatment. Herrenkohl et al. (2008) estimated that child maltreatment occurred in 40% of homes where there was documented intimate partner violence. Other researchers have noted that when child maltreatment occurs in the context of domestic violence, the child maltreatment is likely to be more severe than in families without partner violence (Whitt-Woosley et al., 2014). Finally, when children experience both intimate partner violence between their parents and child maltreatment, they experience significantly more negative outcomes compared to children who only suffer from child maltreatment (Herrenkohl et al., 2008).

These theorists point out that factors may have independent and combined effects on child outcomes. For example, low Socio-Economic Status) SES (that is often accompanied by increased exposure to violence) contributes independently to negative child outcomes as does child maltreatment. Low SES also interacts with child maltreatment so that poor children who are maltreated are at increased levels of risk compared to maltreated children who are not from a low SES family. In other words, the child is being harmed by a combination of effects related to their ecosystem and their microsystem (Cicchetti & Lynch, 1993).

Research Methods

In order to conduct research that is informed by the ecological/transactional model of child maltreatment researchers must utilize wide ranging assessments over multiple systems and across time (i.e., longitudinal studies). The proponents of the theory note that in order to do a complete assessment, we need to gather data from multiple sources and in various contexts or systems. In other words, it is not sufficient to interview only the child and the parent. We also need to gather information from teachers, doctors, social workers, and so on.

Before collecting data across systems, Cicchetti and Rizley (1981) stressed the need for more precise definitions of maltreatment and a separation of maltreatment by type. Because child maltreatment covers an extremely broad range of behaviors, it is important not to group all maltreatment together. In makes sense that the causes and consequences of emotional neglect may be quite different from those of physical or sexual abuse. Furthermore, children who suffer from multiple forms of child maltreatment may well differ from those who suffer from just one form of maltreatment. In addition to better definitions, Cicchetti and Rizley called for better comparison or control groups. They urged researchers to chose control groups based on theoretical grounds rather than convenience. As a final methodological note, they encouraged the use of prospective designs rather than relying on retrospective designs.

Assessment of the Theory as It Relates to Family Violence

The strengths of this theory as it relates to family violence rather than to child maltreatment more narrowly, is that the authors highlight the complexity of human behavior. It is important to remember that acts of violence do not occur in a vacuum. In addition, knowing one thing about a person, or a couple, is not likely to predict whether they will engage in domestic violence. We need to fully consider the histories of the people in the family along with the risk factors and the protective factors within all of the systems they live in. Likewise, simply knowing that a person was the victim of family violence does not tell us what negative effects, if any, they are likely to suffer. The ecological/transactional theory also allows researchers to identify both risk and protective factors that might be relevant for both family violence and child maltreatment. Finally, the ecological/transactional model makes in clear that both prevention and intervention efforts will need to be broad based and to consider many facets of the people and their environments.

What Types of Violence Does It Explain

The ecological/transactional theory is most helpful at explaining acts of violence that are caused by having too many stressors or potentiating factors and too few compensating or protective factors. There will also be cases of violence that are not related to stressors overwhelming protective factors that are not explained or predicted by this theory. The ecological/transactional theory may be better at explaining neglect and physical abuse than sexual abuse.

Practical Applications of the Theory

While it is likely impossible to consider all of the relevant factors in one research study, this theory encourages researchers to broaden their scope and to consider multiple factors that may impact the causes and consequences of child maltreatment. An example of research that is informed by this type of theory is the Prenatal/Early Infancy Project. This program of research was directed at trying to improve developmental outcomes for children born to low-income, single, adolescent mothers. This study was first conducted in Elmira, NY and then replicated in Memphis, TN, and Denver, CO. The researchers considered factors across multiple systems including ontogenic (e.g., the mothers' histories of maltreatment; maternal depression; maternal substance use), microsystems (e.g., mothers' ability to respond appropriately to their children's signals; how parent and child interacted), and exosystems (e.g., social support, interaction with human service providers). They also followed the families across time. The program involved home visits by nurses during pregnancy and throughout the first two years of the babies' lives. The nurses aimed to improve the mothers' social skills, and increase their formal and informal support networks. The parents were also educated about monitoring the health of their infants. As the program expanded to more diverse samples, the researchers also considered the macrosystem by creating teams that were racially and ethnically diverse, addressing more fully the impact of culture on experience (Hattery et al., 2022). Program analysis indicated that the families visited by nurses had better birth outcomes (e.g., fewer preterm deliveries; better birth weights) and fewer reports of child maltreatment (Olds, 1997).

More recently, Wambua et al. (2024) used the ecological/transactional model to examine resilience versus psychosis following adverse childhood experiences (ACEs) including child maltreatment and exposure to domestic violence. They found that the children and their contexts influenced each other and that social support at the microsystem and exosystem levels was particularly important in encouraging resilience. On the ontogenic level, the age of the child at the time of the event was strongly related to their coping ability, with older children having more effective coping strategies. Individuals who were better able to reframe the adverse event and incorporate it into their life also had better functioning. On the microsystem level, economic hardship was associated with increased risk although this was buffered in cases where a family member was able to step in and provide help. Also within the microsystem, substance abuse and mental health problems amongst the caregivers were associated with increased risk for poor child outcome. At the macrosystem level, community support was associated with better child development.

Critiques of the Theory

A common critique in this area of study, applies to this theory as well. Researchers need to improve operational definitions at all levels (Cicchetti & Lynch, 1993). For instance, a very wide range of experiences and events fall under the umbrella term, "violence." Unless we state a more specific definition, it follows that we will not be able to predict a particular outcome. With regard to child maltreatment, unless we clarify what type of maltreatment we mean, how severe the abuse or neglect was, how long the negative behaviors have been occurring, who the perpetrator was and how old the child was at the time, it is very difficult to say what the cause or consequence of the experience was. After examining 29 review articles on child maltreatment that were published between 2017 and 2022, Massullo et al. (2023) concluded that definitional consistency is improving because most researchers used the definitions provided by the World Health Organization (WHO) and the similar definitions provided by the Center for Disease Control (CDC). However, they noted that some researchers were still using other definitions and even researchers using the definition provided by the WHO or the CDC may vary slightly depending on which document or online resource they used to establish their definition.

A criticism that is more specific to this theory is that it may be less explanatory with regard to sexual abuse than to other types of maltreatment. Specifically, while an increase in stressors across systems is associated with increasing the risk for physical or emotional abuse or neglect, it is not strongly associated with increased risk for sexual abuse (Gabinet, 1981).

However, Martinell (2020) argued that the ecological theory could be applied to sexual abuse to understand how factors from each level may influence the likelihood of sexual abuse occurring.

Austin et al. (2020) reviewed risk and protective factors for child maltreatment in each level of the ecological systems model. They concluded that prior researchers had focused on the individual and family levels, but that only recently were researchers tackling the broader levels of the theory. Austin et al. further suggested that more research is needed on both the community and societal levels in order to shape policy interventions that can best serve children and families.

Finally, while the theory clearly lays out the complexity involved in determining the etiology and sequalae of child maltreatment, it is impossible to consider all of those factors within one empirical study.

Conclusions

In conclusion, the ecological/transactional theory of child maltreatment makes it abundantly clear that there is no easy, simple answer or solution to the problem of child maltreatment. Development occurs within a complex set of systems and there are things that increase and decrease risk within each of these systems. Today, there is widespread agreement among researchers and government organizations that child maltreatment is not tied to a single cause or outcome. While authors do not always use the terminology of the ecological/transactional model, across studies, textbooks (e.g., Crosson-Tower, 2022; Kelley, 2011; McCoy & Keen 2022) and government reports (e.g., Center for Disease Control, 2024; U.S. Department of Health and Human Services, 2025; World Health Organization, 2025) multiple factors are considered that cover the levels of the model. For instance, Kelley (2011) breaks risk factors for maltreatment into the following categories: societal, community, family, parental, and child. McCoy and Keen (2022) devote an entire chapter to risk factors, while Crosson-Tower (2022) addresses risk and protective factors within every chapter that addresses a form of maltreatment. Governmental agencies collect and report statistics on a wide range of risk factors and protective factors. The CDC noted in their 2024 report that, "Child abuse and neglect are not caused by a single factor. Instead, a combination of factors at the individual, relationship, community, and societal levels can increase or decrease the risk of violence" (p. 1). Likewise, these sources include information about a myriad of outcomes covering both short and long-term consequences of maltreatment.

Being open to exploring all of the systems that impact child maltreatment might move the field toward a better, and less biased, understanding of what truly puts children at risk. For example, Roberts (2002) noted that while rates of child maltreatment are consistently higher for poor, Black children than for other groups, this does not necessarily mean the parents of these children are more likely to maltreat. It is possible that the differential rates of abuse are related to the way the system treats Black families. Because poor families are more likely to come into contact with social services and Black families are more likely to live in poverty than White families, they are exposed to more mandated reporters (e.g., social workers, police officers), so it may be the case that maltreatment in these families is more likely to be reported than would be the case for middle class families. In addition, the dominant culture in the U.S. has historically stereotyped Black mothers as less competent and caring than White mothers. If social workers, either consciously or subconsciously, hold these views, it may impact which cases they are likely to substantiate as abusive. Finally, it is sometimes the case that poverty is labeled as maltreatment. Parents who may not provide adequate shelter for their children may be doing everything they can, but they simply do not have the resources. In such situations, addressing the inaccessibility of housing would seem a better intervention than removing children from their parents simply because they were poor. When we consider the macrosystem's role in child maltreatment, we need to take into account how people and institutions view and treat people of diverse backgrounds. Robert's findings are echoed by Austin et al. (2020), who noted that, "it is likely not the child's race/ethnicity that places them at an increased risk for maltreatment, but rather structural and systemic racism, discrimination, and implicit and explicit biases that increase the likelihood that Black and American Indian/Alaska Native children will be reported to CPS" (p. 4).

Furthermore, each parent and each child brings with them unique characteristics and experiences that influence both the etiology and sequelae of child maltreatment. These unique families are also impacted by their surrounding communities. Younas Gutman (2022) conducted a meta-analysis of 68 quantitative, published studies addressing risk and protective factors for child maltreatment. They not only noted the most common factors at each level, but documented which type of maltreatment the factors were most associated with. However, they also noted that research on the broader levels (mezzo and macro) was lacking. This complexity is not an excuse to give up, instead it is an impetus to broaden our search and improve our research practices in hopes of uncovering how these many factors interact to affect development. If our ultimate goal is to prevent child maltreatment when we can and to ameliorate the negative consequences when it does occur, a full understanding of the problem is required.

References

Austin, A. E., Lesak, A. M., & Shanahan, M. E. (2020). Risk and protective factors for child maltreatment: A review. *Current Epidemiological Reports, 7*(4), 334–342. https://doi.org/10.1007/s40471-020-00252-3

Bacon, H., & Richardson, S. (2001). Attachment theory and child abuse: An overview of the literature for practitioners. *Child Abuse Review, 10*, 377–397. https://doi.org/10.1002/car.718

Bandura, A. (1977). *Social learning theory*. Prentice-Hall.

Belsky, J. (1980). Child maltreatment: An ecological integration. *American Psychologist, 35*(4), 320–335. https://doi.org/10.1037/0003-066X.35.4.320

Bowlby, J. (1973). *Attachment and loss. Vol. 2, Separation: Anxiety and anger*. Penguin.

Bronfenbrenner, U. (1979). *The ecology of human development: Experiments by nature and design*. Harvard University Press.

Center for Disease Control. (2024). *Child abuse and neglect prevention*. https://www.cdc.gov/child-abuse-neglect/risk-factors/index.html

Cicchetti, D., & Lynch, J. (1993). Toward an ecological/transactional model of community violence and child maltreatment: Consequences for children's development. *Psychiatry: Interpersonal and Biological Processes, 56*(1), 96–118. https://doi.org/10.1080/00332747.1993.11024624

Cicchetti, D., & Rizley, R. (1981). Developmental perspectives on the etiology, intergenerational transmission, and sequelae of child maltreatment. In R. Rizley and D. Cicchetti (Eds.), *New directions for child development: Developmental perspectives on child maltreatment* (pp. 31–55). Jossey-Bass Inc.

Crosson-Tower, C. (2022). *Understanding child abuse and neglect* (10th edn). Pearson.

Fulu, E., Miedema, S., Roselli, T., McCook, S., Chan, K. L., Haardörfer, R., & Jewkes, R. (2017). Pathways between childhood trauma, intimate partner violence, and harsh parenting: Findings from the UN multi-country study on men and violence in Asia and the Pacific. *Lancet Global Health, 5*(5), 512–522. https://doi.org/10.1016/S2214-109X(17)30103-1

Gabinet, L. (1981). "Child maltreatment: An ecological integration": Comment on Jay Belsky. *American Psychologist, 36*(3), 320–322. https://doi.org/10.1037/0003-066X.36.3.320

Gershoff, E. T. (2002). Corporal punishment by parents and associated child behaviors and experiences: A meta-analytic and theoretical review. *Psychological Bulletin, 128*(4), 539–579. https://doi.org/10.1037/0033-2909.128.4.539

Hattery, A. J., Smith, E., Magnuson, S., Monterrosa, A., Kafonek, K., Shaw, C., Mhonde, R. D., & Kanewske, L. C. (2022). Diversity, equity, and inclusion in research teams: The good, the bad, and the ugly. *Race and Justice, 12*(3), 505–530. https://doi.org/10.1177/21533687221087373

Herrenkohl, T. I., Sousa, C., Tajima, E. A., Herrenkohl, R. C., & Moylan, C. A. (2008). Intersection of child abuse and children's exposure to domestic violence. *Trauma Violence Abuse, 9*(2), 84–99. https://doi.org/10.1177/1524838008314797

Kelley, S. J. (2011). Theories and research on child maltreatment. In J. Humphreys & J. C. Campbell (Eds.), *Family violence and nursing practice* (pp. 91–113). Springer.

Massullo, C., De Rossi, E., Carbone, G. A., Imperatori, C., Ardito, R. B., Adenzato, M., & Farina, B. (2023). Child maltreatment, abuse, and neglect: An umbrella review of their prevalence and definitions. *Clinical Neuropsychiatry, 20*(2), 72–99. https://doi.org/10.36131/cnfioritieditore20230201

Martinell, E. (2020). Applying the ecological systems theory to better understand and prevent child sexual abuse. *Sexuality & Culture, 24*, 326–344.

McCoy, M. L., & Keen, S. M. (2022). *Child abuse and neglect* (3rd edn). Taylor & Francis Group.

Olds, D. (1997). The prenatal/early infancy project. In G. W. Albee & T. P. Gullotta (Eds.), *Primary prevention works* (pp. 41–67). Sage publications.

Richters, J. E., & Martinez, P. (1993). The NIMH community violence project: II. Children's distress symptoms associated with violence exposure. *Psychiatry: Interpersonal and Biological Processes, 56*(1), 22–35. https://doi.org/10.1080/00332747.1993.11024618

Roberts, D. (2002). *Shattered bonds: The color of child welfare*. Basic Books.

Sampasa-Kanyinga, H., Nilsen, W., & Colman, I. (2018). Child abuse and work stress in adulthood: Evidence from a population-based study. *Preventive Medicine: An International Journal Devoted to Practice and Theory, 108*, 60–66. https://doi.org/10.1016/j.ypmed.2017.12.029

Tinbergen, N. (1951). *The study of instinct*. Oxford University Press.

U.S. Department of Health & Human Services, Administration for Children and Families, Administration on Children, Youth and Families, Children's Bureau. (2025). *Child maltreatment 2023*. Available from https://www.acf.hhs.gov/cb/data-research/child-maltreatment

Wambua, G., Kilian, S., & Chiliza, B. (2024). "No one will come and help me make my life": Ecological-transactional model approach to resilience among people with a history of childhood adversity. *Social Science & Medicine, 361*, Article 117354. https://doi.org/10.1016/j.socscimed.2024.117354

World Health Organization. (2025). *Child maltreatment*. Available from https://www.who.int/news-room/fact-sheets/detail/child-maltreatment

Whitt-Woosley, A., Gustman, B. D., & Sprang, G. (2014). Lives at risk: Uncovering factors associated with fatal child maltreatment. *Children and Youth Services Review, 47*, 307–313. https://doi.org/10.1016/j.childyouth.2014.10.007

Younas, F., & Gutman, L. M. (2022). Parental risk and protective factors in child maltreatment: A systematic review of the evidence. *Trauma, Violence, & Abuse, 24*(5), 3697–3714. https://doi.org/10.1177/15248380221134634

Chapter 13
Abolitionist Theory

Jill McCorkel and Janis Parker

Name of the theory: Abolitionist Theory
Proponents of the theory: Angela Y. Davis, Leigh Goodmark, and Mariame Kaba
What the theory says: Abolitionist theory critically examines the historical origins and contemporary work of the "carceral system"—a network of institutions that include police, prosecutors, courts, and the penal system. Abolitionists argue that these institutions do not meaningfully address harm, enhance public safety, or deliver justice. Instead, they intensify social inequality and oppression. In the context of family violence, abolitionist scholarship details the numerous ways that the carceral system generates harm and trauma for victims and survivors. The theory advocates for an alternative, community-based system of transformative justice.

Introduction

How should society respond to acts that harm individuals, families, and communities? How can we ensure that our responses to harm and violence reduce the likelihood of additional trauma and harm? How do we facilitate healing for victims and accountability for perpetrators? How do we create a just and equitable world? These are the central questions that animate abolitionist theory and practice. They are not easy

J. McCorkel (✉)
School of Law and Criminology, Maynooth University, Maynooth, County Kildare, Ireland
e-mail: Jill.Mccorkel@mu.ie

J. Parker
Department of History, Villanova University, Villanova, PA, USA
e-mail: janis.parker@richmond.edu

A. Hattery and E. Smith (eds.), *Theories of Family Violence*, Advances in Preventing and Treating Violence and Aggression, https://doi.org/10.1007/978-3-032-17095-8_13

questions to answer. While some might be tempted to say that police and prisons offer the best deterrent to violence and harm, abolitionists reject this perspective. They argue that the "carceral system"–a network of institutions that include police, courts, jails, and prisons–is deeply unjust, profoundly flawed, and ultimately ineffective. Systems of policing and punishment do not address underlying structural sources of violence and harm, including poverty and social and economic inequality. For this reason, a "carceral response"—that is, a punitive system of punishment that warehouses people in jails and prisons—will never enhance community safety, advance social justice, or substantively reduce harm. Moreover, prisons and jails are too often the purveyors of violence and harm.

Abolitionist theory has three objectives. The first is scholarly. Abolitionists substantiate their critique of prisons and policing through detailed, intersectional, and empirical analyses of violence, harm, and inequality. Abolition's second objective is political. Abolitionist theory contrasts safety from security and contends that the former can only be achieved through conditions that facilitate human flourishing. Safety can only be achieved through policies and practices that provide everyone–regardless of race/ethnicity, class, gender, sexuality, religious practice or immigration status–access to quality health care, shelter, food, water, education, the arts, and meaningful work. Abolition's third objective is organizational. Abolitionists believe that safety *from* harm and accountability *for* harm are achieved through care and community. A quote from abolitionist scholar Saidiya Hartman summarizes, "Care is the antidote to violence" (Kaba, 2021, p. 111). Creating and nurturing strong communities facilitates a safe and just world.

In this chapter, we summarize key tenets of abolitionist theory, trace its origins, and identify its contributions to the study of family violence. Abolitionist theory has been particularly influential in the social sciences and humanities, including sociology, criminology, political science, legal studies, social work, and history. It is increasingly prominent in academic and legal analyses of family violence, particularly with respect to intimate partner violence (henceforth IPV) and related forms of gender violence, including sexual assault and rape. Abolition is not only a theory, it's a "survivor-led" social movement. Many abolitionist theorists, scholars, and activists are survivors of gender violence. Their experiences and insights from working within and outside the legal system inform their scholarship, political perspectives, and organizing strategies. Notably, abolitionist theory rejects what it refers to as a "carceral feminist" call for punitive responses to gender violence. We detail the abolitionist critique of carceral feminism and offer examples of abolitionist solutions for combatting family violence. We conclude with a discussion of the strengths the theory confers and the challenges it must yet overcome.

Origins of Abolitionist Theory

The roots of contemporary abolitionist theory are found in abolitionist practice and are traceable to the eighteenth and nineteenth century movement to abolish slavery in the United States. This social movement was led by William Lloyd Garrison (1805–1879), Harriet Tubman (1822–1913), Frances Ellen Watkins Harper (1825–1911), Frederick Douglass (1818–1895) and so many others (Yee, 1992; Quarles, 1991). Yet, it is the esteemed Black sociologist and activist, W.E.B. DuBois (1998/1935) who developed the concept of "abolition democracy" to assert that the legal end of chattel slavery was a necessary but not sufficient condition for the development of a racially just and equitable society. To achieve the latter, DuBois believed that reconfigured institutional structures and new social arrangements were necessary to facilitate Black social, political, and economic advancement. The period of Reconstruction that followed the Civil War fell far short of DuBois' vision. Southern states enacted racially discriminatory criminal laws called the "Black Codes." The Black Codes were nearly identical to their predecessor, the "Slave Codes." The Slave Codes were a system of laws that regulated all aspects of slavery and the lives of enslaved people. In slavery's aftermath, the nearly identical Black Codes made it illegal for African Americans to exercise baseline civil, social, and political freedoms available to white men (Blackmon, 2008). For example, the Black Codes restricted travel, limited access to the courts, and imposed prohibitions on speech, voting, gun ownership, and religious worship. One of the many penalties for violating the Codes was a system of punishment called convict leasing. Formerly enslaved people—convicted for exercising democratic freedoms that were legal and constitutionally protected for whites—were sentenced to perform hard, uncompensated labor on privately owned plantations (Blackmon, 2008). In this sense, the criminal legal system served as a replacement mechanism that restored, at least in part, the social, political, and economic arrangements of slavery. It did so by criminalizing conduct by African Americans that–when performed by whites–was entirely legal. In its earliest guise, abolitionist theory challenged the assumption that the carceral system operated in ways that were politically, economically, and racially neutral. This early analysis proved critical for the development of contemporary iterations of abolitionist theory.

Abolitionist scholarship, writing, and advocacy flourished in the period of the late 1960s through the decade of the 1970s. The Civil Rights movement expanded public awareness regarding the dismal and inhumane conditions inside American prisons and provided extensive evidence of racial discrimination in the application of criminal laws and punishments. In the 1970s, police harassment and subsequent arrest of Angela Davis, a well-known Black intellectual and activist, ignited large, international protests and broadened public awareness about the ways the criminal legal system could be used to squelch political dissent. Davis (2005) adapted DuBois' concept of abolition democracy to identify the ways that the criminal legal system undermines political and economic equality for African Americans and reproduces racial hierarchies and racist ideologies. Building on the intellectual contributions of incarcerated men and women, Davis emphasized that the Constitution's thirteenth

Amendment abolished slavery and involuntary servitude "… except as punishment for a crime." In other words, a criminal conviction all but strips people of the legal rights and protections that are considered essential for the preservation of political democracies.

During the same period, scholars and activists who were part of the Second Wave feminist movement (roughly 1963 to the early 1980s) centered gender violence as one of the key obstacles blocking political, social, and economic equality for women. The legality of marital rape and the routine failure of police and courts to respond to men's violence in the home rendered whatever constitutional rights women might otherwise have enjoyed all but symbolic (MacKinnon, 1989). In 1974, the Free Joann Little campaign, led by Black women, women of color, and queer feminists, linked the struggles for race and gender justice to a broader critique of the carceral system (Thuma, 2019). Little, a Black woman, was serving time in a North Carolina jail when a white correctional officer entered her cell with a weapon and sexually assaulted her. In the course of defending herself from rape, Little fatally stabbed the officer with his weapon. A powerful coalition of feminist, Black power, and civil rights activists coalesced to raise money and support for Little's defense. Incarcerated women—many of whom were, like Little, African American–came forward to share their own accounts of sexual violence at the hands of police and correctional officers, including the officer who had attacked Little. Angela Davis (1998) authored an essay for the campaign that made clear that sexual violence perpetuated against incarcerated women resonated with a broader history of white male sexual violence directed against Black and enslaved women. She argued that both are instances of the rape-racism nexus—a nexus that was reinvigorated in the aftermath of slavery in and through the carceral system. In 1975, a jury found Little not guilty of all charges, and she became the first woman in U.S. to be acquitted for utilizing deadly force to defend against sexual assault (Thuma, 2019).

Despite the early successes of these participatory defense campaigns for "criminalized survivors"—women who were criminally charged for defending themselves from male abusers—abolitionist perspectives were largely ignored by mainstream, predominantly white and middle class, liberal feminist activists. While liberal feminism shared some of abolition feminism's criticisms of the criminal legal system, it rejected abolition's call for community-based alternatives to police and prisons. Instead, liberal feminists pursued legal reforms designed to increase the likelihood that police would make arrests during domestic violence calls and that prosecutors would charge sexual assault cases (Goodmark, 2023a; Gruber, 2021). These reforms centered carceral responses to sexual assault, IPV, and other forms of gender violence. This strategy ignored the problems the carceral system posed for survivors like Joann Little and for Black women, women of color, and LGBTQ2 + people (Goodmark, 2023a, b; Gruber, 2021; Richie, 2012). Since the early 1970s, feminist abolitionists have emphasized that when Black women, women of color, and queer people are the victims of interpersonal forms of gender violence they also become uniquely vulnerable to various forms of state violence. While the criminal legal system may offer relief to some survivors of gender violence, it exacerbates harm for many others. Kaba (2021) and Richie (2012) argue that in the latter case, the system compounds trauma and harm by discrediting victims' experiences and criminalizing their survival strategies (see also Combahee River Collective, 1997; Goodmark, 2023a).

The 2020 police murders of George Floyd in Minneapolis, Minnesota and Breonna Taylor in Louisville, Kentucky reignited scholarly and public interest in abolitionist theory. Abolitionist theory has since moved from margin to center, informing debates about the chronic nature of police violence, the costly failures of mass incarceration, and the ongoing criminalization of African Americans and people of color in the United States. As journalists, policymakers, and concerned members of the public have struggled to understand why an average of 1000 Americans–disproportionately people of color–are shot to death by police each year, abolitionists emphasize the symbiotic relationship among the carceral system, racial inequality, and violence. Prison scholar and leading abolitionist Ruth Wilson Gilmore (2007, p. 261) formulates it this way: "Racism… is the state-sanctioned or extralegal production and exploitation of group-differentiated vulnerability to premature death."

Key Tenets of Abolitionist Theory

Abolitionist theory is engaged with three projects: (1) scholarly analysis of the carceral system, (2) pursuing a politics of "transformative justice" while rejecting carceral responses to harm, and (3) developing collective organizing strategies that anchor care and accountability in the context of community. Each project has its own interrelated set of key terms and concepts. In this section, we review key terms and tenets of contemporary abolitionist theory.

Scholarly Analysis of the Carceral System

Abolitionist scholarship compiles and analyzes social science and historical data to critically examine the origin of police and prisons, analyze the influence of race, class, gender, and sexuality on laws, legal practices, and legal and extra-legal outcomes, and evaluate the extent to which police and prisons facilitate or undermine the health and safety of all people and communities. Decades of social science research demonstrates that the carceral system is deeply flawed, racially discriminatory, and narrowly focused on the crimes of the poor rather than those of the wealthy (Reiman & Leighton, 2023). Abolitionists argue that the persistence of racial discrimination is not a discrete flaw or fixable error. Rather, they contend that the carceral system is designed to protect the interests of white elites at the expense of racial/ethnic minorities and the poor. It preserves a system of racial, ethnic, and class-based hierarchy that originates in the social arrangements of chattel slavery.

The concept of "criminalization" is central to this argument. In abolitionist theory criminalization takes two forms. The first involves criminal laws, like that Black Codes, that make it illegal for one group to engage in a set of behaviors that are otherwise legal for others. The second is the use of harassment, surveillance, and violence by law enforcement directed against racial/ethnic minorities and the poor. For example, numerous studies demonstrate that African Americans are more likely to be stopped and searched by police even though those searches are *less likely* to produce evidence of a crime compared to searches of whites (Carvalho et al., 2021). In both instances, the system *presumes* Black criminality while simultaneously denying or minimizing criminality among whites. Abolitionists argue that criminalization leads to racially disproportionate rates of arrest, conviction, and incarceration for African Americans, particularly when compared to whites (Davis et al., 2022; Kaba, 2021, Richie, 2012).

Research shows that racially disproportionate rates of arrest, conviction, and incarceration do not reflect group differences in crime participation. African Americans are no more crime-involved than whites (Sohoni et al., 2021). This leads to a second key tenet of abolitionist theory: the criminal justice system does not actually deliver justice. It is fundamentally unjust to discriminate on the basis of race, ethnicity, class, gender, and other constitutionally protected categories. Discrimination in the application of law is one prominent form of injustice that plagues the current system.

A second form of injustice is the failure to act on criminal harms that disproportionately impact one group and not others. Gender violence is one such example. Crimes of gender violence disproportionately impact women and girls and are often ignored or dismissed by police and prosecutors (Goodmark, 2023a; Richie, 2012). For example, just a tiny fraction of all rapes reported to police end in a conviction. One reason: law enforcement in many jurisdictions do not bother to take the simple first step of testing rape kits. A recent study found that nationwide there are hundreds of thousands of rape kits that have gone untested (Kennedy, 2025). On the basis of these and other empirical and historical examples, abolitionists conclude that the system is not designed to actually solve crime, hold perpetrators accountable, or keep individuals and communities safe. For these reasons, abolitionists reject the moniker "criminal justice system." They instead use the phrases "criminal legal system" and "criminal punishment system" to emphasize that the system does not deliver justice to people and communities experiencing harm.

The Politics of Transformative Justice

The second project of abolition is political. Given the volume of empirical and historical data demonstrating the persistence of race, class, and gender inequality, abolitionists reject policy proposals that aim to reform the criminal legal system. Mariame Kaba (2021, p. 95) is blunt in her estimation of the odds of reform success: "We cannot reform police. We cannot reform prisons. We cannot." Her pessimism is based on the constancy of police violence despite decades of civil rights investigations, enhanced training programs, and civil lawsuits (among other reforms). Kaba's pessimism is also informed by her knowledge of policies that were initially conceived of as reforms that, once implemented, became inhumane and ineffective. For example, prisons were once considered a humanist reform to corporal punishment and convict leasing.

However, decades of research, litigation, and first-person accounts reveal that they are anything but humane in their treatment of incarcerated people.

The ultimate political goal of abolition is to replace the punitive carceral system with a community-based system of "transformative justice." Transformative justice centers communities as the sites for responding to harm. It prioritizes healing (for both survivors and perpetrators), repair of harms that occurred, and accountability for harm (Battle & Powell, 2024; Kaba, 2021). In this model, community members work collaboratively to provide support and protection for victims and survivors. Care and protection of victims and survivors are the priorities of transformative justice. Beyond this, the transformative justice model seeks to identify and understand the individual and structural factors that produced the harm. This means moving beyond merely identifying an individual's blameworthiness (i.e., did s/he or didn't s/he commit a criminal harm?). How might poverty, mental health crises, and past traumas have contributed to the harm that occurred? Did the violence originate in racist and/or misogynistic beliefs? This is a broader analytical inquiry than what presently exists in the criminal legal system. In the transformative justice model, community members, victims, survivors, and perpetrators must investigate all the conditions that generated the harm. This allows communities to develop an informed set of strategies and interventions to decrease the likelihood of the harm recurring (Kaba, 2021; LaVarco, 2023).

Collective Organizing

Given that strong and robust communities are central to achieving transformative justice, it follows that a third project of abolitionism is collective organizing. Scholars Brittany Battle and Amber Powell (2024) explain that the popular abolitionist slogan, "we keep us safe" reflects a commitment to achieving safety and justice in and through the community. The abolitionist distinction between security and safety is useful for understanding this point. In the carceral system, security is outsourced to private companies and state institutions like police, jails, and prisons. Security makes it more difficult and less desirable to attack and harm a particular target, regardless of whether that target is a person or property. An example might be a gated community that hires a private security company to patrol its borders, or a local retail business outfitted with cameras and warning signs that say, "shoplifters will be prosecuted." Security does not eliminate the impulse to steal, it only makes stealing from that particular neighborhood or store less appealing.

In contrast, safety is achieved internally, emerging through a network of strong, reciprocal, and nurturing relationships that form communities. Safety, in the community context, is accomplished through mutual aid. It materializes when neighbors come together to share resources, skills, emotional support, knowledge, and experience. Instead of securing targets, communities fortify human creativity, empathy, joy, connection, and talent. Safety prevents harm from occurring by eliminating the sources–poverty, loneliness, violence, alienation, oppression–that produce harm. Abolitionists believe that the impulse to harm others all but disappears in social contexts that encourage close bonds among interconnected networks of friends, family, and neighbors.

Contributions to the Study of Family Violence

Family violence encompasses a range of harms within the context of intimate relationships, including but not restricted to IPV, child neglect/abuse, sexual assault, and elder abuse. Gender and sexual violence are often at the center of these abuses and trauma. For abolitionists, the complexity of family violence and the generational legacies of trauma it leaves in its wake demand a radical shift away from carceral responses. In this section, we summarize the abolitionist critique of carceral feminism and its misplaced faith in the criminal legal system. We highlight abolition's contributions to two key areas of family violence scholarship: IPV and child welfare. We conclude this section with a discussion of abolition's practical interventions on behalf of survivors of IPV and offer an example of a Philadelphia-based effort to prevent gender-based violence.

Critique of Carceral Feminism

In a pivotal paper entitled "Whose Safety? Women of Color and the Violence of Law Enforcement," Annanya Bhattacharjee (2001) offered a comprehensive critique of mainstream, "carceral" feminism's support for punitive responses to gender violence. Echoing many women of color activists before her, Bhattacharjee argued that calling for heightened policing and punitive sanctions created additional layers of harm and vulnerability for survivors of color, LGBTQ2 + survivors, and others (Bhattacharjee, 2001; Davis et al., 2022). Her principal concern was the widespread support the 1994 Crime Bill occasioned among mainstream, liberal feminists. The bill, which included the Violence Against Women Act (VAWA), increased spending on police and prisons and "solidified state control over responses to gender violence" (Davis et al., 2022; Kim, 2020). VAWA offered little in the way of community-based options to redress harms. In centering criminal penalties for perpetrators of violence, VAWA failed to address the fact that many survivors face challenges and have needs that extend beyond the exercise of carceral vengeance and retribution.

VAWA harmed survivors in at least three ways. First, it introduced laws and policies that had the effect of overtly criminalizing victims. For example, many states passed laws that made it a crime for a parent to allow a child to witness abuse in the home. Given the intimate and complex nature of IPV, it can be all but impossible for the parent who is the target of an abusive partner to shield their abuse from view.

These laws meant that victims of IPV, primarily women and mothers, were subject to criminal prosecution even as they were unable to protect themselves from the violence of their abusers (Richie, 2012; Goodmark, 2023a).

Second, VAWA legislation exposed many survivors, especially women of color, women living in poverty, and LGBTQ2 + people to various forms of state violence, including police brutality, incarceration, and loss of child custody (Bhattacharjee, 2001; Davis et al., 2022; Gruber, 2021; Kaba, 2021). For example, in 2023, a Los Angeles sheriff's deputy shot and killed Niani Finlayson in her home after she called 911 for help as her former boyfriend attacked her.

For abolitionists, a carceral response merges the individual violence perpetrated by abusers with institutional violence perpetrated by agents of the state.

A third way that the carceral system harms survivors is in its inability to deliver safety, accountability, and healing. Most perpetrators–even those who are convicted and punished by the system–rarely receive the kind of therapeutic programming that would diminish the likelihood of their engaging in future harms, much less improve the quality of their intimate and familial relationships (Barocas et al., 2023). Further, the structure of plea arrangements and expansive prosecutorial discretion actively discourage perpetrators from taking accountability for their actions. Instead, perpetrators are encouraged to minimize or deny harm and challenge survivor testimonies in order to receive a more favorable outcome in court (Davis et al., 2022; Goodmark, 2023a). The absence of accountability and rehabilitation exacerbates survivor trauma and renders the healing process unduly arduous and complex.

Contributions to Family Violence Scholarship

Abolitionist theory has made important contributions to several subfields in the family violence literature. In this section, we highlight abolition's impact on two such subfields: IPV and child welfare. In both areas, abolitionist theories address what legal scholar Dorothy Roberts (2022) identifies as "carceral entanglements" between the criminal legal system and civil society (see also Poor, 2023). Carceral responses to IPV and child welfare further ensnare and perpetuate harm to many vulnerable populations including women of color, LGBTQ + people, immigrants, and communities combating poverty.

Abolitionist theory has become increasingly prominent in research and policy literature on IPV (and other forms of gender violence). Its appeal is due to the growing number of studies demonstrating the myriad ways that carceral responses have exacerbated harm for survivors.

Recent years have also seen public outrage over criminal charges filed against women who defended themselves from lethal violence. Prosecutorial attempts to criminalize survivors have targeted women like Marissa Alexander who attempted to defend herself against her estranged husband by firing a warning shot into an empty room; like CeCe McDonald, a Black trans woman who fought and killed her attacker; like Tracy McCarter, who killed her husband during a IPV episode; and so many more (Goodmark, 2023a; Kaba, 2021; McCarter & Sisay, 2023).

Leigh Goodmark (2023a, p. 9) argues that to avoid criminalization "… survivors of violence had to perform their victimization in very specific ways: they had to be perfect victims." Among other requirements, "perfect victims" are not supposed to fight back or display aggression. The system continues to frame Black women like Alexander, McDonald, and McCarter—all of whom were defending themselves from lethal violence— as "imperfect" and thus criminally blameworthy.

The current system requires victims and survivors who seek protection from an abusive partner or family member to engage with police, prosecutors, and other carceral actors.

Alternatives to this system are few and far between. Most remain enmeshed within the criminal legal system (Goodmark, 2018; Poor, 2023). For example, survivors of IPV are required to interact with law enforcement to secure a civil protective order (CPO). Thus, access to "non-carceral" remedies still requires carceral intervention. Even family law systems, which are a branch of civil law, are reliant on the criminal legal system (Goodmark, 2023b). For example, violations of domestic violence protective orders are criminal offenses even though they are civil orders issued in family court. Thus, the alternatives offered by the family law system still expose victims of IPV to heightened risk of criminalization and related carceral harms (Goodmark, 2023b). The entanglement of family law and the criminal legal system undermines the ability of civil remedies to operate as an effective alternative for victims of IPV (Poor, 2023).

In addition to its influence on IPV, abolitionist theory is also becoming pivotal in research and policy debates regarding the child welfare system. The child welfare system, or what Dorothy Roberts (2022) calls the "family-policing system," facilitates harmful state intrusion into marginalized communities and families under the guise of care (see also Davis et al., 2022). Roberts' use of the phrase "family-policing system" foregrounds the ways that the system responds punitively to families in crisis and challenges the accuracy of commonly used terms like "child welfare system" and "child protective services." Roberts argues for an abolitionist framing of the family-policing system because it centers the entrenched carceral nature of the state's attitude(s) toward children and families, especially when those children and families are racial/ethnic minorities and/or living in poverty. According to Roberts (2022, p. 24), "Far from promoting the well-being of children, the state weaponizes children as a way to threaten families, to scapegoat parents for societal harms to their children, and to buttress the racist, patriarchal, and capitalist status quo."

Building on abolitionists' insights about the ineffectiveness of family law alternatives for responding to IPV, Roberts (2022) cautions against simply diverting resources from formal carceral institutions—like the police—to civil agencies like Child Protective Services (CPS). The family-policing system is an inextricable component of the larger carceral state and therefore linked to other forms of family violence, including IPV. As Maya Schenwar and Victoria Law (2020) observe, reformist alternatives have contributed to increased surveillance and policing of targeted families. This does nothing to address trauma or reduce harm. It often makes it worse.

Parents, overwhelmingly Black women, other women of color, and poor women, trapped in IPV situations are at risk of losing their children to foster care, even if they try to locate resources as domestic violence survivors (Roberts, 2022; Schenwar & Law, 2020). If child "protective" services determine that the non-abusive parent—i.e., the parent experiencing abuse—exposed their child to domestic violence, officials can cite the parent for "failure to protect" and remove the child from the home (Goodmark, 2023b). Reform mechanisms like mandated reporting deter some survivors under age 18, especially LGBTQ + children, from seeking help for fear of what might happen to their family if reported to child services (Schenwar & Law, 2020). From Roberts' (2022) vantage, the "carceral entanglements" between criminal and civil institutions have become so entrenched and ineffective that they both warrant abolition.

Abolitionist theory demands that scholars, policymakers, and activists critically examine the logic behind relying on police and the courts to resolve the harm and trauma of family violence. What makes the state a suitable actor to intervene in moments of crisis within families and between intimate partners? In responding to this prompt, abolitionists reject the state's "arbitrary authority" and instead argue that "... the pretext of ending gender violence allows the state to determine the nature of the problem, to decide on 'reasonable' solutions, and to categorize people as either deserving to be free from injury or not" (Davis et al., 2022, p. 111). This applies to the family-policing system as well. State institutions and actors determine whether certain parents and children are deserving to be free from intervention, from separation, or not. Research demonstrates that race/ethnicity and racism are central to these determinations. As Roberts (2022) notes, state agents working in the family punishment system often perpetuate racist tropes and historical stereotypes about Black pathology and Black parenthood to justify family separation. For Roberts (2022), Goodmark (2023b), and other abolitionist scholars, carceral responses to the harms of IPV, child abuse, and child neglect brings additional pain, trauma, vulnerability, and marginalization to victims and survivors.

Practical Abolitionist Interventions

One of the misconceptions about abolitionist theory is that it offers sweeping condemnations of the criminal legal and family punishment systems but fails to put forward tangible policies to address violence and harm. This is untrue. Abolitionists have advocated for a variety of discrete policy interventions and facilitated numerous community-based strategies to prevent violence. In this section we profile two abolitionist interventions. The first is a policy intervention directed at freeing incarcerated survivors of gender violence. The second is a Philadelphia-based violence prevention program targeting men and masculine-identifying people.

Among the most notable and promising abolitionist policy interventions are campaigns to free incarcerated survivors of IPV and gender violence. One of every 15 women in prison is serving a sentence of life or 50 or more years (Nellis, 2021). The vast majority are survivors. Their criminal convictions are often directly or indirectly an outcome of gender violence and abuse. Abolitionists propose the use of executive clemency to bring immediate relief to incarcerated survivors. Clemency is an umbrella term that refers to the power to grant different types of legal mercy from the executive branch. The form of clemency proposed by abolitionists is commutation of sentence. Commutation reduces the length or terms of a criminal sentence. In state systems these decisions are made by the office of governor and in the federal system it is the office of President. For survivors serving life without parole or "virtual" life sentences of 50 years or more, clemency may be their only hope of returning home.

Clemency is not without its flaws. Its beneficiaries are most likely to closely conform to what Goodmark (2023a) characterizes as "perfect victims." The trope of the "imperfect victim"–a survivor, often a woman of color, who fought back, acted aggressively, used drugs, or was living in poverty–reduces the odds of success for many commutation applicants.

Commutation decisions are highly political and idiosyncratic and are most likely to be granted in "exceptional cases." For example, New York Governor Andrew Cuomo granted just 21 commutations out of 7,500 + applications submitted over an eight-year period from 2011 through 2019 (Zamouri, 2023).

To avoid the pitfalls of exceptionalism and categorizing survivors as "worthy and "unworthy," abolitionists have proposed that incarcerated survivors be eligible for mass clemency. In New York, their efforts directly contributed to the passage of the Domestic Violence Survivors Justice Act in 2019. The legislation allows survivors convicted of most crimes the opportunity to receive a reduced sentence (either retroactively or at the moment of sentencing) based on their abuse histories and related criteria. Criteria include: (1) establishing that they experienced "substantial" abuse at the time of the offense, (2) the abuse was a "significant contributing factor" to the offense, and (3) the sentence that was imposed was "unduly harsh." By early 2023, 40 survivors were granted retroactive modification of their original sentences (Komar et al., 2023). Although some abolitionists have critiqued this legislation for not going far enough, it was the first of its kind in the country and represents an important milestone in survivor-based advocacy.

Abolitionists also pursue on-the-ground strategies to prevent gender violence. One notable example is Masculinity Action Project (henceforth MAP), a Philadelphia-based education and prevention initiative that is premised on two critical assertions: (1) gender violence is informed by and facilitated through traditional notions of masculinity, and (2) traditional forms of masculinity are harmful to everyone (Gender Justice Fund, 2025). MAP operates under the auspices of a bilingual, city-wide domestic violence program. While the domestic violence program is focused primarily on providing counseling and transitional housing to victims and survivors of IPV, it also acknowledges the need for community-based violence prevention efforts that engage perpetrators of harm, as well as men and masculine-identifying people more generally.

MAP began in the early 2000s as a yearly rally every October during domestic violence awareness month. Its goal was to encourage men to take action to end domestic violence. The rallies proved so successful that by 2016, MAP evolved into a full-fledged, community-based organization. Today MAP hosts a series of workshops for men and masculine-identifying individuals designed to encourage critical reflection regarding masculinity norms and socialization and to facilitate internal change. They offer training programs to enable men to effectively identify, call out, and disrupt gender violence, harm, and other kinds of toxic behaviors. Additionally, MAP aims to bring men as active allies into broader movements for gender justice. MAP hosts a "masculine ally month" which offers programming, in partnership with local feminist organizations, on specific topics related to gender justice and gender violence. In addition to learning from feminist abolitionist organizations and organizers, MAP participants fundraise to support local campaigns for gender justice.

Although it is impossible to know how many incidents of gender violence MAP programming has prevented from happening, it is clear the organization is making a positive impact in Philadelphia. It offers a non-carceral space for men and masculine-identifying people to take accountability for harmful actions, to understand how socialization and cultural norms may have contributed to those actions, and to make positive change at both individual and structural levels. As Kaba (2021) has noted, there is virtually nothing in our culture that encourages people to take accountability for the harms they have caused, much less ways to make amends for that harm. MAP serves as a useful abolitionist model for not only facilitating accountability for gender violence, but creating the conditions to prevent gender violence from occurring in the future.

Challenges and Critiques of Abolitionism

There are three major criticisms of contemporary abolitionist theory. The first concerns the theory's ability to substantively grasp the scale and scope of harm, particularly for those most vulnerable to violence. Two additional criticisms are procedural. Some legal scholars, philosophers, and policymakers have expressed skepticism regarding abolition's ability to deliver results (Levin, 2024). They note that abolition offers no concrete mechanisms to replace police and prisons with community-based alternatives. Further, critics argue that by focusing on a "pie in the sky" goal, abolitionists miss opportunities to enact practical reforms that would confer immediate benefits to people who are the victims of violence, as well as those who have engaged in criminal harms.

One of the most persistent criticisms of abolition comes in the form of a question about gender and violence: in the absence of police, who will protect women and girls from sexual assault and intimate partner violence? The question presumes that law enforcement functions to prevent or at least discourage gender violence. This is a dubious assumption given decades of research suggesting that most gender violence does not get reported to police and, when it does, it often fails to trigger arrests, prosecutions, and convictions of perpetrators (Battle & Powell 2024; Goodmark, 2023a).

Feminist abolitionists respond to this critique in two ways. First, abolitionists like Kaba (2021) emphasize that many of the leading architects of contemporary abolitionism are themselves survivors of gender violence. Lived experience confers for survivors a clear and commanding grasp of the nature and extent of gender violence. Second, abolitionists argue that critics frame the question of gender violence too narrowly. That is, critics conceptualize gender violence as interpersonal. This perspective fails to acknowledge that gender violence is also perpetuated by state actors like police, prosecutors, and jailers (Davis et al., 2022). Prosecuting survivors for defending themselves against their attackers is one such form of gendered state violence. Feminist abolitionists contend that defunding or abolishing police and prisons alleviates one form of gender violence while opening alternate avenues for effectively responding to interpersonal forms of violence.

A second line of critique emerges from a perspective known as "criminal law minimalism." Minimalists are critical of mass incarceration and the excesses of the criminal legal system but contend that abolition's utopian vision does not yield clear guidelines for how to hold perpetrators of harm accountable while reducing the likelihood of future harm. Slogans like "we keep us safe" do not address the very real and immediate harms that some individuals and groups present. What, for example, is the abolitionist response to heavily armed militias committed to racial terrorism? A third and related concern among minimalists is that abolitionists do not pursue practical, achievable reforms that could substantially improve criminal legal outcomes (Levin, 2024).

For the most part, abolitionist theorists acknowledge that there is no easy formula or blueprint for achieving transformative justice from one community to the next. These are processes and solutions that must be collaboratively deliberated, enacted, and evaluated in and through community. As Kaba (2021, p. xx) says, "We'll figure it out by working to get there." Additionally, there is nothing in abolitionist theory that would prevent advocates from adopting a "both/and" rather than "either/or" approach to reforms. Gilmore's (2007) call for "non-reformist reforms" allows abolitionists to pursue material changes to the system that improve conditions in real time while simultaneously serving to shrink the footprint of criminalization and mass incarceration.

Conclusion

Abolitionist theory begins with a question: how can we make the world safe, just, and equitable? To answer it, abolitionist theorists emphasize the experiences and perspectives of victims and survivors of family and gender-based violence. Abolitionist scholars contend that for most survivors, police and prisons have not made them safer, healed their trauma, or addressed the variety of harms that dovetail victimization including access to safe and affordable housing, employment, childcare, education, and counseling services. Even worse, many survivors find themselves in the carceral system's crosshairs and at risk of criminal prosecution, incarceration, and loss of child custody. Through detailed analysis of empirical and historical data, abolitionist scholars demonstrate that the negative encounters survivors have had with the criminal legal system are not the exception. They are the norm. For this reason, abolitionist theory rejects entirely the argument that the criminal legal system should be the primary vector for responding to violence and harm. At best, it might provide some measure of security for those who can afford it. It will never facilitate public safety.

Abolitionist theory proposes instead a system of transformative justice that is located within communities rather than embedded in state systems. Abolitionist scholarship has yet to fully detail what such a system would look like; a system of transformative justice may look and operate differently from one community to the next. For abolitionists, variation is a good thing as it reflects specific community needs, values, strengths, and aspirations. In this framework, community is not simply a network of social relationships. It is an ongoing, empathetic practice of care and accountability—a practice that abolitionists believe will ultimately confer liberation, freedom, safety, and flourishing for all people.

References

Barocas, B., Avieli, H., & Mills, L. G. (2023). Restorative justice treatment for domestic violence crimes: A qualitative study. *Criminal Justice and Behavior, 50*(12), 1805–1826.

Battle, B. P., & Powell, A. J. (2024). 'We keep us safe!' Abolition feminism as a challenge to carceral feminist responses to gendered violence. *Gender & Society, 38*(4), 523–556.

Blackmon, D. A. (2008). *Slavery by another name.* Anchor Books.

Bhattacharjee, A. (2001). Whose safety? Women of color and the violence of law enforcement. In *A justice visions working paper.* American Friends Service Committee and Committee on Women, Population, and the Environment

Carvalho, A. A. S., Mizael, T. M., & Sampaio, A. A. S. (2021). Racial prejudice and police stops: A systematic review of the empirical literature. *Behavioral Analysis in Practice, 15*, 1213–1220.

Combahee River Collective. (1997). A black feminist statement. In L. Nicholson (Ed.), *The second wave: A reader in feminist theory* (pp. 63–70). Routledge.

Davis, A. Y. (1998). JoAnne Little: The dialectics of rape. In J. James (Ed.), *The Angela Y. Davis reader* (pp. 149–160). Blackwell Publishers.

Davis, A. Y. (2005). *Abolition democracy.* Seven Stories.

Davis, A. Y., Dent, G., Meiners, E., & Richie, B. E. (2022). *Abolition.* Haymarket Books.

DuBois, W. E. B. (1998/1935). *Black reconstruction in America, 1860–1880.* Free Press. Gender Justice Fund. (2025). *Masculinity action project.* https://www.genderjusticephilly.org/map

Gilmore, R. W. (2007). *Golden gulag.* University of California Press.

Goodmark, L. (2018). *Decriminalizing domestic violence: A balanced policy approach to intimate partner violence.* University of California Press.

Goodmark, L. (2023a). *Imperfect victims: Criminalized survivors and the promise of abolition feminism.* University of California Press.

Goodmark, L. (2023b). Why centering the family court system won't decrease criminalization of intimate partner violence—and why that's a problem. *Virginia Journal of Social Policy & the Law, 30*(1), 56–66.

Gruber, A. (2021). *The feminist war on crime: The unexpected role of women's liberation in mass incarceration*. University of California Press.

Kaba, M. (2021). *We do this 'til we free us*. Haymarket Books.

Kennedy, P. (2025). *The secret history of the rape kit*. Vintage.

Kim, M. E. (2020). The carceral creep: Gender-based violence, race, and the expansion of the punitive state, 1973–1983. *Social Problems, 67*(2), 251–269.

Komar, L., Gonzalez, C., Isaacs, E., Mogulescu, K., & Szlekovics, M. (2023). *Sentencing reform for criminalized survivors: Learning from New York's Domestic Violence Survivors Justice Act*. The Sentencing Project. https://www.sentencingproject.org/reports/sentencing-reform-for-criminalized-survivors-learning-from-new-yorks-domestic-violence-survivors-justice-act/

LaVarco, S. (2023). Reimagining the violence against women act from a transformative justice perspective: Decarceration and financial reparations for criminalized survivors of sexual and gender-based violence. *New York University Law Review, 98*(3), 912–961.

Levin, B. (2024). Criminal law minimalisms. *Washington University Law Review, 101*(6), 1771–1803.

MacKinnon, C. (1989). *Toward a feminist theory of state*. Harvard University Press.

McCarter, T., & Sisay, S. (2023). Prosecutors must use their immense discretion to end the criminalization of survivors of gender-based violence who act in self-defense. *CUNY Law Review, 26*(204), 204–230.

Nellis, A. (2021). *In the extreme: Women serving life without parole and death sentences in the United States*. The Sentencing Project. https://www.sentencingproject.org/app/uploads/2022/08/In-the-Extreme-Women-Serving-Life-without-Parole-and-Death-Sentences-in-the-United-States.pdf

Poor, E. M. (2023). Disentangling the civil-carceral state: An abolitionist framework for the non-criminal response to intimate partner violence. *New York University Review of Law & Social Change, 47*(2), 273–337.

Quarles, B. (1991). *Black abolitionists*. Grand Central Publishing.

Reiman, J., & Leighton, P. (2023). *The rich get richer and the poor get prison* (13th edn). Routledge

Richie, B. E. (2012). *Arrested justice: Black women, violence, and America's prison nation*. New York University Press.

Roberts, D. E. (2022). *Torn apart: How the child welfare system destroys black families–and how abolition can build a safer world*. Basic Books.

Schenwar, M., & Law, V. (2020). *Prison by any other name: The harmful consequences of popular reforms*. The New Press.

Sohoni, T., Ousey, G., Bower, E., & Mehdi, A. (2021). Understanding the gap in self-reported offending by race: A meta-analysis. *American Journal of Criminal Justice, 46*(5), 770–792.

Thuma, E. L. (2019). *All our trials: Prisons, policing, and the feminist fight to end violence*. University of Illinois Press.

Yee, S. (1992). *Black women abolitionists: A study in activism, 1828–1860*. University of Tennessee Press.

Zamouri, I. (2023). Self-defense, responsibility, and punishment: Rethinking the criminalization of women who kill their abusive intimate partners. *UCLA Journal of Gender and Law, 30*(1), 203–270.

Chapter 14
Where Theories of Family Violence Fall Short: A Case for Singlehood and Chosen Families

Katelyn E. Foltz and Kris Marsh

- **Name of the theory**: Family Violence, Singlehood, Intersectionality, Respectability Politics
- **Proponents of the theory**: Patricia Hill Collins, Kimberlé Crenshaw, Bella De Paulo
- **What the theory says**: Sociology is a comprehensive science of social action that pursues universal truths about an infinitely complex world even though that objective is ultimately unattainable. In that quest, sociologists develop "pure type" concepts that focus attention on the key aspects of social action. Science, as a form of social action, can be examined as a pure type. That analysis shows that science is limited in what it can prescribe as an ultimate ethical basis for social action leaving the determination of social values to the political realm of social action. The key to moral conduct is the creation of a fully open debate within the political realm of societies.

Introduction

In this chapter, we critique the theories of family violence, as these theories are predicated on narrow notions of what a family is or should be. Instead, we offer singlehood, family-of-one, chosen families, augmented families, and more inclusive

K. E. Foltz (✉)
University of Mississippi, Oxford, MS, USA
e-mail: kefoltz@olemiss.edu

K. Marsh
University of Maryland, College Park, MD, USA
e-mail: kmarsh1@umd.edu

A. Hattery and E. Smith (eds.), *Theories of Family Violence*, Advances in Preventing and Treating Violence and Aggression, https://doi.org/10.1007/978-3-032-17095-8_14

definitions of family as potential solutions to family violence. An expansive definition of family, including those single and living alone, might serve as a safe family formation (family-of-one) from some forms of family violence. Drawing from feminist theory, intersectionality, and respectability politics, we highlight the patriarchal and racist foundations of family today that are entrenched in power.

Heteropatriarchal families are often privileged in these discussions; however, we aim to acknowledge, promote, and advocate for families that do not fit into traditional definitions to reduce violence. It is worth noting that being single is often stigmatized and, while we challenge theories of family violence, we also need to challenge the idea of singlehood as taboo. Finally, we conclude the chapter with policy recommendations for a more inclusive society comprised of various family types that does not overlook singlehood. Chief among these policies is alleviating structural barriers that deter people from living in an alternative family structure, a structure that could reduce violence. This paper is primarily a discussion on policy that grows from the current state of theory and as a result, policy is not responsive to evolving definitions of families including those that are single and living alone as well as chosen families.

Assessing the Theories

Family Violence. Much important theorizing and research has been done in assessing domestic violence and family violence over the past 50 years. Seminal authors such as Straus(2017), Walker (2016), Browne (2008), and Renzetti (1992) have shaped the understanding of theories of family violence and how society maintains conditions for family violence. This research has been important in theorizing methods to reduce instances of this violence or prevent it from occurring. While this literature is foundational to family violence, it could benefit from other theories, such as notions of singlehood, intersectionality, and respectability politics, which can in turn help us understand theories of family violence in more nuanced ways.

Singlehood. With singlehood growing globally, either by choice or circumstance, coupled with theories of family violence, thought provoking questions are raised. Kislev and Marsh (2023) argue that singlehood is no longer considered a transitory phase or a mere demographic indicator.

Singlehood can, and should, be a status of choice and identity (DePaulo, 2015; Kislev, 2019; Klinenberg, 2012) and should thus be studied through an intersectional lens.

Intersectionality. The field of family violence has assessed how this violence does not impact each family and individual uniformly. This chapter calls for a more heavily focused approach on the theory of intersectionality to provide a more nuanced understanding as well as to help undergird theory-based related policy (Collins & Bilge, 2020; Combahee River Collective, 1983; Taylor, 2017). In its most basic definition and drawing from that given by law professor Kimberlé Crenshaw, who coined the term, intersectionality is a "lens through which you can see where power comes and collides, where it interlocks and intersects" (Crenshaw, 2020). Familial violence and intimate partner violence look different in Black and Brown families and couples (Hattery & Smith, 2007), low-income families and couples (Lubker, 2004), and LGBTQIA+ families and couples (Renzetti, 1992). However, one thing these theories fail to do is imagine a world in which romantic and familial relationships are not at the center of many people's lives.

Respectability Politics. Generally, respectability politics is the misguided idea that Black people should change to fit in or conform to mainstream (in this case, white) ways, manners, behaviors, and appearances to assimilate better in a predominantly white society. This behavior is also touted as a purported protective measure from prejudice, discrimination, and racism. Collins (2004) points out that in the spirit of respectability politics, Black women often forsake themselves and submit to Black male dominance. The result can be unfulfilling, even toxic relationships where family violence may ensue in the name of maintaining a respectable image of a good wife and mother (Collins, 2004; Landor & Barr, 2018). Furthermore, Collins (2019) asserts that families (and marriages) can protect and perpetuate social inequalities.

What needs to be more fully interrogated is the term "family" within the theories of family violence. In some spaces in modern society, the center of a family is *usually* a heterosexual couple or, at minimum, a romantic partnership. When taking a step back, is it possible that this very definition creates the conditions for this violence to occur? Is the presence of a family (as presently defined) a risk factor for this violence? We argue that much could be accomplished by broadening the definition of family, to include chosen families, augmented families, and families of one. Doing so would allow for family to be ruled, not by patrilineal name transfer and blood, but by choice. This simple definitional shift requires a radical reimagining for many in society, one that we argue could be monumental in violence reduction.

Policy and Societal Impacts

Drawing from this narrow vision of what constitutes a family, we turn to the 1968 work of Andrew Billingsley, a scholar who pioneered a new approach to studying Black families, that affirms cultural "difference" and praises the strengths of Black families, rather than focusing on "problem" (i.e., female-headed) families. He argued that a dichotomous approach to characterizing families—middle-class married couples and poor single-headed households—underestimates variations among Black families. Billingsley (1968) identified three categories of Black families: primary families (two-parent), extended families (other relatives, in-laws), and augmented families (non-related individuals). While Billingsley provides a broader view of what constitutes a family, a narrow vision of family can shape not only how we continue to understand family violence, but how we structure every institutional response to it. Today, family structures for many are evolving. However, family definitions in policy vary from state to state and some continue to operate on "traditional" definitions instead of evolving with the times.

Traditional theories of family violence emerged during a period when the "nuclear family" dominated both academic discourse and policy making. As Collins (1990) demonstrates through her groundbreaking work on *Black Feminist Thought*, this narrow focus never adequately captured the diverse ways that people, particularly those in marginalized communities, create and maintain family bonds. Yet, these theories and short-sighted definitions, void of diversity, often drive institutional responses to family violence.

Billingsley's (1968) early recognition of augmented families offers an alternative framework for understanding family formation. However, as Marsh (2023) documents, policymakers still largely ignored these insights, continuing to base protections and services on "traditional" family definitions, ignoring chosen families and families-of-one. This theoretical myopia carries real consequences. For example, psychologist Bella DePaulo (2006) identifies systematic discrimination against single people—what DePaulo terms "singlism"—across institutional policies and practices. It is worth raising the question: in what ways might this discrimination create additional barriers to seeking help, accessing support services, and receiving assistance for family violence if the victims do not fit "traditional" family models or are single and considered a family-of-one?

Today's policy landscape reveals systematic exclusions that particularly impact single, chosen, and augmented families. The policy implications extend far beyond family violence and extend to other areas such as economics and law. For example, legal scholar Dorothy Brown (2021) demonstrates how tax policies, insurance structures, and housing regulations all privilege "traditional" family formations while penalizing alternative arrangements. These penalties accumulate over time, creating what economist Darrick Hamilton (2020) identifies as systematic barriers to economic stability and wealth building for diverse family formations.

Going one step further than economic policy and laws, we must consider how family violence might require the engagement of the healthcare system, an institution that can be steeped in antiquated notions of family. Healthcare policies also present particularly stark examples of institutional failure for those not in "traditional" family units. Hospitals routinely deny visitation rights to chosen and augmented family members, and insurance policies can exclude them from coverage. Social welfare scholar Tina Sacks (2018) shows how these exclusions create cascading effects that impact both immediate care and long-term health outcomes. A single adult experiencing family violence might find themselves unable to access crucial support services simply because their closest family relationships fall outside of "traditional" definitions.

Looking to the Future in Four Phases

Moving beyond these systemic failures requires comprehensive policy reform that recognizes and protects all family formations. The path forward begins with legal recognition reform.

Current legal frameworks must expand to encompass chosen and non-traditional family bonds. Drawing from sociological research, this means creating new categories of legal recognition that extend beyond blood, marriage, and adoption (DePaulo, 2023; Kislev, 2019; Marsh, 2023).

These categories must be flexible enough to accommodate diverse family structures while providing clear legal standing for chosen and augmented family relationships.

We need straightforward procedures that allow people to document their chosen family relationships while maintaining appropriate safeguards against abuse. These procedures should be accessible through multiple channels, from healthcare facilities to social service agencies, ensuring that people can establish legal recognition when and where they need it most. For example, a domestic violence statute could expand its definition of "family" to include documented chosen family relationships. The statute might read: "any person related by blood, marriage, adoption, or legally documented chosen family relationship." This would allow chosen family members to seek protective orders and ensure that violence between chosen family members carries the same penalties as a "traditional" family type.

Healthcare policy reform presents another crucial arena for change. Current healthcare systems, structured around "traditional" family definitions, create particular hardships for non-traditional families facing violence. This means requiring insurance providers to cover chosen family members with the same provisions currently extended to legal spouses and blood relatives. It means establishing clear protocols for medical decision-making that recognize chosen and augmented family relationships. Most importantly, it means training healthcare providers to understand and respect diverse family formations. Specifically for family violence, current screening could include varying family structures by including screening questions to include chosen family members, people you live with as family, or anyone you consider family regardless of legal relationship.

Economic policy reform must address both immediate barriers and long-term wealth-building potential and how this might intersect with financial abuse. Tax codes must be revised to eliminate marriage penalties and create equivalent deductions for single taxpayers. For example, equalizing tax treatment would remove this economic disincentive to leaving intimate violent partnerships or getting into a "respectable" family formation for possible financial gain.

Similarly, if chosen family members could file jointly or share certain deductions, abuse survivors could maintain economic stability through their chosen family support networks rather than remaining financially dependent on abusive partners. Related, social security and pension systems must expand to recognize chosen family relationships in survivor benefits and inheritance rights. When a victim leaves an abusive partner, they should still have access to their partner's social security or pension benefits. In cases where there is potential to lose access to their partner's social security or pension benefits, chosen family members could designate each other as beneficiaries. This way survivors could build independent retirement security through their support networks, reducing a form of financial abuse (a similar measure should be in place for tuition remission for chosen or augmented family members of university professors).

Likewise, financial abuse as a form of elder abuse often exploits isolation and limited support networks for the aging population. Single older adults or those in non-traditional families face higher risks because financial institutions may not recognize their family-of-one nor their chosen family members as legitimate contacts. These same institutions might exploit the possible vulnerabilities of this demographic if they are not able to advocate for themselves. Implementation of these reforms requires careful phasing over time.

The first phase engages with various scholars that point out the racial and cultural variances in notions of who and what constitutes family. Such an engagement praises the strengths of various family formations, especially a family-of-one, chosen families, and augmented families, while encouraging scholars, and social institutions to rethink how we engage with the term "family" (Billingsley, 1968; Marsh, 2023; Moultrie, 2021) and what implications this might have for family violence and related policies. As has been highlighted, there are a number of social, political, and financial benefits that result from being called a family, from cell phone family plans to favorable income tax arrangements (Brown, 2021; DePaulo, 2006; Marsh, 2023).

Singles should be considered a family-of-one. Likewise, chosen and augmented families should be legally recognized. Institutionalizing a family-of-one, chosen families, and augmented families allows people to establish family units with friends (and themselves) in a legal manner to access benefits ranging from preferential cell phone plans to more substantive benefits in the realm of asset and wealth management as a potential mechanism to prevent and/or overcome family violence.

From a family violence perspective, legal recognition of diverse family structures creates crucial protective mechanisms. For instance, a family-of-one recognition could enable single people to designate trusted chosen family members as emergency contacts and financial monitors, reducing vulnerability to financial abuse and elder abuse that disproportionately targets isolated individuals. Current systems that only recognize "traditional" family structures can inadvertently increase abuse risk by forcing people to choose between safety and losing family-based benefits, or by failing to recognize the legitimacy of families-of one and chosen family support networks that could provide prevention, protection and intervention.

The second phase focuses on immediate relief measures. Emergency protocols can be established through executive action while more comprehensive legislation is developed. Front-line staff in key institutions—the hospitals, social service agencies, law enforcement—must receive training on recognizing and respecting families-of-one as well as chosen and augmented family relationships. Basic documentation systems can be created using existing administrative frameworks, providing immediate protection while more comprehensive systems are developed.

In the context of family violence, these immediate relief measures become particularly urgent safety interventions. Emergency protocols must include provisions for chosen family members to seek protective orders and emergency shelter placement together, recognizing that separating chosen family units during crisis can eliminate crucial support systems and increase vulnerability to continued abuse. Training for front-line staff should specifically address how to identify family violence within non-traditional family structures—such as financial abuse between chosen siblings or intimate partner violence in augmented family households—and how to conduct safety planning that leverages chosen family networks rather than dismantling them.

Documentation systems must enable rapid recognition of chosen family relationships during emergency situations, allowing chosen family members to make medical decisions for abuse victims, access emergency housing together, and receive the crisis intervention services. Without these immediate protections, victims in non-traditional family structures face the additional trauma of having their support systems invalidated precisely when they need them most, often forcing them to choose between accessing help and maintaining their family bonds.

The third phase involves deeper structural reform. Comprehensive legislation must be passed at federal, state, and local levels to establish permanent legal recognition for diverse family formations. Administrative systems must be overhauled to implement new recognition protocols. Service providers must develop comprehensive support programs that meet the needs of all families. This phase requires sustained commitment from policymakers and institutional leaders, backed by scholarship, dedicated funding streams, and clear accountability measures.

Within the family violence prevention and response framework, this structural reform phase must fundamentally reconstruct how legal and social service systems address abuse within diverse family formations. Comprehensive legislation should establish specialized domestic violence courts trained to handle the complexities of chosen and augmented family violence cases.

Administrative overhauls must create interagency protocols that allow protective services, law enforcement, and healthcare systems to share information about chosen family relationships during investigations and interventions. Service providers must develop trauma-informed programs that recognize the unique dynamics of abuse for various family types—such as therapeutic interventions for chosen family units experiencing violence and specialized shelter programs that can accommodate entire chosen family networks. This comprehensive approach requires sustained investment in research on family violence patterns within diverse family structures, funding for specialized training programs, and accountability measures that track outcomes across all family types rather than defaulting to traditional family metrics that render non-traditional family violence invisible.

The fourth phase focuses on cultural transformation. As sociologist Eric Klinenberg (2012) demonstrates through research on single adults' support systems, policy change alone cannot create truly inclusive institutions. Public education programs must help shift societal understanding of what constitutes a family. Professional training programs must embed inclusive practices in institutional cultures. Community support networks must be developed to ensure lasting change. Overall, efforts must be made to directly address and combat the "taboo" surrounding singlehood as well as chosen and augmented families.

In addressing family violence, this cultural transformation phase through public education campaigns must actively celebrate the resilience and strength of these family formations. For example, in recent years there has been a rise in movements that center singlehood globally. Many women are following ideologies presented by the "4B movement," (Lee & Jeong, 2021). This movement comes from a movement in Korea that centers around four ideals, which in Korean all start with the letter "b": no marriage, no childbirth, no dating, no sex (Rashid, 2024). This movement is a direct response to gender-based discrimination and became increasingly popularized in the United States after the recent election of Donald Trump in November 2024 (Rashid, 2024). While this movement may seem radical to some, these social movements help push the norms in society in ways that could ease the stigma surrounding being single by choice.

Resource allocation plays a crucial role in successful implementation. Federal funding must support both program development and ongoing operations. State and local governments must provide matching funds to ensure comprehensive coverage. Private sector partners must contribute through both direct support and policy compliance. Innovation funding can help develop new approaches to family recognition and support.

Accountability measures ensure these reforms achieve their intended effects. Community accountability boards, composed of diverse stakeholders including a family-of-one, chosen families, and augmented family members, must oversee implementation. Regular compliance audits track institutional progress. Impact assessments measure outcomes across different communities and family formations. These accountability measures must be backed by enforcement mechanisms with real consequences for non-compliance.

Evaluation frameworks must capture both quantitative and qualitative measures of success. Drawing from research on stress and support systems in various communities (Woods-Giscombé, 2010), we must assess not just numerical outcomes but lived experiences. This means tracking how many people establish legal recognition for a family-of-one, chosen family, and/or augmented family relationships, but also understanding how these relationships function in times of crisis, of which family violence can be an example. It means measuring improvements in healthcare access and economic stability while also documenting how different communities experience these changes and how this might intersect with family violence. Success requires careful attention to intersecting identities and needs. As Collins (2021) reminds us, families serve multiple social functions, from providing emotional support to transferring wealth between generations. Families can also function to perpetuate and prevent violence. Our evaluation metrics must consider how well reformed policies serve and address these various functions across differing family types. This includes examining how reforms impact historically marginalized groups, ensuring that new systems do not inadvertently recreate old patterns of exclusion.

Long-term sustainability demands ongoing adaptation and refinement. Regular community feedback mechanisms must inform policy adjustments. Research partnerships with academic institutions can help identify emerging needs and evaluate program effectiveness. Professional organizations must update their standards and practices to reflect expanded understanding of family relationships. Each of these elements contributes to creating lasting institutional change.

Institutional leadership must demonstrate sustained commitment to inclusive practices. Professional training programs must prepare new generations of service providers to understand and support diverse family formations. Community organizations must build capacity to advocate for continued progress. These elements combine to create the infrastructure needed for lasting change.

The path forward requires both patience and urgency. While some changes can happen quickly through administrative action, others demand longer-term cultural transformation. As Landry and Marsh (2011) demonstrate through their analysis of evolving family structures, meaningful change often occurs gradually through sustained effort over time. Yet this gradual pace cannot become an excuse for inaction. People facing family violence need protection now, regardless of how their families are structured.

Creating truly inclusive family violence policies requires fundamentally rethinking how we understand and support families in our society. The reforms outlined here represent not just policy proposals but a vision for institutional transformation. This transformation demands sustained commitment from academics, policymakers, institutional leaders, and community members alike. Only through comprehensive reform can we create systems that truly protect all families from violence while supporting the diverse ways people create meaningful relationships and support systems in their lives. For example, domestic violence shelter systems would need to transform to accommodate various family types—perhaps a group of five siblings escaping financial abuse from a sixth member, or a single person with their chosen parent, chosen children, and chosen siblings seeking safety from an abusive ex-partner who has been stalking the entire chosen family network. This would require not only physical space redesigns but also new intake protocols that recognize complex family dynamics, therapeutic programming that addresses collective trauma within various family systems. Such transformation illustrates how meaningful reform extends far beyond simply changing eligibility criteria—it demands reimagining the fundamental assumptions about family relationships that underlie how we design, fund, and operate violence intervention services.

Success in these reforms would mean that no one faces additional barriers to safety simply because their family doesn't fit traditional definitions. It would mean that a family-of-one, chosen family, and augmented family relationships receive the same recognition and protection as blood or legal ties. Most importantly, it would mean that our institutions finally recognize and support the many ways people create family bonds in contemporary society.

The stakes could not be higher. Every day that current policies remain unchanged, people face increased vulnerability to violence simply because their family relationships fall outside "traditional" definitions. The reforms proposed here offer a path toward more inclusive and effective protection for all families. The question is not whether such change is needed, but whether we have the collective will to make it happen.

References

Billingsley, A. (1968). *Black families in white America*. Prentice-Hall.

Brown, D. A. (2021). *The whiteness of wealth: How the tax system impoverishes Black Americans—and how we can fix it*. Crown.

Browne, A. (2008). *When battered women kill*. Simon and Schuster.

Combahee River Collective. (1983). The Combahee river collective statement. *Home Girls: A Black Feminist Anthology, 1*, 264–274.

Collins, P. H. (1990). *Black feminist thought: Knowledge, consciousness, and the politics of empowerment*. Unwin Hyman.

Collins, P. H. (2004). *Black sexual politics: African Americans, gender, and the new racism*. Routledge.

Collins, P. H. (2019). *Intersectionality as critical social theory*. Duke University Press.

Collins, P. H. (2021). Intersectionality and epistemic justice. In *The Palgrave handbook of critical race and gender* (pp. 231–252).

Collins, P. H., & Bilge, S. (2020). *Intersectionality*. John Wiley & Sons.

Crenshaw, K. (2020). Kimberlé Crenshaw on intersectionality, more than two decades later. In *African American policy forum*. Columbia Law School. Retrieved February.

DePaulo, B. (2015). *How we live now: Redefining home and family in the 21st century*. Simon and Schuster.

DePaulo, B. (2023). *Single at heart: The power, freedom, and heart-filling joy of single life*. Apollo Publishers.

DePaulo, B. M. (2006). *Singled out: How singles are stereotyped, stigmatized, and ignored, and still live happily ever after*. Macmillan.

Hamilton, D. (2020). The moral burden on economists: Darrick Hamilton's 2017 NEA presidential address. *The Review of Black Political Economy, 47*(4), 331–342.

Hattery, A. J., & Smith, E. (2007). *African American families*. Sage Publications.

Kislev, E. (2019). *Happy singlehood: The rising acceptance and celebration of solo living*. University of California Press.

Kislev, E., & Marsh, K. (2023). Intersectionality in studying and theorizing singlehood. *Journal of Family Theory & Review, 15*(3), 412–427.

Klinenberg, E. (2012). *Going solo: The extraordinary rise and surprising appeal of living alone*. Penguin.

Landor, A., & Barr, A. (2018). Politics of respectability, colorism, and the terms of social exchange in family research. *Journal of Family Theory & Review, 10*(2), 330–347.

Landry, B., & Marsh, K. (2011). The evolution of the new Black middle class. *Annual Review of Sociology, 37*, 373–394.

Lee, J., & Jeong, E. (2021). The 4B movement: Envisioning a feminist future with/in a non-reproductive future in Korea. *Journal of Gender Studies, 30*(5), 633–644.

Lubker, D. K. (2004). Socioeconomic status and domestic violence. *International Journal of Global Health and Health Disparities, 3*(1), 85–91.

Marsh, K. (2023). *The Love Jones cohort: Single and living alone in the Black middle class*. Cambridge University Press.

Moultrie, M. (2021). Making myself. *Journal of Religious Ethics, 49*(2), 314–336.

Rashid, R. (2024, Nov. 14). *As 4B takes the world by storm, South Korea is grappling with a backlash against feminism*. The Guardian. https://www.theguardian.com/world/2024/nov/15/4b-south-korea-feminist-movement-donald-trump-election-backlash

Renzetti, C. M. (1992). *Violent betrayal: Partner abuse in lesbian relationships*. Sage Publications.

Sacks, T. K. (2018). *Invisible visits: Black middle-class women in the American healthcare system*. Oxford University Press.

Straus, M. A., Gelles, R. J., & Steinmetz, S. K. (2017). *Behind closed doors: Violence in the American family*. Routledge.

Taylor, K. Y. (2017). *How we get free: Black feminism and the Combahee river collective*. Haymarket Books.

Walker, L. E. (2016). *The battered woman syndrome*. Springer Publishing Company.

Woods-Giscombé, C. L. (2010). Superwoman schema: African American women's views on stress, strength, and health. *Qualitative Health Research, 20*(5), 668–683.

Index

A. Hattery and E. Smith (eds.), *Theories of Family Violence*, Advances in Preventing and Treating Violence and Aggression, https://doi.org/10.1007/978-3-032-17095-8

T

U

V

W

The manufacturer's authorised representative in the EU is Springer Nature Customer Service Centre GmbH, Europaplatz 3, 69115 Heidelberg, Germany. If you have any concerns regarding our products, please contact ProductSafety@springernature.com

Printed and bound by CPI Group (UK) Ltd, Croydon, CR0 4YY
17/09/2026
02218458-0003